The Flying Firsts of
Walter Hinton

The Flying Firsts of Walter Hinton

From the 1919 Transatlantic Flight to the Arctic and the Amazon

BENJAMIN J. BURNS

McFarland & Company, Inc., Publishers
Jefferson, North Carolina, and London

LIBRARY OF CONGRESS CATALOGUING-IN-PUBLICATION DATA

Burns, Benjamin J., 1940–
    The flying firsts of Walter Hinton : from the 1919 transatlantic flights to the Arctic and the Amazon / Benjamin J. Burns.
    p.   cm.
    Includes bibliographical references and index.

    ISBN 978-0-7864-6447-0
    softcover : acid free paper ∞

    1. Hinton, Walter, 1888 or 9–1981. 2. Air pilots, Military — United States — Biography. 3. NC-4 (Aircraft) 4. United States, Navy — Aviation — Biography. 5. United States, Navy — Aviation — History. 6. Aeronautics — Competitions — History — 20th century. 7. Transatlantic flights — History — 20th century. I. Title.
TL540.H48B87 2012
358.40092—dc23
[B]   2011049522

BRITISH LIBRARY CATALOGUING DATA ARE AVAILABLE

©2012 Benjamin J. Burns. All rights reserved

No part of this book may be reproduced or transmitted in any form or by any means, electronic or mechanical, including photocopying or recording, or by any information storage and retrieval system, without permission in writing from the publisher.

On the front cover: *inset* Walter Hinton, crew member of NC-4, 1919 (Library of Congress); Hinton poses next to the Fairchild plane that he and his co-pilot flew to small towns all over the country to promote aviation (Burns collection)

Manufactured in the United States of America

McFarland & Company, Inc., Publishers
Box 611, Jefferson, North Carolina 28640
www.mcfarlandpub.com

To my wife, Beverly Hall Burns, who, with her intelligence
and editing skills, made it more than it would have been, and
to my four wonderful children — Blakely Burns Meyers,
Bethany M. Burns, Benjamin J.H. Burns and James C. H. Burns, for
their constant encouragement to tell Walter Hinton's story to the world.
It was my lucky day when Beverly told a mutual friend
before I had even met her: "There's the man I'm going to marry."

Acknowledgments

Librarians, archivists, and museum historians — bless them all. I got tremendous aid, comfort, and cooperation from libraries, archives, and museums across the land. From the Library of Congress, the National Archives and the Smithsonian and the Naval History Museum in Washington, D.C., and from the National Naval Air Museum in Pensacola, Florida, to graduate student librarians at Wayne State University and the folks in the Grosse Pointe and the Van Wert Brumback libraries, folks who helped dig out useful information.

The definitive book on the Great Atlantic Air Race of 1919 is still Richard K. Smith's *First Across*. His meticulous research and collection and copying of documents made the path easier to follow. There are thousands of pages of documents relating to the flight of the NCs in the National Archive locations around Washington, D.C. Smith copied all those he used and they are in the facility at Suitland, Maryland.

I have to thank my wife, Beverly, for reading my first clumsy drafts and pointing out gaps and discrepancies. Now an accomplished attorney, in a previous life she was one of the best newspaper copy editors I have ever met.

I also thank a chemistry professor at Pennsylvania State University whom I have never met. Dr. Barbara Garrison was doing genealogical research when we met via e-mail. She is a distant relative of Walter Hinton's real mother, who died when he was an infant. She provided census data and other key bits of information that helped me track down other Hinton kin. She is a terrific researcher and she gently pushed me to finish the manuscript so she could read it. I thank her for that.

Table of Contents

Acknowledgments — vi
Preface — 1
Prologue — 5

1. In the Beginning — 7
2. November 10, 1888, to February 12, 1908 — Van Wert, Ohio — 15
3. And See the World — 20
4. June 1917 to May 8, 1919 — 30
5. Chatham, Massachusetts, Chatham Naval Air Station — 52
6. With the NC-1 and NC-3 — 65
7. May 16–17, 1919, Aboard the NC-4 — 76
8. May 16–17, 1919, Aboard the NC-1 — 82
9. May 16–20, 1919, Aboard the NC-3 — 89
10. Brits Fly for Honor: March 28, 1919–May 18, 1919 — 99
11. British Bombers Compete: May 13–26, 1919 — 109
12. Lisbon and Beyond — 116
13. Ballooning into Canada — 131
14. Hopping Down to Rio — 156
15. Exploring the Amazon Basin — 174
16. Hinton the Celebrity — 192
17. Touring the Country for the Exchange Clubs and Beyond — 206

Epilogue — 220
Chapter Notes — 233
Bibliography — 243
Index — 247

Preface

Flying is an act of faith. Whether it is faith in the human at the controls or faith in a higher power is your business, but few people fail to experience some reflective thought when that huge jet barrels down the runway, they are pressed back in their seats with all tray tables stowed and seats in the upright positions, and they are suddenly, seemingly quite unnaturally airborne.

And yet since recorded history mankind has dreamed of conquering the heavens and flying like the birds. Boys and girls from ancient times looked at birds in flight and asked, why not me? As a six-year-old with the willing assistance of my eight-year-old brother, I constructed a rude contraption of long, light sticks and cloth, strapped the angel-wing affair to my back, and launched off the flat shed roof on our farm in Michigan's Thumb country. Luckily it was a low roof and my momentum from running across the roof carried me to a soft, grassy spot about nine feet below and about six feet from the shed. It was hardly a repetition of Orville and Wilbur at Kitty Hawk, but right in the grand tradition of some of the fools who perished over previous centuries with schemes of flying. That was my last personal attempt to "slip the surly bonds of earth." But it didn't end my fascination with "dancing the skies on laughter-silvered wings."

A few years later my brother Jim and I learned that at a small, grass airport several miles down Pratt Road near our farm outside Memphis, Michigan, there were a half dozen yellow Piper Cubs, basic but reliable little planes in the late '40s and early '50s that could carry two or three people, depending on how much they weighed. So we organized an expedition of friends and hiked to the airport that sported a Quonset hut left over from some World War II factory, a tired windsock, and several pilot/mechanics who flew and repaired their own planes. The guys were friendly to the awkward farm boys who wanted to fly and after several hours of nagging one of them agreed to take two of us up, probably just to shut us up and get rid of us. My brother and I stepped forward as our two friends got cold feet and hung back.

So, up we went. It was incredible. You really haven't flown until you get in a small plane that is like a fragile, bubble of safety as you are buffeted by stray breezes and the craft pops up and down like an elevator that is angry at its occupants. But we concealed our terror while experiencing the delight of flying for the first time. It was also our last time at that particular airport as the young pilot, a survivor of World War II, decided to give us a real thrill and simply cut the engine and went into a dive from about 3,000 feet up. Sort of like riding a roller coaster down the big hill, but there is no noise from the vehicle other than the occupants screaming. He started it up in plenty of time to level out and wing in for a safe landing at the converted cow pasture. And pointed out casually that the plane seemed to do that on a regular basis and he was darned if he could figure out why. Our friends, who had said they would take the second ride, had witnessed the fake stall and dive and decided it was not a good day to fly.

And after we recounted our adventure that evening to surprised parents, we were permanently grounded and forbidden to go anywhere near the airport. I never did learn to fly, but I have always been fascinated by the men and women who defy gravity to "wheel and soar and swing" in space. I have been particularly interested in those early aviators, aeronauts and birdmen, who never knew whether their plane was going to get off the ground and, once they were up, never knew for sure whether they would get back safely. Today, government agencies would ban flying if they were confronted by the attempts to invent aviation near the beginning of the 20th century.

So when I learned, while serving as a mid-level editor at the Miami Herald bureau in Fort Lauderdale, that the man who had been a pilot on the first plane to span the Atlantic lived nearby, I assigned a reporter to do a feature on the fellow and determined to meet him.

Walter Hinton was the quintessential early aviator. He was modest about his accomplishments and he would only reluctantly confirm any fact he felt might damage the reputation of another. He was a natural flyer and nothing in his childhood, spent not far from Dayton where the Wright brothers lived, hinted at his gifts.

I spent more than 40 hours interviewing him in 1967 and 1968 and after that hundreds of hours researching that first transatlantic flight in 1919. I sorted through documents at three National Archives locations in Washington, D.C. I corresponded with or interviewed all of the survivors of that U.S. Navy expedition. I read the logs of the mission. Then I put my materials aside for decades and pursued a career in the newspaper business. In 1999 in preparation for the end of the century, a noted television news anchor hosted a television documentary claiming the 1927 solo Atlantic hop of Charles Lindbergh was the first step to today's space missions. I thought, "Poor research." Ninety-one men had crossed the Atlantic by air when Lucky Lindy took off on his solo flight and Walter Hinton was pilot of the first plane. I was reminded that the world has largely forgotten Walter Hinton and the men who were the real first step toward conquering space. So I spent additional hours gathering more details on the mission. I interviewed all the relatives of Hinton I could locate and some who claimed to be relatives, but weren't. I read all the books on the subject, including the official Navy version *The Triumph of the NCs*, published in 1920, and the excellent *First Across*, by Richard K. Smith, which won the 1972 History Manuscript Award from the American Institute of Aeronautics and Astronautics. Smith's meticulous collection of original documents gathered at the National Archives facility in Suitland, Maryland, were invaluable to this work.

This, then, is Walter Hinton's and my version of that first flight and Hinton's other aviation adventures — lost in the Canadian Arctic and believed dead; first flight to Rio de Janeiro from New York; first aerial exploration of the Amazon and a nationwide tour promoting aviation and airports for the Exchange Clubs. I have tried to reconstruct Walter's story using direct quotes where I had them and left out quote marks if I don't know that is exactly what the person said. I have tried to simplify times by using standard time zones where it makes sense rather than Greenwich Mean Time in most cases, distances by using miles rather than nautical miles, and miles per hour rather than knots.

Prologue

The white-haired old man stood on the 23rd floor balcony overlooking the Fort Lauderdale beach as a young woman with long blonde hair jogged along the water's edge. Engrossed in her progress as she trotted, the young man almost missed what the 80-year-old was saying. Walter Hinton said, "You know I was a pilot of the first plane to fly over that."

"But I thought Lindbergh was the first to fly the Atlantic in 1927," the reporter said, showing off the scant knowledge of early aviation that may have drawn him this feature assignment for the *Miami Herald Tropic Magazine*—interview a man named Walter Hinton, who made a number of pioneering flights, including the first from New York to Rio de Janeiro, Brazil, and the first aerial mapping of the Amazon River valley, which earned him the splendiferous nickname "The White-winged God on the Big Bird."

Walter Hinton, a plain-spoken man, who grew up on an Ohio farm hard by the Indiana border, repeated his point. "We flew over the Atlantic in 1919 — the first across by air."

Hinton's gray eyes twinkled and he laughed as he looked at the great, blue ocean warping out to the horizon toward the Bahamas and beyond.

> There were dozens of men who flew it before Lindbergh. He was the first to fly it solo, non-stop. We were the very first in a four-engine, Navy-Curtiss flying boat in May 1919. There were six of us on board and we were part of a three-plane mission, but we were the only one to make it. The others went down at sea. The first nonstop flight was about a month after us when Alcock and Brown flew it a Vickers-Vimy bomber and crash-landed in an Irish bog.
>
> Lindbergh always said our mission was tougher than his because airplane engines weren't reliable in 1919, gasoline frequently had dirt in it and if a motor ran for 10 hours we took it apart to find out why. We were aiming at a half dozen specks of islands out there.

Hinton said, gesturing east — the Azores — "and Lindbergh aimed at a continent."

"So tell me about it," the reporter invited. And the pair moved inside Hinton's beach front condominium to revisit a story the old man had told many times in a flat, nasal, Midwestern, no-bragging fashion born of farm life before the turn of the 20th century when there were no electric lights, indoor plumbing, or running water. Hinton was born to Millard Hinton and Effie Garrison Hinton in 1889 on a farm near Van Wert, Ohio, a small town at the confluence of three rivers in a flat, fertile countryside near the Indiana border. A hundred miles away in Dayton, Orville, 18, and Wilbur Wright, 22, were publishing the neighborhood *West Side News*, which specialized in local news, folksy stories and items cribbed directly from a magazine called *The Youth's Companion*. They wouldn't get seriously interested in flying until 1899.

The gliding experiments of Chicagoan Octave Chanute in the Indiana dunes along Lake Michigan, a local Van Wert man's attempts at flying off hills and barns and the Wright brothers success at Kitty Hawk were all fodder for the young Hinton's imagination. An indifferent student who probably never graduated from high school, Hinton was an able mechanic and saw no future in farm life. When he was 18 he boarded a horse-drawn wagon and rode the 20 miles into Fort Wayne, Indiana, where he signed up to join the Navy and see the world. While serving aboard the cruiser *Seattle*, which carried six JN-9 (Jenny) seaplanes, he found an aviation book as he stood watch one night on the bridge. He was caught reading it on duty by Lt. Com. Kenneth Whiting, a naval Academy graduate and one of the first naval aviators. Rather than reprimand the seaman, Whiting asked Hinton if he would like to learn to fly. Hinton said yes, and in 1917 was one of the first enlisted men to be sent to the Naval Air Station at Pensacola to become a pilot. Hinton turned out to be a natural flyer. If it could get airborne, he could fly it and he could get planes airborne that frustrated other fliers. In a time when aviators crashed on a weekly basis, Hinton logged hundreds of hours without a serious mishap. He was promoted to flying instructor and taught another Naval Academy graduate, Lt. Commander Richard E. Byrd, how to fly, cementing a lifelong friendship with the man who some years later became a famous aviator and Arctic explorer.

Byrd, already a man who felt he was predestined for greatness, made elaborate plans with Hinton for an Atlantic attempt. They continued their discussions when both of them flew submarine patrols out of Halifax, Nova Scotia, in the waning days of World War I. When Commander John Towers opened the Navy's transatlantic section, one of the first test pilots he picked was Hinton, who transferred to Rockaway Naval Air Station for his appointment with history.

1

In the Beginning

"Aviation in itself is not inherently dangerous. But to an even greater degree than the sea, it is terribly unforgiving of any carelessness, incapacity or neglect."

— Capt. A.G. Lamplugh[1]

May 8, 1919

The noise was deafening. Walter Hinton and co-pilot Elmer Stone were sitting barely a foot and a half in front of and a few feet below four unmuffled 12-cylinder engines thundering in unison as they drove one of the world's largest airplanes through the air north toward Nova Scotia on the first leg of their bid to cross the Atlantic by air first.

Hinton and Stone stuffed handkerchiefs over their ears under their thin leather flying helmets to try to block the roar. They couldn't hear Commander Albert Cushing Read's orders. Read, also the navigator, relied on hand signals. Read sat six feet in front of them in a cockpit that looked like an open manhole in the bow. He sat on a stool that doubled as the plane's toilet. When Read wanted to communicate orders, he had three choices: wave his arms and point, crawl back through a low, narrow tunnel and tug at the pilots' legs or pound on the hull and point. The hull pounding didn't help much because vibrations from 48 barking cylinders on the Liberty engines overpowered puny human efforts.

Hinton, 31, a junior grade lieutenant, was one of the best multi-engine test pilots in the Navy. Stone, who sat in the co-pilot's right-hand seat, was the first officer in the Coast Guard to win his aviator wings. Stone, 32, outranked the one-time Ohio farm boy, but defered to Hinton with Putty Read's approval because of Hinton's special knack for getting planes into the air and crippled planes back on the water in one piece.

The NC-4 they were flying had only been tested for five hours before being put into service on this mission. This first 737-land-mile leg to Halifax was its own shakedown cruise. If anything went wrong in the air, it would be Hinton's job to get them down safely.

Hinton and Stone flew in rough formation. The command ship NC-3 was in the lead, the NC-1 to its port and slightly behind, and the NC-4 is trailing both flying boats off to starboard. Rising and falling slowly as if cresting invisible ocean waves, the flying boats plowed through the air currents until 2:30 in the afternoon. By then the NC-4 lagged a half-mile behind the others because its center pusher engine had failed. No oil was getting to its pistons. The engine, called a pusher because the propeller is at the rear of the engine, lost oil pressure first and then the spark died. This Liberty engine took two Detroit automotive engineers six days to design at the Willard Hotel in the nation's capitol after they were hastily called to Washington in 1918 to provide an engine that could power a transatlantic plane. It was rated the most reliable engine in aviation at a time when engines which run for 10 hours without failing are taken apart to see why. The L-12s were built by the Packard and Ford Motor car companies in Detroit. They were tested by mounting them atop trucks driving through the streets of that city.

Hinton in flying garb (U.S. Navy photograph).

The trio of giant, bi-wing flying boats, which resemble someone's mechanical interpretation of pelicans or construction scaffolding grafted on to Dutch wooden shoes, headed north from Jamaica Bay on Long Island toward Newfoundland, the hopping-off place for the Navy's entry in the "Great Atlantic Air Race." Newfoundland's only claim to a launching point to try to best the ocean is like the real estate salesman's mantra: location, location, location. It is the closest place in North America to Europe. Every mile counts. So if you wanted to string the first Marconi radio cable or fly the

1. In the Beginning 9

Atlantic, that was where you went. Newfoundland is a world apart. It doesn't even keep the same time as other North American continental cities. Before 1919 most residents had never seen an airplane. The closest European landfall was the Portuguese Azores 1,384 miles distant. The closest mainland European landfall was Cabo da Roca, not far from Lisbon. The other choice was Ireland, some 1,600 miles from Newfoundland. The forbidding land of spring storms, giant icebergs, hardy fishermen and tilted rocky pastures attracted five groups of fliers hoping to achieve fame and fortune by being first across the Atlantic.

The U.S. Navy officially proclaimed that their mission was a scientific expedition and they were not part of the contest to be first to cross the Atlantic by air and win the $50,000 *London Daily Mail* prize. But the prize for the Navy if it were first across the ocean barrier was much greater than money. It would establish national pride, worldwide renown and the importance of naval air power at a time when Congress was in a military budget-cutting mood in the post–World War I world. The headlines and news coverage would

A dirigible like the C-4 that was lost at sea hovers over the three NCs as they make ready for their takeoff (U.S. Navy Photograph).

be worth more than money in promoting naval aviation to a world bloody and bowed as 19 million lost their lives and 21 million more were wounded or gassed in the War to End All Wars. On this day in May 1919, the statesmen and politicians of the globe were gathered at the French palace of Versailles to divide up the world and guarantee that the aggressive Germans will never again be a threat to peace. President Woodrow Wilson, the first U.S. president to travel abroad while in office, was among them with his dream of a League of Nations that can solve disputes without sacrificing men, women and children to war.

The NCs were accidentally nicknamed the Nancies by a reporter, who misunderstood a press briefing officer when he said, "NC," and the woman's name stuck. They almost defy description. The open-cockpit flying boats cost $60,000 each to build, stood 24 feet 6 inches high, and looked like Rube Goldberg inventions, erector sets that have been cobbled to Dutch wooden shoes. They have been described as "pregnant waterfowls." They had high double gray rudder tails, swollen gray bodies and wings yellowed from varnish coating five layers of dope on the Irish linen fabric that was laced tightly on the wings. Three hollow spruce booms braced by steel cables linked the tail assembly to the rear of the boat. A seven-eighths-inch-wide spruce beam ran down the middle of each 12-foot-wide wing to provide a narrow walkway for repairs in flight. Both mechanics and engineers carried telephone lineman harnesses so they wouldn't fall off while working outside the plane in the air. If a mechanic or engineer stepped off that track he could have crashed right through the fabric. The upper wings, at 126 feet, were as long as those on a modern Boeing 707 jet and both sets of wings, which sat on top of the hull, were designed to be discarded if necessary after a crash landing at sea, hopefully turning the hull into a seaworthy boat. The upper wings were 14 feet higher at the center and 12 feet higher at the tips of the lower wings. The keels were oak or rock elm, the main structure western spruce, and the deck planking spruce or cedar. "You can't fly that without oars," one newsman said presciently before the take-off from Rockaway Naval Air Station.

The 45-foot-long boat hull was made of thin sheets of laminated spruce and it was divided into six water-tight compartments by bulkheads connected by a narrow, two-foot-wide tunnel that snaked past nine 200-gallon gas drums that should provide enough fuel to bridge the Atlantic. An additional 91-gallon gravity-feed gas tank was in the upper wing and fuel was pumped 16 feet up to it from the drums in the hull by small windmill propellers and piped from there to the engines. Fully loaded, an NC weighed 28,500 pounds and could get up to 60 miles per hour on the water and 90 miles per hour in the air without help from a tail wind. The cruising speed was 77 miles per hour and the stalling speed 67 miles per hour; the pilots had to fly carefully and maneuver within that narrow range.

1. In the Beginning 11

The pilots had dual controls that looked like automobile steering wheels, with dashboard gauges including turn indicators, two inclinometers, air speed indicators, a ball-and-turn indicator, two compasses, an altimeter, oil pressure and temperature gauges for each engine, water temperature gauges, ignition switches to start and shut off each engine, and a master switch to kill all the engines at once. The pilots sat directly under and in front of the center 400-horsepower, 12-cylinder tractor engine. Two other similar tractor engines on the wings faced forward, pulling the craft. A fourth pointed to the rear, pushing. There was an upside-down U-shaped crawl tunnel on the hull under the pusher to discourage the mechanic or engineer from standing up and being decapitated. Even so, one mechanic lost a hand when he stood up too close to a prop during flight preparation. He staunched the blood flow with his other hand, climbed down and was driven to the infirmary. He was off the mission.

The propellers on all three Nancies were Olmsteads, a new type designed to give better performance and higher speed. They had never been tested. There were no mufflers on the engines, just exhaust ports. The pilots' only protection from the elements were two tiny windshields — less than 24 inches wide and 18 inches high. The commander of the craft guided the flight and

All the NC crews lined up for photographs before the take off from Rockaway, Long Island, New York (U.S. Navy Photograph).

stoods in a manhole-shaped cockpit in the nose. He sat down when he wasn't navigating because the wind buffeting him at 60 to 70 miles per hour was too cold. His cone-shaped seat, 18 inches across at the top, was covered by a thin oil-cloth-covered cushion. It had a supply of waxed paper bags to contain waste since it doubled as a toilet. Small weather balloons were supplied for the other function. The commander had an air speed indicator, a Navy compass, a drift indicator, a course and distance indicator, a bubble sextant, a chart board, a pair of dividers, one pencil compass and an 18-inch parallel rule, a stopwatch, a log book and a pair of six-power binoculars. In addition he had an anchor, a towing bridle and lines to cast to harbor towboats. There were three flashlights and four liquid fire extinguishers on board. Two flare holders pointed downward from each side of the bow to be fired in case of a night landing. They were activated by a red button on the pilots' dashboard.[2]

The commander was linked to the pilots by a radio intercom that worked fine on dry land with the engines shut off. But it was overwhelmed by the noise of the engines and the vibration of the plane. Think of standing within a few feet of a jet engine or Niagara Falls. Shouting does no good. Communication was by hand signals and notes. There was a compartment immediately behind the pilots with a resting bench and a hatch cover.

The mechanic and flight engineer sat in a compartment near the rear of the gas drums and the radio man was in a compartment further back. The compartment had a sliding hatch cover that could be closed against the weather. The engineer had an Aldis lamp hooked to the main battery to light his compartment, an oil pressure gauge and tachometer for each engine, and a water temperature thermometer. The radio aerial was a 200-foot-long cable that could be reeled out once the plane was high enough. It was weighted with a lead fish to make sure it trailed behind the craft. It had to be reeled in as the plane landed or the aerial would be torn off by the weight of the fish hitting the water. The radio operators had a radio compass to hone in signals from ships at sea and carry spare batteries and radio tubes. The Navy described these noisy behemoths as "rugged and comfortable craft designed and built in accordance with standard Navy practice."

If the commander wanted to give an order, to reach the radio operator, engineer or mechanic, he had to crawl back or one of them had to crawl forward. The connecting intercom also did not work when the planes were underway. Each crew member had been allowed five pounds of personal effects. Each got a Thermos bottle of coffee, a hot water bottle and two regulation ham sandwiches — "there is not too much ham and they are not too good."[3]

The NC-4 (or Four), which in the early going had proved the fastest of the three flying boats, continued to struggle along on its three engines, the idled propeller of the pusher causing additional drag. Lt. Commander Read,

Hinton and Read are in their flying clothes and Coast Guard Lt. Elmer Stone is in his dress uniform before the flight (U.S. Navy photograph).

the commander/navigator of the Four, spied the smoke of the *McDermut*, the first station ship designed to help keep them on course, off to port; he turned and pounded on the hull and waved to Hinton and Stone. Station ships and weather ships were positioned 50 miles apart and formed a chain of communication when the cumbersome craft headed out across the Atlantic. The *McDermut* crew acknowledged Read's direction with a wave. They were about a mile behind the Three and the One as they fly over the ship, which, according to prearranged orders, was now steaming north, pointing the way to the *Kimberly*, 50 miles further along. A canvas numeral "One" was prominent on the *McDermut* deck and sailors and deck crew cheered and waved their hats and their arms. Halfway to the *Kimberly* the center tractor engine on the Four exploded in a cloud of steam and showered Hinton and Stone with hot water. A connecting rod arched lazily end over end into the ocean below. The Four could fly on three engines. It couldn't on two. Read motioned to the pilots to take her down. They were already attempting to prolong the glide to make the touchdown as smooth as possible. When Read crawled back to the aft compartment, Herbert Rodd had already sent out radio signals. Radio operators Lt. Harry Sadenwater aboard the One and Lt. Robert Lavender aboard the Three acknowledged. The *McDermut* radio operator advised Rodd to radio their location when the Four touches down. Rodd reeled in his radio antenna cable. There were whitecaps on the sea below as Hinton guided the Four down. The Four's engineer, Lt. James Breese, and the mechanic, Ensign Eugene "Smokey" Rhoads, buckled themselves in. Read scuttled back to his command compartment and turned his back at splash down as he and the nose disappeared in spray. The waves were running eight to ten feet. The Four, taxiing now on two engines, rode them like the early hills on a roller coaster. It is a fairly smooth but stomach-churning ride. Up and down, up and down at about five miles per hour. Rhoads, a Pennsylvania Dutchman and an old-time sailor, was a last-minute replacement as the mechanic aboard the Four. Everyone called him Smokey. He crawled forward, tugged at Hinton's knee, and offered up a can of stewed tomatoes. "It is the best thing for sea sickness, Meester Hinton," Rhoads said. Hinton and Stone both refused the offering.[4] It appeared that the mission was over for the Four unless they could get at least one replacement engine and repair the oil problems on the other. Read plotted a course for the Chatham Naval Air Station on Cape Cod in Chatham, Massachusetts, about 80 miles east. They were about 20 miles further out than he had estimated while the Four was in the air. The pilots took half-hour turns at the controls keeping the craft in synch with the seas running toward the coast. It gave Hinton a chance to think about how a Van Wert, Ohio, farm boy from mid–America wound up aboard a crippled transatlantic flyer chugging steadily like an ocean-going roller coaster toward land.

2

November 10, 1888, to February 12, 1908 — Van Wert, Ohio

"Beware, dear son of my heart, lest in thy new-found power thou seekest even the gates of Olympus.... These wings may bring they freedom but may also come thy death.

— Daedalus to Icarus[1]

Walter Hinton shucked a corncob and threw it at the galvanized bucket. It made a satisfying clang. He was angry. The crops were in, the hay was in the barn and his 16th birthday was coming up in a couple weeks. His father, Millard Hinton, had told him at breakfast that morning before leaving for work in Van Wert that he wasn't going to make good on a promise to buy a horse and buggy for Walter if he stayed and worked the farm for a year. Millard said he couldn't afford it; he didn't have the money.

Walter, never a particularly good student, had been working on the 80-acre farm on Ridge Road near Convoy, Ohio, since he dropped out of school after the sixth grade. But this year — 1906 — his father had said to manage the farm while he worked in town and he would get Walter a horse and buggy. Walter diligently cared for the cattle, sheep and hogs and was finishing his fall chores by removing cobs from corn shocks that had been stacked in the fields. Clang, another shucked cob hit the bucket.

Walter was sweet on Bertha Bayles, from a nearby farm, but he felt his lack of transportation to get to Van Wert, six miles distant, hampered his social life. Another corncob clanged off the bucket. There wasn't much going on in Convoy of a weekend. It was mainly grain elevators and a railroad track. What was he going to do?[2]

Van Wert, Ohio (population 11,000), was and is middle America. It isn't that far from Dayton where the Wright brothers had their bicycle shop and were experimenting with flying.

Surrounded by flat, fertile Ohio fields filled with corn, soybeans and other grain crops, it sits halfway between Lima, Ohio, and Fort Wayne, Indiana, 30 miles to the west. A few years later Ridge Road, which is the main street in downtown Van Wert, was designated part of the Lincoln Highway, the first transcontinental pike in the nation. But from 1888 to 1908 Ridge was still a dirt road following an east-west line toward Fort Wayne along the high ground. It was planked in spots to allow passage in the boggiest areas, but was frequently impassable between Convoy and Fort Wayne during spring thaws or the rainy season. The county got 34 inches of rain a year. The streets of Van Wert were still mostly dirt, even downtown in front of the ornate county courthouse and the first county library in the nation, the Brumback Memorial Library, a castle-like structure, where adults and young boys and girls could read and "yearn beyond the skyline where strange roads go down."[3]

Van Wert had been founded 71 years earlier in 1835 and named for Isaac Van Wart. The altered spelling is blamed on a clerical error, but no one knows whether it might have just have been an Ohio recording clerk who figured Van Wart didn't sound that attractive for potential settlers. It was no fault of anyone in Van Wert. The county had been incorrectly named Van Wert in 1820.

Van Wart's claim to fame was he was a New Yorker of Dutch heritage, who spoke and read little English. During the Revolutionary War, while he and two cousins were manning a security checkpoint, they were approached by a man bearing a pass from General Benedict Arnold. That man was the British Major John Andre, a spy in civilian clothes carrying the plans to West Point in his boot.

The three cousins couldn't read the pass so they searched Andre and found the plans. Van Wart and his colleagues were instant heroes and Andre was subsequently hanged. General Arnold fled to England one step ahead of arresting officers and lived out his life in disgrace. The U.S. government thanked the trio by making them grants of money and presenting them with tracts of land and struck special medals in their honor.

In 1820 the Ohio legislature decided to honor the three by naming counties after them in the northern part of the state, a little-populated area that included a vast place called "The Great Black Swamp." Thus (John) Paulding, (David) Williams, and (Isaac) Van Wert counties were born. Van Wert County was blanketed by dense forests and mosquitoes from the swamp. That made growth slow until the swamp was drained to provide rich black farmland.

Walter Hinton was born November 10, 1888, to Millard Madison Hinton and Effa J. Garrison Hinton. Millard and Effa, better known as Effie, had been married on June 17, 1885, and Hinton's sister Florence was born that same year. Effie contracted measles and died while pregnant when Hinton was two so he never really knew his mother. She was 23.

Millard, a handsome man with a full head of hair and a moustache, had mixed success as a farmer and worked various jobs to supplement the farm income. For a while he was foreman in an oil well supply company and purchased timber for sucker rods used in pumping. The nearest neighbor lived a half-mile down the road, and Florence and Walter walked a mile and a half to the nearest elementary school. When the children weren't in school they frequently worked daylight to dusk. Not long after Effie's death, Millard remarried, his bride a 29-year-old spinster, Louvinia F. Hinton, because he needed a mother to care for his children. But Louvinia never really did care much. Louvinia fancied herself an artist and gave singing lessons then spent the money on clothes for herself. There is a picture of her in a Chinese brocade with a notation by Walter Hinton on the back: "She charged 50 cents an hour for lessons and paid $1.50 for the dress. Big money in those days."[4] Louvinia got pregnant once and complained about her burden throughout the pregnancy until late in her term when she had a miscarriage. Then she complained about losing the baby. Florence became Walter's mother figure and protector. When Walter failed to split the logs for the stove and instead went off playing in the fields, Florence would step in and do the chore when she heard the noon whistle, so Millard, who by now was working at one of the Van Wert stave factories in town that made barrels, wouldn't whip Walter when he got home for his lunch. Walter might show up hours later proudly carrying a rattlesnake he had killed in the woods. Florence never talked much about her relationship with her stepmother, but she called her "a whiner."

Walter was smart and had an inventive mind. His logical bent came across in his letters: clear, concise and to the point. He could make almost any gadget work and could figure out and fix any machine, but he didn't care for the regimen of school.

Another corncob clanged in the bucket. Walter was furious. He had never gotten along particularly well with his father or his stepmother. There was obviously no future for him on the farm. He packed his things and left.

With no job, no high school diploma and few prospects, he eventually turned to his sister, Florence, who had married Clarence Slade and lived on another farm near Convoy, a few miles west of Van Wert. Clarence had married Florence because Clarence's father said she was "perfectly acceptable" and they needed help with the cooking, cleaning and farmwork. Clarence and Florence took Walter in, giving him a room high up under the eves of the two story, tin-roofed house. The move created a rift because Millard had calculated his son would come crawling back as cheap farm labor. Millard was angry with Florence for spoiling his plan. And they didn't speak for months. After a few months Clarence grew weary of having another young man in the house and started prodding Walter to find work and another place to stay or to go out and see the world.

In 1907 and early 1908 the newspapers in Van Wert and across the nation were full of stirring accounts of Theodore Roosevelt's "Great White Fleet," which the pugnacious president had assembled, painted white and sent on a world cruise to impress and intimidate other nations with U.S. naval power, particularly the Japanese. The 16 battle ships and assorted support craft gave TR a 21-gun salute when they sailed out of Hampton Roads, Virginia, on December 16, 1907. The voyage covered 45,000 miles around the world in 14 months. It lasted until February 22, 1909, and was viewed as a highly successful exercise in international public awareness of the Navy. It was part of TR's "Speak Softly and Carry a Big Stick" or "gunboat diplomacy."

The January 23, 1908, *Van Wert Times* carried the page-one story: "Third Stage of Voyage, The Big Battleship Fleet Sails for Magellan Strait" under a one column headline. "To the booming of guns and the cheers of thousands on accompanying pleasure craft the warships sailed from Rio de Janeiro bound for Punta Arenas on the Magellan Strait," the unnamed correspondent reported. There were rumors the Japanese would put mines in the Straits of Magellan, the winding, 370-mile-long watercourse that was from two and a half to 70 miles wide and ran below South America from west of Punta Arenas to the Pacific.

That was it—danger, adventure, travel, foreign lands. Naval recruiting posters of the era by artists like Henry Reuterdahl, who took part in the Great White Fleet mission, made the sea sound glamorous. Reuterdahl, a short, blocky, bespectacled man, was listed as an artist/correspondent on the White Fleet mission, but there is little doubt he was a spy gathering military intelligence for the admirals back in Washington.

"I didn't see much opportunity in becoming another farmer so I decided to join the Navy and see the world," Hinton said.[5] Hinton and several friends headed for Fort Wayne, the nearest place to sign up. Whether they covered the 30 miles on foot or hitched rides with teamsters hauling goods to the nearest big city on sleds and in wagons is not known. It was February and there was still ice and snow on the ground. A few years later, Clarence and Florence, who by that time had a daughter Marjorie, also left. They headed to Michigan where Clarence heard the fishing and hunting was good and settled on a farm between three lakes near Olivet in south central Michigan.

On February 12, 1908, Walter Hinton passed the Navy aptitude tests and was sworn in as a common seaman. He was shipped east for basic training to Norfolk naval base with 12 other raw recruits from Fort Wayne. At least three others from Van Wert failed to be accepted by the military and went home.

In Norfolk Hinton found a lot of foreign-speaking people, a lot of Norwegians, old sailing ship people who had been in the service for years. He learned some basic lessons about naval life from them—"no thievery from the ditty box, a sense of honor, no tale bearers and no one to testify at court martials."

He got 90 days of training before reporting to his first ship, the U.S.S. *Olympia,* which served as Admiral George Dewey's flagship at the Battle of Manila Bay during the Spanish American War. Hinton later served on the tender *Dixie* and the destroyer *Wainwright.* The Ohio farm boy was seeing the world.

3

And See the World

"If you are looking for perfect safety, you will do well to sit on a fence and watch the birds; but if you really wish to learn, you must mount a machine and become acquainted with its tricks by actual trial."

— Wilbur Wright[1]

The world of 1908 was an exciting place for a 20-year-old seeking adventure and different vistas than that offered by the flat farmlands of western Ohio. The naval base at Norfolk, Virginia, was a bustling new world hard by the Atlantic Ocean and populated by old salts from a dozen lands, who had learned their seamanship under sail.

U.S.S. *Olympia*, once the proud flagship of Admiral George Dewey, was made famous by his victory in the 1898 Spanish-American War against Spanish forces at Manila Bay in the Philippines. By 1908 the *Olympia* served as summer cruise vessel for the future captains and admirals of the fleet — midshipmen from Annapolis.

While the ship that helped establish the U.S. as a world naval power was relegated to training Naval Academy cadets, when in port it was still popular with visitors a decade after its Philippine triumph. The curious wanted to know where Dewey stood on the deck when he gave his famous May 1, 1898, order: "You may fire when ready, Gridley." It was an order Capt. Charles V. "Steve" Gridley and five other ship's captains carried out with dispatch and little loss of American life. Within hours they had sunk the Spanish fleet, shown the world they were a force to be reckoned with, and won a promotion for Dewey to Rear Admiral.[2]

All the 1908 crew members of the *Olympia* were familiar with the story and soon tired of pointing the spot out to visitors where Dewey had stood, so one day Hinton and a fellow seaman traced Hinton's foot on the deck and marked it with brass headed screws. After that when visitors asked where Dewey had stood, the pair would point to the footprint and say, "Right there." When they asked where the other footprint was, the two would say, "Oh, he had his other foot on the rail."[3] Today if you could visit the 344-foot-long ship at the Independence Seaport Museum in Philadelphia, you would find two footprints marked on the deck; possibly one of them is still Hinton's.[4]

While Hinton didn't get to take part in the last days of the Great White Fleet Mission from mid–December 1907 to February 22, 1909,[5] nor get to see much of the world outside the western hemisphere during the next decade, he shared in the jingoistic excitement of "gunboat diplomacy" that originated with Teddy Roosevelt.

There was no pretense of walking softly during those years. American military actions were a reprise of the Spanish-American War. If a country offended U.S. honor — real or imagined — or threatened U.S. commercial and banking interests, it risked a visit from U.S. Navy gunboats and playing host to a contingent of Marines, there to protect national interests and U.S. citizens.

While Hinton was working his way up the ranks of enlisted men, two other Ohioans — Orville and Wilbur Wright — from their bicycle shop in Dayton and on the Atlantic shores at Kitty Hawk, North Carolina, were quietly revolutionizing the world of heavier-than-air flying machines. Such machines had left the ground before the Wrights' 1903 historic flight, but the aviators had been unable to fly them in anything but a straight path and had no ability to balance them in the slightest wind. What the Wright brothers brought to aviation was the ability to maneuver an aircraft — the big breakthrough. While most of the nation's press was focused on the claims and pretensions of Alexander Graham Bell's aviation inventions, the French, and Samuel Langley, the Secretary of the Smithsonian Museum, the Wrights quietly improved the craft they flew at Kitty Hawk. When asked, while doing a flying test at a field outside Dayton, what practical use there was for an airplane, Wilbur reportedly had a one-word answer: "War," he said. By 1906 the Wrights had won patents for their original wing designs. But that fact went unnoted by the nation's media.[6]

By 1908 the Wrights had plenty of competition from serious inventor/aviators, sham inventors and would-be aviators, some of whom were perfectly willing to expropriate the brothers' patented features that made airplanes flyable in a variety of wind and weather conditions. One of their chief competitors was Glenn Curtiss, of Hammondsport, New York, a former motorcycle racer, who started working with Bell and then split off on his own. New aviation records were being set every day for distance, time in the air, altitude and speed. This was simply because engines were getting lighter and stronger and men were daily learning more about the mysteries of flight. If there had been plaintiff's product liability attorneys in 1908, aviation would never have gotten off the ground. It was dangerous. Engines died in mid-air. Wings and tails fell off. Everyone crashed or had accidents. The brave souls involved in aviation were learning aerodynamics on a trial-and-error basis. Many were injured and numbers died. It was only a question of how hard the plane hit and whether the pilot survived. The flying machine frequently didn't.

Curtiss became famous the year Hinton joined the Navy when he piloted a plane called June Bug for a distance of more than seven-tenths of a mile in a straight line. He won $10,000 from the *New York World* in 1910 for the first successful flight from Albany to New York City. Curtiss hedged his bet by attaching pontoons to his craft in case the engine quit on his journey down the Hudson River so he could effect a water landing. Orville Wright attached a canoe to the bottom of his flyer just in case he wound up in the drink when he made a demonstration flight around the Statue of Liberty in New York Harbor.

While Curtiss fought with the Wright brothers over his legal rights to use ailerons, which the Wrights claimed were covered by their patents, he pioneered the design of the floatplane and the flying boat. Naval aviator Eugene Ely made the first successful takeoff and landing from the U.S. Navy ship *Pennsylvania* in a Curtiss plane at San Francisco in 1910. Ely wore a football helmet of the era and an inflated bicycle tire because he could not swim.[7]

While Walter Hinton was learning to be a sailor and working his way up the ranks of enlisted men on board the cruiser *Wainwright* and later on the *Seattle*, other members of the transatlantic mission crews and support staff—almost all Academy graduates—were learning aviation. These included lieutenants John Towers, Patrick N. L. Bellinger, Holden Richardson and Kenneth Whiting.

John Henry Towers, a son of the Confederacy from Rome, Georgia, graduated from the Naval Academy in Annapolis as a midshipman in 1906, the year that bandmaster Charles A. Zimmerman composed a new march to replace the customary "Home Sweet Home" at the Farewell Ball. The march was entitled "Anchors Aweigh" and later, with words added, became the official Navy song.[8]

In 1911 the Navy assigned the Annapolis graduate to go to Curtiss' facility at Hammondsport, New York, to learn to fly. Towers wrecked a plane on his first flight. While Towers' nickname was "Hattie" at the Academy the enlisted men he served with called him "Smiling Jack," not because of a sunny disposition, but due to his single-minded focus on the project at hand that made him seem taciturn.[9]

The training procedure on the shores of Lake Keuka in New York for the single-seat aircraft developed by Naval Aviator No. 1, Lt. Theodore Gordon Ellyson, better known as "Spuds," was to have the student taxi across the field with the throttle's foot-pedal blocked so the student couldn't get up enough speed to take to the air.

Ellyson told Towers: "Don't worry. I have a wedge jammed under the pedal and you can push it all the way down without getting enough power to take off."

Towers, 5' 10" and 150 pounds, got into an airplane for the first time, the engine was started and he pushed down hard on the pedal. "The plane bumped cross the field like a scared rabbit. Towers later said, "Before I realized it, I found myself about 30 feet high, then remembered I wasn't supposed to be there. Hastily pushing forward on the control wheel, I headed for the ground at a steep angle and hit with a splintering crash." The plane "cartwheeled into a ball of broken sticks and wire." Towers, who had a broken foot, said, "I was lucky to be only slightly injured."

Later the aviators calculated that Ellyson, who weighed 25 pounds more than Towers, had sufficient bulk to keep the plane on the ground and Towers didn't.

When Curtiss later asked the officers to pose beside the Navy's first plane, the A-1, to commemorate its initial flight test, Ellyson told Towers, "Ditch your crutches in the grass where they won't show. (We) don't want anyone to think they might get hurt in one of Mr. Curtiss's machines."[10]

In late August, with Towers off crutches, Ellyson deemed his student was ready to fly solo, but because the engine sounded suspicious the pair took it up for a pre-flight test.

The engine lost power as the plane lifted into the air. Ellyson flew it straight to try to get enough altitude to turn around. After two miles he started a turn and the engine died. He advised Towers to dive clear as soon as the plane touched down on the water, but the plane flipped onto its back and carried both men down with it. They were in the water for two and a half hours while a motorboat towed the machine ashore. Both were stiff with the cold, but otherwise uninjured.[11]

In September a stern-looking Towers was the cover boy of *Aero*, America's aviation weekly, because he earned his license by learning to fly in 10 weeks.

The Navy then packed up their two planes and moved them to Annapolis where the aviators were greeted with so little enthusiasm that their hangar was downrange from the rifle range and not a safe place to be when errant midshipmen practiced on Wednesdays.

In November, while making a turn in the A-1 at 70 feet, Towers was sent into a steep bank by a gust of wind. It plunged toward the water in a steep spiral. Towers tried to jump clear as it hit, but got caught in the wires and went down with the plane. When it surfaced he struggled out of the wire tangle and strapped himself to the pontoon. He had to wait 45 minutes before being rescued with a puffy black eye, bruised thigh and a wrenched ankle.[12]

But that wasn't the worst of Towers' flying accidents. On June 28, 1913, while flying as an observer aboard a Wright B-2 biplane piloted by Ensign William Devotie "Bill" Billingsley near Annapolis, they were confronted by a rain squall. As Billingsly, a good pilot, flew around the edge of the storm about six or eight miles from home, a strong following wind suddenly lifted the tail. After falling 130 feet the plane bucked and threw Billingsly forward against the controls, disabling them and increasing the throttle, pushing it into a faster, steeper dive. Billingsly plunged to his death, his arms spread and whirling as he fell. Towers also fell out of the plane, but grabbed an upright brace and hung on with both hands. He kicked at the steering gear to get the plane back in operation, but the craft, darting and shifting, dived almost straight down and then turned nearly belly up in a somersault, tearing Towers' right hand off the brace. Towers clung with his left as the twisting, turning plane fell at various angles before crashing into the ocean engine first. Towers blacked out as the lower wing struck the water.

When he came to, he lashed his good arm to the pontoon and 45 minutes later heard a rescue launch approaching in heavy afternoon mist. As the boat moved off in another direction, Towers heard barking and the two sailors in the boat came back. Towers' fox terrier mascot was on board and must have smelled him and set up the alarm that saved him.

Towers refused to be taken ashore and directed the search for Billingsly for 20 minutes before the boat crew ignored his orders and took him to the Naval Academy dock. Towers was bruised all over and had torn a rib from his breastbone on his left side where he had hung on during the fall. A kidney had been ruptured and his liver torn loose, but he walked up the hill to the Naval Hospital. Billingsly was naval aviation's first fatality and his death cast a pall over the program. His body was recovered a week later. Towers was put on rest and recuperation leave for 90 days. One of the first aviators to survive such a crash, he reported his findings to Curtiss, who then developed seat belts much like those in use today, to hold pilots and passengers in the open cockpits when the crafts turned over.[13]

With the weather in the mid–20s on the Atlantic shore, in early 1912 the naval aviators packed up their gear and headed for San Diego, where Curtiss had a training camp on North Island.

Towers took on the daunting task of teaching Lt. Holden Chester Richardson, a native of Shamokin, Pennsylvania, to fly in early 1912 at a Curtiss training camp on the island near San Francisco. It wasn't daunting because Richardson was a slow learner, it was because of his bulk. Richardson tipped the scales around 200 lbs and couldn't fit his shoulders inside the yokes of the pilot's seat. Nicknamed "Big Dick," they could only take him up early in the day when there was enough breeze to lift the craft with Richardson on board. On Richardson's second solo hop, he crashed in the Pacific and wrecked a plane, but was uninjured.[14]

Richardson graduated from the Academy in 1901 and distinguished himself with his engineering ability aboard ships. He was sent to the Massachusetts Institute of Technology to get a master's degree in naval construction. He was then sent to Washington where he developed an experimental glider, pontoons, hulls and the first Navy catapult. He was the fifth naval officer to fly solo and the service's first engineering test pilot.[15]

Patrick Neison Lynch Bellinger, a dashing, handsome, dark-haired man, was Towers' classmate at Annapolis. P. N. L. Bellinger hailed from Cheraw, South Carolina. He entered the Naval Academy in 1903 and graduated in 1907. Like Towers, he took part in the around-the-world cruise of the Great White fleet aboard the USS *Vermont*. He later trained in and commanded a submarine, the C-4, before being assigned to aviation duty at the Naval Academy in November 1912. Towers taught him to fly.[16] Towers confessed that Bellinger was the hardest man, other than Richardson, he ever taught to fly, but said, "Once he learns how to do something, he never forgets." Bellinger developed into an excellent pilot and the pair became good friends.[17]

On June 13, 1913, Bellinger set an altitude record in a Curtiss plane by pushing it up to 6,200 feet. Towers had told him any pilot that got a craft above 2,000 feet would probably get his name in the paper. Bellinger told the story this way: "The higher I went the more I realized tht my direction control was not as good as usual and, before long, the plane seemed to be wallowing in the air. Then with a terrific lurch, the right wing seemed to disappear. As I instinctively pushed down on the control, I thought: Friday the 13th — that was it. The plane headed down and, as I glanced fearfully to the side, I was amazed to see that the wing was still there. I tried all of the controls and everything was fine, but I had the hell scared out of me, and headed for home.... I had raised the seaplane record to 6,200 feet.... In the days of pusher planes and shoulder yoke controls, when successful flying required a real feel of the air, [it] was an awesome altitude.... It wasn't until a couple of weeks later that I discovered that I had stalled."[18]

In 1914 Towers and Bellinger were part of the aviation sections of the U.S. expeditionary force assigned to punish Mexico for arresting two Navy seaman at dockside. Bellinger arrived in Vera Cruz aboard the U.S.S. *Mississippi* and was in charge of the airplane section. Hinton was also at Vera Cruz, aboard the *Seattle*, that carried half a dozen Jenny planes and a catapult. He was assigned to send flag signals from a hotel rooftop to his ship in the port. At night the signal men used lights on the end of poles. "That tended to draw rifle fire," Hinton said.

While flying over enemy lines, Bellinger drew rifle fire and when he landed back at the port his crew found holes in the fuselage and wings. It was the first recorded case of a U.S. aviator taking enemy fire. Another extremely competitive support crew then poked holes in Tower's plane fuselage with a screw driver to try to wrest the claim from Bellinger, but that was discounted by Towers.

On another occasion Bellinger was several miles inland on a reconnaissance flight when a connecting rod broke in the engine with a tremendous noise. Bellinger coaxed the shaking plane toward the beach in a glide and when he got there he and his observer looked down to a squad of Mexican riflemen below. While it appeared for a while they would be captured or shot, the plane drifted out over the ocean on a gust of wind and a picket boat swept in and saved them.[19]

Bellinger became the darling of the press while in Vera Cruz. He gave airplane rides to as many correspondents as he could accommodate, played water polo with famed war correspondent Richard Harding Davis and J. B. Connelly and dined with Jack London and his wife at a local hotel. Davis, Connelly and others wrote flattering articles about Bellinger in *The Saturday Evening Post* and *Colliers*, but that didn't set particularly well with some top Navy brass who had little use for aviation.[20]

In the summer of 1914 Towers was sent back to Curtiss' facility at Hammondsport to serve as a test pilot for the flying boat *America*, which department store scion Rodman Wanamaker proposed as the ship to first cross the Atlantic. Retired British Naval officer John Cyril Porte was scheduled to pilot the craft that had a 72-foot upper wing span, a hull of 35 feet and two 160-horsepower engines.

Towers felt the plane was seriously underpowered and would not get off the water fully loaded, so they developed a plan for three engines that could generate 480 horsepower. The outbreak of war in Europe in July ended the plans and the British government bought the *America* and three sister ships from Curtiss to use for submarine patrol.[21] Towers' dream of conquering the Atlantic was put on hold.

By 1915 Bellinger was back at Pensacola enjoying the good life. For example, when the society leaders of Pensacola held a special charity costume ball, Bellinger agreed to take part as a sultan with a "harem." Lt. Holden Richardson was designated as his eunuch. Bellinger rigged a siphon bottle of scotch and soda to resemble a Turkish pipe and drank freely throughout the evening.

The next morning after breakfast — April 16 — he was summoned to test a new catapult design, the first such test since Lt. Ellyson had done it in 1912. Bellinger threw up and then vomited again when he arrived at the hangar. Richardson spotted the hungover pilot and said he was in no condition to make this test. It was Richardson's job to fire the catapult.

Most of the crews were assembled for a formal picture on the steps in Washington, D.C. Read is at the far left in the front row. Secretary of the Navy Josephus Daniels is to his right, then Lt. Commander John Towers, Assistant Secretary of the Navy Franklin D. Roosevelt and P.N.L. Bellinger. Hinton is in the back row at the far right (U.S. Navy photograph).

Bellinger said he felt fine, got in the plane, and taxied out to the coal barge. The catapult was mounted on and Richardson tripped the mechanism. "There was a glorious feeling. Everything worked beautifully," Bellinger said. "As soon as I was in the air, I was a well man."

A week later on April 23, in a Burgess-Dunne, AH-10, Bellinger set a new altitude record for a seaplane in a flight of one hour and 19 minutes to 10,000 feet.[22]

During this same period Hinton had achieved the rank of quartermaster and had been transferred to the *Washington*, later renamed the *Seattle*. Hinton served on board the *Seattle* when it sailed to Haiti to attempt to help quell a rebellion set off July 27, 1915, by President Vilbrun Guillaume Sam when he executed 167 political prisoners without warning. That provoked angry mobs in Port-au-Prince, which tracked Sam down at the French embassy where he had taken sanctuary. Ignoring French diplomats, the mob tore Sam to pieces and then paraded his parts through the street on poles.

The first contingent of sailors and marines landed the next day, beginning 19 years of U.S. occupation of the second oldest independent nation in the western hemisphere.[23]

It was while serving on board the *Seattle*, a 504-foot-long armored cruiser that carried five or six Curtiss Jenny planes, that Hinton came into contact with two other officers who later played key roles in the first transatlantic flight — Lt. Albert Cushing "Putty" Read and Lt. Kenneth Whiting.

Putty Read was a small, quiet, bird-like man, with the characteristic reticence of his Lyme, New Hampshire, heritage. He got his nickname from his pale complexion, not from the leg wrapping puttees that went with uniforms of that era. He graduated from the Naval Academy in 1907 and spent eight years on surface ships reading everything he could about flying before being sent to Pensacola for flight training in 1915. After he soloed, he was designated Naval Aviator No. 24 and made numerous catapult takeoffs aboard the U.S.S. *Carolina*, the first ship provided with aircraft.

In many ways Read was like Towers, "impressive principally as a man who has something on his mind. He talks almost not at all," one reporter observed. "He answers questions almost monosyllabically. He is decidedly not given to chatter."[24] Another described him as "the Calvin Coolidge of the Navy. He speaks about 130 words a day and weighs 130 lbs. In a clutch Read is a terrier."[25]

Lt. Kenneth Whiting, born in Massachusetts and reared by the waters of Long Island Sound, had a feel for the sea. He was another small, short, serious officer. He weighed under 150 pounds and would try anything once. He could be cagey, sharp and tough.[26]

His mother, a dominating red-haired woman, nixed his desired career in art and won Whiting an appointment to the Naval Academy in 1899. But unlike Read, he wasn't studious. He flunked the entrance exams to the Academy. His mother forced him to study for a year and arranged another appointment. Whiting flunked out. His mother secured a third appointment. Like most early aviators, he accepted danger as a daily occurrence.

While stationed at Manila Bay in the Philippines in 1909, he decided to prove that a sailor in an emergency could escape from a stricken sub in shallow water via the torpedo tubes and survive to summon help. A year earlier another sailor perished when he attempted such an escape using the high air pressure to blast him out. As skipper of the mini-sub *Propose*, Ensign Whiting submerged his craft at the bottom of Manila Bay in 30 feet of water. He ordered his crew to close the inside torpedo door behind him, stripped to his shorts and climbed inside the greasy 18-inch diameter chamber, lying on his back with his arms over his head. He pushed with his heels on the torpedo loading rack and when his knees were inside his men shoved him the rest of the way in and closed the door. The crew then started the outer cap engine and, as the door opened, sea water filled the tube. Before it covered his face, Whiting took a deep breath and the door swung open, dragging his hands and elbows out of the tube. Whiting pushed and pulled himself out of the tube and swam to the surface. It had taken 77 seconds. The submarine blew its ballast tanks and surfaced and found Whiting floating on his back. He wrote simply in the ship's log: "Whiting went out the torpedo tube as an experiment." However, word leaked to the press and various embellished accounts circulated about the feat. The modest Whiting refused to talk to reporters or discuss the affair.

When Whiting asked for a transfer to aviation he was called a fool for entering what was viewed as a dead-end career. Whiting was one of the last aviators taught to fly by the Wright brothers. While flying with Orville near Dayton in 1914 on a training flight, the pair nearly died when one wing fell off their hydroaeroplane and it crashed into the Miami River. Both men swam ashore.[27]

Whiting was put in charge of the Pensacola Naval Air Station in November 1915 and qualified as a naval air pilot the following spring. In March 1917 he joined the *Seattle* as senior naval aviator, charged with installing catapults aboard her and three other ships. He took his aviation texts with him when he went aboard and they were the reason he got to know Walter Hinton.

4

June 1917 to May 8, 1919

"Flying is so many parts skill, so many parts planning, so many parts maintenance, and so many parts luck. The trick is to reduce the luck by increasing the others."
— David L. Baker[1]

Flight Preparations

Engrossed in reading the aviation text book, Walter Hinton didn't see the officer arrive on the bridge of the armored cruiser *Seattle*. A Navy quartermaster, Hinton shouldn't have been reading an aviation text or anything else. He was supposed to be standing watch, but it was a long night shift, the Caribbean weather was warm and tranquil, and the four-stack ship was at anchor in Guantanamo Bay. Actually it wasn't the 29-year-old Hinton's reading material at all. The book, a textbook on naval aeronautics, belonged to the officer who had just come on deck—Lt. Kenneth Whiting, who was in charge of the five seaplanes that were designed to catapult off the deck. These were the naval version of the Curtiss Jennies from World War I rigged with pontoons. The bi-wing planes each accommodated two persons seated in tandem and were powered by 150-horsepower Wright-Hispano engines. Each had a maximum speed of 93 miles per hour and could climb to 4,550 feet in 10 minutes with a range of 268 miles. The crew would launch the planes off the *Seattle* with a catapult.[2]

Hinton's job as quartermaster was to work on the bridge, correcting charts, notices, buoy changes, lighthouse notices and the like, but there had been little of that to do this night, so he started reading one of Whiting's books. He was fascinated with the new field of aviation.

Whiting startled Hinton when he made his sudden midnight appearance, but he surprised him even more when he didn't chew him out for reading on the watch. "Hinton, would you like to get into aviation?" Whiting asked.

Hinton immediately said yes.[3]

Hinton discovered aviation manuals while on night watch aboard the *Seattle* (U.S. Navy Photograph).

"They're going to experiment with some enlisted men as pilots, and if you put in your application, I'll see it through," Whiting said. "I can't promise you you'll get to fly, but I can recommend it."[4] With the U.S. building toward entry in World War I, the Navy knew it was going to need more pilots and there were simply not enough candidates coming from the officer corps to handle the need. That was partially because the "gun officers," as they were called, believed aviation was a dead end for career officers looking for promotion.

Earlier that year Whiting had helped rescue two fellow pilots who were flying radio tests in an N-9 float plane. When the plane stalled at a low altitude and crashed into the harbor, Whiting took the admiral's barge and raced to the rescue. One officer was just dazed by the crash, but the other, Lt. Robert A. Lavender, had both arms broken and was freed from the wreckage just before it sank. Lavender was later the radio operator aboard one of the NC's on the transatlantic mission.[5]

Hinton put in his papers the day after he and Whiting talked and Whiting, who was being transferred to Pensacola, arranged for him to be one of 10 in the first class of enlisted men to take tests to become pilots. Eight were Navy petty officers and two were Marine sergeants. Hinton outscored them all on the tests. On April 6, 1917, he reported to the Naval Air Station at Pensacola, Florida.

Pensacola was an ideal location for naval aviation training, a mostly temperate climate with flat, sandy beaches on the bay, protected by barrier islands, Santa Rosa and Perdido Key, from seasonal foul weather blowing off the Gulf of Mexico.

The Spanish settled there in the 1750s and named the city for the Panzacola Indian tribe that lived in the area. When Hinton reported there, he found a city platted by the British in 1765 that was a world apart from the Midwest where he grew up. Pensacola didn't grow much until after the Civil War when builders looking to exploit the yellow pine forests in the area for lumber export provided railroad links with the North and the West in the 1880s. When Hinton arrived in April 1917, the Louisville and Nashville Railroad Company Marine Terminal on Commendencia Wharf, built in 1892, was still bustling, providing a link between the railroad and ships loading pine boards and fish in refrigerated railroad cars. City Hall, facing Ferdinand Plaza, had a Spanish architectural style that looked exotic to an Ohio native. Downtown streets were brick paved and the ten-story American National Bank building towered over anything from Hinton's hometown.

Pensacola Naval Air Station was opened in 1914 at the site of an abandoned Navy yard, which had been built where a 17th-century Spanish fort had been located.[6] Lt. Commander John Towers was in charge of the group that selected the site. Commander Henry C. Mustin was commanding officer and the station had nine officers, three instructors, 12 mechanics, 11 other enlisted men, and seven seaplanes, housed in portable tent hangars along the water's edge. But by 1917 the Navy was spending as much as $400,000 a year on construction at the facility.

There were so many Navy men pouring into Pensacola that there was a housing shortage and the local newspaper called the community "a barracks for servicemen."[7]

The young women of Pensacola, North Florida, and eastern Alabama were attracted to the men in uniform and vice versa. Only one class from 1914 through 1923 graduated without a Pensacola bride. Hinton was one of those statistics. He was moving up in the Navy. He made warrant officer shortly after his arrival in Florida, then warrant boatswain, then ensign. He no longer had to dream about owning a horse and buggy. He bought a car, a six-cylinder 1914 Chandler, a high-quality, medium-priced vehicle, that had been built in Cleveland, Ohio.

He cut a handsome figure in his uniform and his quiet reticence was taken for strength of character. He met and married his first wife Sally Adline, a New York native, a beautiful, young brunette, who was called Addie. It was a whirlwind romance and the pair went to New Orleans for the ceremony on November 17, 1917.[8]

4. June 1917 to May 8, 1919

The need for pilots dramatically increased the demand for instructors who could teach would-be pilots to fly. Nearly 1,000 pilots completed their training between April 1917 and November 1918. Hinton was a natural at flying and his innate sense of mechanics made him invaluable with the eccentric machines they learned on. After he arrived at Pensacola he wrote a letter to a childhood friend in Van Wert: "Was just wondering if you were drafted and what your opinion of the war might be. I have been flying for three months now and like the work." He wrote on the back of a picture of a Jenny seaplane:

> This is the type of seaplane I fly, 100 horse power motor, 1400 rev[olutions] per minute, 53 ft. wide, 29'10" long, weights 2400 lbs. loaded and will climb at the rate of 2,000 ft every ten minutes. As soon as I finish my test in this I will get a 200 horsepower machine good for a hundred miles per hour. This one flies at 70 miles per hour. May be sent to France any time. I have a Chandler six and nicely located here but will be glad to fly in France.
> As Ever, W. Hinton.[9]

Hinton never got to France. He was promoted to twin-engine flight instructor then chief instructor of the twin-engine division. One of his twin-engine students was an Annapolis graduate, Lt. Commander Richard E. Byrd, a member of an influential Virginia political family. Ironically it was Byrd who had signed the paperwork certifying Hinton as naval aviator No.135. Byrd went on in later years to become famous as an Arctic and Antarctic explorer and adventurer.

Byrd had been retired in March 1916 as a junior lieutenant, forced out of the Navy because of a foot injury that caused him to limp and made it painful to stand for long periods. But when the U.S. declared war on Germany in April 1917, he used his influence to go back on active duty. His first job was mobilizing the Rhode Island state naval militia, which he did energetically while campaigning for something more exciting. Then Byrd was transferred to Washington to a desk assignment handling transfer papers for enlisted men. Appealing personally to Secretary of the Navy Josephus Daniels, he got appointed as secretary to the naval commission of training camp activities. He spent his time signing the paperwork that proclaimed others as qualified pilots. That wasn't what he wanted either, but it gave him the excuse to visit Pensacola to inspect training camp activities and he convinced his old colleagues there to let him train to fly in the fall of 1917.[10]

Byrd's instructor was one of Pensacola's best — Hinton, who made temporary boatswain in November 1917, and in February 1918 he was promoted to ensign. "Byrd was an average student," Hinton, who trained 100 or more pilots at Pensacola, said. "He plunked down in the ocean because he would level off too high on landings in the Gulf. He would do everything, but wreck the plane. But each time he would learn something about it."[11]

Most crashes at Pensacola occurred when the wind died and the surface of the ocean became mirror smooth, according to Hinton. The students couldn't tell where the surface was. "Some would try to land 50 feet in the air and some would fly right into the sea." That would cause the folks on shore to hoist the red flag, indicating a crash, and they would rush a speedboat out at 45 mph to rescue the survivors.[12]

One of the instructors who survived such a crash, according to the *Pensacola News Journal* on January 9, was Lt. P.N.L. Bellinger. The student he was training dropped the craft 50 feet into shallow water. Bellinger was just bruised, but the student's leg was broken. The Wright planes with pusher engines were killing aviators and finally the pilots simply refused to fly them.

The idea of a transatlantic flight in a multi-engine craft came up after Byrd soloed. One day Byrd asked his instructor, "Hinton, would you like to fly across the Atlantic?" Hinton asked, "In what?"[13]

"The Navy is building four giant seaplanes as long-range submarine hunters," Byrd said. "And they're too big to be transported on ships—they have to be flown across. Suppose I was lucky enough to be a navigator and you the pilot? We might as well see what we can do about getting in on it."[14] Byrd and Hinton made elaborate plans and schemed to be part of the crew.[15]

Byrd and Hinton's first plans were to fly an H-16 flying boat with a three-man crew powered by two 400-horsepower engines and carrying enough five-gallon cans of gasoline to see them across. They would require two station ships with weather balloons aloft to use as markers and a saw to cut off the wings if the flying boat went down at sea. It was similar in many respects to a 1914 proposed aerial crossing by Rodman Wanamaker that Towers and a British officer John Cyril Porte would have flown.

"Nothing will be left undone and I will place every effort, heart and soul on this, in hopes that we may be fortunate enough to make the trip," Byrd wrote in his proposal to the Navy.[16] There is no record of any reply from naval authorities.

Byrd loved the idea of being the first to fly the Atlantic and when the Virginian was offered the chance to command the Naval Air Station at Halifax, Nova Scotia, and supervise coastal patrols for German submarines, he grabbed it. And he used his influence to get Hinton assigned first to Washington, D.C., for duty in the office of naval operations and then to Halifax on August 30, 1918, as his operations officer at the Canadian post. There they continued to plot ways to be on a transatlantic mission. Byrd engineered Hinton's promotion to lieutenant on September 12, 1918. While Hinton, like every other pilot, had had his share of equipment failures at Pensacola, Hinton had developed a reputation as the man who had logged hundreds of hours without a serious mishap.

4. June 1917 to May 8, 1919   35

That fall in Halifax, Hinton experienced a life-threatening crisis in the air. He was patrolling off Halifax just before dusk and a small, wooden propeller blade that made his gas feed to the engine froze and broke. The pieces flew back into his pusher-type propeller and the prop came apart in mid-air, sending fragments down through the bottom of the plane. Hinton thought, "My God, here we are alone miles at sea." He, his mechanic, and his machine gunner prepared to ditch in the cold, gray North Atlantic. With one propeller broken, the plane was almost impossible to steer as it kept wanting to nose up, Hinton said. He fought the nose down to keep the plane level as it landed in the water.

Luckily for the crew, a nearby destroyer had seen the plane descending. It steamed up as they were landing, threw them a line, and towed them slowly back to Halifax. They didn't arrive at the naval base until after nightfall and when the destroyer released the line as they approached the beach, the plane sank and the three aviators had to swim the last 30 yards in the cold bay waters.[17]

A few weeks later while on a training flight at 2,000 feet with two students and a mechanic on board a twin-engine craft, another propeller "went to pieces in the air." A broken crankshaft was the cause. A fire started in that engine and Hinton cut off the fuel and sideslipped the plane to a landing so the flames would carry away from the crew. He taxied the flying boat back to base on the remaining engine. Was it hard to land with one engine out? "No, it wasn't difficult to land. You just glide down. I frequently cut off one engine in a training flight just to see the students' reaction."[18]

One day while patrolling 50 miles off Halifax over rough seas, Hinton's crew spotted a ship which didn't show its colors after being signaled. So Hinton decided to go down and take at look at the name on the stern to see if it was German. When he turned the plane over, the check ball in the wing tank blocked the air vent and became stuck, so when he leveled off the engine quit. He quickly lost air speed and headed down into angry seas. As the plane struck the water, it jarred the ball loose and the engines started again. Knowing the plane would never be able to survive in the rough water, Hinton gunned the engines. As the engines revved the left wing dipped and the wing float was torn free, spinning the plane in a 180-degree turn so it was headed in the opposite direction. Hinton kept accelerating and got clear of the water, but now he was flying with one heavy wing so he sent the mechanic out on the starboard wing. The mechanic crawled out and fastened himself to a strut. His weight balanced the plane. Hinton leveled off and they limped back to Halifax.[19]

By the summer of 1917 German U-boats, operating in wolf packs, had been sinking ships carrying a million tons of war supplies a month. Rear

Admiral David W. Taylor, chief of the Bureau of Construction and Repair, concluded that the Allies needed planes that could stay aloft for considerable lengths of time, harassing German submarines and driving them away from their easy prey.

Admiral Taylor asked his staff to produce aircraft that at that moment didn't exist — planes that could stay up for 16 hours and could span the Atlantic and thus avoid the problem of storing the huge craft on ships. The longest flight to that date had been about 1,200 miles near an airport, not over an open ocean. Lt. Commander Jerome C. Hunsaker and Lt. Commander George Westervelt turned to Glenn Curtiss, of Hammondsport, New York, for help. Curtiss had designed the *America* for Wanamaker in 1914 to span the Atlantic and that flying boat had been sold to the British and used in the war, to good effect.[20]

In July 1918 *The London Daily Mail* publisher, apparently sensing the end of the war would come in a matter of months and realizing there was going to be an incredible surplus of planes on the market when hostilities ceased, renewed a $50,000 prize for the first plane to span the Atlantic. It drew immediate interest and helped focus the Atlantic crossing as "the most talked-about and most glamorous goal of postwar aviation."[21]

Meanwhile U.S. Navy planners agreed at a September meeting that the minimum acceptable standard for a plane's capabilities would be a flight from Newfoundland to the Azores and then to Portugal. Other routes were considered and rejected as plans moved forward included Newfoundland to Greenland, Iceland and then England. The weather on those routes was deemed too unsettled and there was a lack of suitable ports; South America to Africa was rejected because of inaccessibility of the point of departure; and Newfoundland to Ireland was dropped because it was not practical to have an overseas flight of 1,675 nautical miles. The Navy kept under wraps the fact that the only practical route for the NCs was from Newfoundland to the Azores and then to Portugal until a week before the planned take off. Towers worried in an April telephone conversation with Capt. E. E. Irwin that the Navy would be criticized if they waited much longer to clear up the route question.[22]

Holden Chester Richardson, 41, the principal hull designer, by this date weighed 245 lbs. The 1901 Annapolis graduate was generously described as medium height and portly. He later earned a master's degree from the Massachusetts Institute of Technology. He got his first ride in a plane in 1911. He completed his aviator's training while on detached duty at the Naval Aeronautical Station, Pensacola, and was designated Naval Aviator #13 on April 12, 1915. Richardson helped design improved pontoons for Naval aircraft and was detached from his work at Pensacola to supervise the construction and inspection of the NC flying boats and then test fly them at Rockaway. His hull design for the NCs proved controversial.[23] Critics thought the hull should be longer in proportion to the wing span. Cyril Porte, who had been slated to fly the *America* with Towers in 1914, reportedly said: "It is very interesting," and laughed all the way back to London.[24]

Even Glenn Curtiss didn't like the hull and he tried to add side fins to the design to stabilize it without consulting Richardson. Richardson nixed the side fins and said they would keep the wing tips out of the water with pontoons. Towers, in a typical understatement, characterized the plane as odd.[25] With all the design changes on the planes as construction took place, the Navy later calculated that each cost about $150,000.

The key to a plane's performance is disposable lift — how much weight can a plane get into the air and then how far can it fly.[26] The teams of engineers and designers went to work. By July 1918 the first machine, the NC-1, took shape, but it failed to impress a British technical expert who was visiting the U.S. as part of an inspection group. "The hull of this machine was examined, and it is the design of a naval constructor. The machine is impossible, and is not likely to be of any use whatever."[27] The hulls of the four NCs were built at three different sites — two of them boatyards, one in Rhode Island and the other in Boston. Other parts were made a variety of other sites.

It wasn't the first time the British were wrong in writing off American aviation designs. By the end of September 1918 the components of the NC-1 with a three-engine configuration were shipped to Rockaway Naval Air Station for assembly and a week later the giant craft was assembled.

Rockaway Naval Air Station was built on 94 acres of land loaned by New York City to the federal government during the early days of U.S. involvement in World War I. It originally had a blimp hangar, another for servicing HS-2 flying boats and a 165-by-110 foot hangar built to house two of the NCs.[28] Special trucks were built to move the giant machines on their cradles from the hangars to the ramps leading to Jamaica Bay.

The NC-1 had its first test on October 4, 1918, with Richardson at the controls. While its first flight was not notable — she was aloft for 30 seconds — it drew a cheer from among the Navy and Curtiss witnesses on the shoreline. Five more short tests were flown that day.

By October the end of the war was in sight and, on October 31, Lt. Commander John Henry Towers, who had hoped to take part in the Wanamaker flight in 1914, renewed his quest to first across the Atlantic. In a memo to the Chief of Naval Operations, he asked for the assignment and said, "I believe the U.S. Navy should make a determined effort to make the flight because: the first airplane of any type was built in America, the first successful seaplane was built in America and the U.S. Navy was the first branch of any government to use a seaplane successfully.

"I understand a citizen of a European country is having a plane constructed in the U.S. and it appears he has a possibility of success.

"The prestige gained in aviation by the United States in the early stages of aviation, and now being regained, should be held, and the first flight across the Atlantic will go down as an epoch making event."[29]

The citizen of a European country that Towers referred to was a Swedish pilot named Hugo Sundstedt, who had made tentative plans for a transatlantic flight in 1916 before the U.S. entered World War I. His plans were shelved with the U.S. entry into World War I, but had been revived after the armistice. He proposed to fly an enclosed cabin, twin 220-horsepower Liberty engine plane equipped with 32-foot-long pontoons from Newark, New Jersey, to St. John's, Newfoundland, before hopping off for Ireland, utilizing the jet stream to speed his flight. The plane would carry a crew of four—Sundstedt, co-pilot U.S. Army Lt. Paul Micelli, and two mechanics.

Towers recommended a spring 1919 start in his memo and suggested he be given the command because of his 1914 duty with the *America*, which he was on until he was ordered abroad in August 1914 "and because I am the senior aviator, in point of aviation service, on aviation duty."[30] The mission was approved and Towers was given the assignment.

Towers, who had been in the forefront of naval aviation from the beginning, had friends in high places—notably the Assistant Secretary of the Navy, Franklin D. Roosevelt. Roosevelt, a distant cousin of Theodore Roosevelt, had grown up hearing the stories of TR's exploits. FDR saw the adventure of sponsoring the first aerial crossing of the Atlantic as a way for the Navy to make a big splash, akin to what Dewey accomplished in Manila Bay. It would put U.S. naval aviation on the map and in the history books.

At 10:50 AM on November 7, with a crew of seven, Richardson and Dick McCulloch, a naval Reserve pilot handpicked by Towers for the mission, flew the One to the Washington Navy Yard for review by top brass. But it was not without mishap. The trip to Washington and Hampton Roads, Virginia, took two days. The One lost its center engine when its radiator started leaking and the mechanics were unable to repair it in flight. Rather than try to fly overland across the Maryland Peninsula on two engines, Richardson landed the One in ten-foot Atlantic ocean swells near Barnegat Inlet in New Jersey. The radiator was repaired and more time was lost as they didn't have a bucket on board to refill the radiator with sea water. Meanwhile several crew members got seasick from the rolling and pitching. An hour later, after a minute of taxiing in the swells, the One took to the air and arrived at Anacostia Naval Station five hours later.[31]

On Monday, November 11, Germany accepted an armistice ending the war. There would be no need for the giant NC bombers in Europe. But the proposed flight took on even greater importance as a demonstration of the importance of naval air power to help preserve the service's budget for aviation.

On November 14 the British Royal Aero Club announced they were lifting the wartime ban on the race to span the Atlantic. By spring 1919 there were 11 potential British entries and the 10,000 pounds offered by the *Daily Mail* had been increased by 3,000 pounds by the Ardath Tobacco Co. and a business man.[32] Only four ever reached Newfoundland, the closest place on the North American continent to Europe, and a fifth by the Short Aviation Company, which planned to fly west to east against the prevailing winds. The rules of the *Daily Mail* contest that the flight be non-stop excluded the Navy mission, but more important than the money was the projected prestige of being first.

In late November, having heard that the Brits had set a record for the total number of passengers aboard a Handley Page bomber flight with 41 men, the Navy brass decided to better that mark and loaded 50 persons on board the NC-1 for a short flight. When they returned to shore they counted heads and discovered they had 51. Harry D. Moulton, machinists mate, 2nd class, the first aerial stowaway, disappointed that he hadn't been chosen for the flight, secreted himself among the gas tanks on board over an hour early in order to take part.[33]

In December 1918, on Byrd's recommendation, Hinton, with his renowned skill on multi-engine craft, was transferred to Rockaway Naval Air Station on Jamaica Bay on Long Island to help with the testing of the NC's. He and Sally moved into a house on Long Island a few miles from the base.

At the same time, Byrd was still trying to figure out any way he could to wangle an assignment as part of the mission and he pulled whatever strings he could. He offered the navigation instruments he had developed and himself to Washington Navy officials. They accepted the instruments and turned down Byrd, but he was assigned to work with the support staff.

It was not clear how the pilots and crews were selected. But there was definitely Navy politics involved. Some of Towers' choices were selected for the mission; others were turned down. Byrd apparently had offended some of the old-time Navy brass and was not considered. Eventually the naval powers advised everyone who had applied that only sailors who had remained stateside during World War I would be appointed to the crews. This supposedly eliminated Byrd since he had served in Halifax, but of course that didn't address why Hinton and other crew members had been chosen since some served in Europe and Hinton had also served in Nova Scotia.

Rockaway Naval Air Station was swarming with mechanics, pilots, support staff and, per Jack Towers' usual custom, at least one mascot dog, a Jack Russell terrier, when Hinton arrived there in January 1919. Buildings were still being completed, supplies were being delivered and modifications continued daily on the seaplanes.

Meanwhile Sundstedt was having his own problems getting the Sunrise ready for the transatlantic mission. He couldn't find a hangar for his plane and appeals by influential businessmen to Navy brass to use an empty hangar on Long Island were deliberately ignored. On the day the Sunrise was finally launched in Bayonne, New Jersey, differing engine speeds caused her to taxi at a diagonal from shore and she crashed into a dock, nicking a plane wing. After repairs on her first trial flight from Newark Bay, she drifted north as the huge nine-foot propellers refused to turn. She drifted most of the afternoon as the mechanics tinkered with repairs. The Sunrise was finally towed back and the frozen crew went to the Puvonia Yacht Club where they were staying to warm up.[34] In March Sundstedt agreeably let a Russian amateur pilot take the controls of the Sunrise and he proceeded to wreck the craft beyond repair. Towers breathed a sign of relief.

But Towers was having his own problems at Rockaway. In late March, the first of a series of disasters occurred. Since the hangar would only hold two of the giant planes, the NC-1 ws anchored in the bay and on March 27 a gale hit; the One dragged her anchor and a wing struck the ramp of the marine railway, dropping the port wing into the sea where it was pounded to pieces by the surf.[35]

With Navy Secretary Daniels in Europe at the peace talks with President Wilson, Roosevelt decided to further put his stamp on the mission in April by going to Rockaway for a flight. In spite of poor flying weather Richardson and McCulloch took FDR up for a nine-minute flight in the Two. The pilots had difficulty controlling the plane in the turbulent air, but Roosevelt, who was seated directly behind the pilots, seemed unaware of the control difficulties as it bounced out to the Narrows, up New York Harbor, across Brooklyn, and back to the base.[36]

On April 18 a second competitor for the transatlantic prize dropped quite literally out of the race. British Major J.C. P. Wood and his navigator, Captain C.C. Wylie, left the Thames River to ferry their modified Nort Shirl torpedo biplane to the jumping-off place in Curragh, Ireland. They planned to fly against the prevailing westerly winds from east to west. They crossed England, but, 22 miles out of Holyhead, Wales, their engine stalled and they had to ditch at sea. When the plane was finally towed almost a day later into Holyhead, it was found to be damaged enough to require a major overhaul. They were out.

The NC-3, scheduled to be Commander Towers' flagship, didn't take to the air until April 23, just days before the scheduled May 1 departure date for Trepassey, Newfoundland, that upper-level Navy officials had decreed and the

Four was not even fully assembled. That same day mechanics stripped the wings off the Two, which was to have been Lt. Marc Mitcher's to command, and transferred them to the storm-damaged One.

Two top British test pilots — Harry Hawker and Frederick P. Raynham — were already in Newfoundland with their airplanes, ready to fly as soon as the weather cleared and a third, a Handley Page bomber to be flown by another top pilot and war veteran, John Alcock, was aboard the freighter *Digby*, at sea on its way to Newfoundland. At least three other entries were getting their craft ready in England for shipment across the Atlantic.

The 12-hour days the workers were putting in became 24-hour days as they labored around the clock with watchful eyes on the news from the British aviators in Newfoundland where a dozen reporters had joined the British race contestants in St. John's, the capital city.[37] They were working with the knowledge that the 68 ships that would be involved in supporting the flight and serving as a chain of guides across the Atlantic would leave port by April 30 for assignments from Cape Cod to Lisbon and could not be held on station indefinitely because they would run short of fuel.

The Four, finally assembled, made her first flight on April 30.

With storms reported along the eastern seaboard on May 1, a Saturday morning, the three NCs were positioned on the apron by the bay for commissioning even though the One with its salvaged wings from the Two was still not flyable. The mission was organized like a surface ship division with an overall commander — Towers — and captains of each airship — lt. commanders Bellinger and Read. It was to be the only time in naval history that aircraft were treated the same as ships. It was only then that each crew member learned which plane he was to fly on.

Towers would put his flag on the Three and command it. Richardson and McCulloch would be the pilots. Lt. Commander Robert A. Lavender, who had handled developing the radios for the division, would be radio officer. Lt. Braxton Rhodes, the biggest of the group, would be the engineer and Chief Boatswain Lloyd R. Moore would be a second engineer. Lt. Byrd, who still harbored hopes he would get to take part in the adventure, would fly with the Three as far as Trepassey Bay, working with the navigational instruments he had developed.

Aboard the One, Bellinger would command and navigate. Mitscher, who had sacrificed command of the Two to provide wings for the craft, would be the pilot and Lt. Louis T. Barrin would be the co-pilot. The radio officer would be Lt. Harry Sadenwater, Chief Machinist's Mate Rasmus Christensen and Chief Machinist's Mate C. I. Kessler would serve as engineers.

Lt. Commander Read, one of the best navigators in the Navy, would command the Four. The Coast Guard's first pilot, Lt. Elmer Stone, and Lt.

Walter Hinton would serve as pilots. Herbert C. Rodd would be radio operator and Lt. James L. Breese, a childhood friend of FDR's who had worked with development of the Liberty engines, and Chief Machinist's Mate Edward H. "Harry" Howard would serve as engineers.

When the pilots of the Four got aboard, Stone, the senior officer in terms of rank, climbed into the right-hand seat, normally reserved for the co-pilot. "Elmer, you're in the wrong seat," Hinton said. "No, I'm not," Stone said. "You have a lot more experience on this craft than I do so you'll be the chief pilot." Both men looked toward Read in the forward navigator's cockpit, who had heard the conversation. Read nodded his approval of what Stone said. And that's the way it was.[38]

The crews were drawn up in formation in front of their planes, a bugler played "To the Colors," U.S. flags were raised on stern tail assem-

Albert Cushing Read (International Film Service).

blies, and commissioning pennants put up on wing struts, the Naval Jack — blue with a white diamond center design with a fouled anchor — at the bows while Towers read his orders placing him in command of Seaplane Division One. Navy movie cameramen recorded the ceremony for history, while artists sketched the scene as New York newspaper reporters took notes and got quotes. They had found Towers difficult to pry news material from and Read also reticent, so they gravitated to Bellinger and Richardson, who were more likely to say something quotable.

After the ceremony everyone went back to work bolstered by additional Curtiss employees from their Garden City, New York, plant. Shortly after midnight on Sunday, when most of the Curtiss employees had gone home, a spark from an electric pump moving fuel from a barrel to an NC tank started a fire. Christian spotted it first and he and others sprayed chemicals on the drum, but the fueling hose came loose from the plane tank and spewed gas on the hangar floor. It exploded "with a great whoosh," sending flames under the Four's tail and the starboard wing of the One. Before the fire was put out the

Four's lower horizontal stabilizer and elevator was damaged and the One's starboard wing fabric had burned away, leaving charred spars and ribs. The wing was beyond repair.

The crews went back to work sandpapering, replacing wing fabric, varnishing and doping the Four. The Three was in worse shape, but Bellinger and his crew were convinced she could be salvaged and Monday morning they started the task of taking the starboard wings from the cannibalized Two to replace the damaged wing of the One.

That same day two aviators stunting in an HS-1 over the air base stalled and came out of a dive too late to avoid hitting the 75-foot-tall blimp hydrogen gas storage tank. Both were killed as the plane burned, but the fire didn't ignite the volatile gas inside. And in another incident, a pair of sailors headed to New York City from the base were injured in an truck accident.

Meanwhile, the weather on the eastern seaboard continued to be foul with limited visibility. So Towers' plan to leave on Tuesday with the Three and Four and let the One catch up when it was repaired was aborted. Towers did get a telegram from Roosevelt prematurely congratulating him on getting the planes repaired and ending with, "I wish I were with you."[39]

On Wednesday the bad weather continued, but there were predictions the front would move out Thursday. Meanwhile, mishaps continued to occur as mechanics, Curtiss workers and men not familiar with the craft swarmed over them.

The red button on the pilots' dashboard of the Four drew a curious finger from a sailor and two flares on the bow designed to light night landings shot to the floor and skidded into cans of paint, starting another fire which was put out quickly.

That same afternoon Chief Mechanic Howard crawled through the small tunnel on the fuselage of the Four designed to protect a person from the after propeller of the pusher engine and stood up without thinking where he was. The oak blade neatly chopped off his left hand at the wrist. Howard held the bleeding stump, slid down the fuselage and walked to a car and Bellinger raced him to the base hospital. Howard's transatlantic flight was over. Towers replaced him with Pennsylvania Dutchman Eugene Saylor Rhoads despite Howard's pleas to be included.

On Thursday, May 8, the flight crews got up and into their one-piece leather flying suits at 4 AM. Hinton and Stone carefully placed extra handkerchiefs in their outside pockets to put over their ears when they finally got on board. While last-minute checks were made on the NCs, the C-4, a blimp, left Rockaway at 45 miles per hour for a flight to New Haven, Connecticut, to drop leaflets promoting the purchase of Liberty Bonds for the "Victory Loan" campaign. The weather reports from the *Baltimore* in Halifax were discouraging until 9:20 AM when clearing reports started coming in from along the New England coast. At 9:20 AM. Towers gave the order — take off at 10 AM.

About 500 persons had gathered to witness the historic leave. Starter switches to the 12 engines were flicked on as engineers in the aft compartments checked their gauges for water and oil temperature and pressure. Pilots turned on 8-volt ignition master switches and the 12-volt switches to start each motor. After the engines roared to life in a deafening crescendo, they were set at idle as the giant planes rested on their cradles at the top of marine railway tracks running into Jamaica Bay.

On hand to watch were Captain Noble Irwin, director of naval aviation, and Commander George C. Westervelt of the Construction Corps, who had been a key developer of the NCs and who also, as a pilot, hoped to be on the mission. But Westervelt had recommended his colleague Richardson get the honor of flying on the mission and when he was offered a chance like Byrd to fly as far as Trepassey, he demurred and asked them to give the seat to Ensign C. J. McCarthy, who worked on the engine configurations for the craft.

Before taking off the commanders of the three planes issued prepared statements to the press. Towers spoke first:

> I have been in the flying game too long to venture a very strong prediction regarding the result of even short flights. However, we are ready, and if the power plants hold out, I know of nothing which will prevent us from reaching the other side. I have been asked many times if we are going into this venture from patriotic, scientific, or sporting standpoint. There is little patriotism connected with the lucky chance to be a member of the overseas crew. Everyone in the air service of the Navy is anxious to go, for it will be good sport, though in no way a sporting venture. It is a scientific experiment, and if we get no further than Rockaway Point, the undertaking will be worthwhile for the reason that we have made big strides in the heavier-than-air machines.
>
> The Navy Department and the entire field have worked untiringly and have left nothing undone to equip the planes for the long flights. We are going to do our best. Guesses aren't worth much, but if you want mine, here it is: we'll get there.

Lt. Commander Albert Cushing Read, the small, fox-faced son of a New England Baptist minister, spoke next:

> Whether we get there or not, we are going to get some fun out of it, especially the commanding officers, who are also the navigators. The trip will be a most unusual and interesting problem in navigation. If any of the machines do not arrive on the other side it will be on account of some entirely unpreventable failure in material or the unforeseen development of unfavorable weather conditions, matters which may happen regardless of the amount of care devoted to preparations. We leave with the assurance that all hands are pulling for us. America is

with us and I believe all countries want to see this experiment a success. Good wishes help.

Bellinger, who had not donned his bulky flying suit over his handsome forest-green uniform with its gold wings above the breast, but had left the clumsy affair aboard the One, remained in character: "With the help of God, and in spite of the devil — we'll get there."

Irwin presented each of the flyers with four-leaf clovers. Hinton put his in his uniform pocket under the flying suit. Towers gave the order to mount up at 9:50 AM "Board your craft."[40] The crews headed for their planes. Breese, having a last-minute thought about the long trip ahead, sent an ensign to get some weather balloons. The only toilet facility on board was the seat the commander/navigator would be sitting on and paper bags.[41]

The Three, pushed by a tiny tractor built specially for the job that looked like a modern-day forklift, slid down the runway onto the calm waters of Jamaica Bay. The One and Four followed and Bellinger, arms over his head, pantomimed two hands shaking to the crowd and yelled, "Sure," when someone hollered: "Do you think you'll make it?" Both Breese and Rhoads felt the effects of hangovers earned celebrating the night before. Breese's headache was multiplied by the roaring engines. Rhoads said he felt fine.[42]

In V formation with the Three in the lead, the bi-winged trio taxied

The NC-4 in mid-air. Note the head of Lt. Commander Albert Cushing Read in the front navigator's cockpit (U.S. Navy photograph).

slowly out into the bay, the engines ticking noisily at over 1,300 revolutions per minute (rpm). Towers stood up in his manhole-shaped cockpit. He had pinned a red, white and blue ribbon to his flying suit that 40 Brooklyn school girls sent him for good luck. The colors match the tail fins of the craft, which are still flying the U.S. flag.

Towers faced the trailing flying boats and waved his hand forward at 9:59 AM like a troop commander sending his men over the top into battle. The rear cockpit hatches slid shut to protect the men and radio equipment from water and spray. Hinton and Stone each pulled open two throttles. All throttles now open, the rpms leapt to 2,800. The three giant craft charged across the bay, trying to reach planing speed of 50 miles per hour (planing speed is the speed at which a craft's hull rises to the surface and the water pressure pushing upwards holds it on top of the water). Horns honked, spectators cheered, and the sirens and whistles of the air station blasted the air. But no one on board could hear them over the engine thunder. The hulls of all the flying boats disappeared beneath the spray as gravity at first overpowered speed and lift. It looked like three sets of giant wings moving over the water. Read, like Bellinger and Towers, crouched with his back to the water breaking over the bow. A sheet of spray flew back half blinding Hinton and Stone hunched down on their wooden seats behind glass windshields smaller than a legal notepad that barely protected the dashboard compasses. Cold water trickled down the inside of their flying suits, dampening the fleece lining and the several layers of clothes they wore underneath. Water beaten to fine mist by the huge Olmstead propellers trailed hundreds of feet behind.

Inside, the planes were divided into compartments by five watertight bulkheads. The commanders — Towers, Bellinger and Read — sat in pits in the bows on cushioned stools. Each had a small chart table, a new instrument called a bubble sextant, a drift indicator based on a design by an Italian airship captain, a compass, notepads and rulers. A narrow tunnel about two feet wide and four feet high ran the length of the starboard side of the craft. Immediately behind the commander/navigator was a place where a pilot or crewman could stretch out and even nap. Byrd was crowded into this space with Towers, and McCarthy took this space with Bellinger. The Four didn't carry an additional man.

This area was open to the underside of the pilots' dashboards and the controls. Each pilot sat on a cushion on a slatted wooden seat with a steering wheel much like those in trucks of that era. The controls were linked so two pilots could wrestle with them together in bad air. Behind them were nine 200-gallon aluminum barrels of aviation gas. A small propeller pumped gas from the drums to a gravity tank on the upper wing, which fed fuel to all the engines. Aft of the drums, which looked like steel barrels but were considerably lighter, was the crowded rear cockpit containing the engineer, the mechanic and his tools, and the radioman and his equipment. A speaking tube allowed the crew to communicate on the ground, but it didn't work well in flight because of engine noise. Similarly, a telephone headset rig worked primarily when the engines were off. The radiomen had switches which were supposed to allow them to talk to the other planes or stations within 20 miles. A bull's-eye symbolizing an international force was painted on the upper wings, which were made of cotton layered with several coats of dope, giving the wings a yellowish cast.

Hinton got the Four up on plane first. She was faster and lighter than the older crafts. He waited for Richardson to take the Three up, as the lead ship. At last all three of the 25,000-pound craft were up. Two minutes later, the flagship Three — per Navy protocol — lifted off. Hinton took the Four up at 10:04 and five minutes later the One lumbered clumsily into the air last. In wobbly formation, like giant pelicans patrolling for food, the planes climbed west toward the Statue of Liberty and New York City, slowly and ponderously gaining several hundred feet of altitude. The wind was from the north-northwest at about eight miles an hour. After two minutes they were at 1,000 feet. In the aft cockpit of the Four, Breese and Rhoads slid open the hatch and stuck their heads out to watch the sights below while Rodd reeled out his radio's 250-foot-long trailing antenna, a lead fish pulling it down and away from fouling the tail. Following Towers' lead, the flying boats made a wide turn to the south and formed a loose V.[43]

Stone took the heavy controls that were linked in tandem while Hinton wiped off his goggles then Stone then cleared his. Read, Bellinger and Towers waved white handkerchiefs at the crowd below as the seaplanes headed east back over the air station, Rockaway Beach and Jacob Riis Park. The three continued climbing to about 2,000 feet and leveled off along the south shore of Long Island as they headed toward Montauk. At Montauk the sun broke out and from his post in the bow Read watched the One and the Three with their doped yellow wings shining against the blue water of the Atlantic. Towers ordered his pilots, Holden "Big Dick" Richardson and Dick McCulloch, to turn north as they reached the tip of Long Island and pointed toward Block Island ahead on the horizon. They passed over the island at 12:15 and headed for Monomoy Point at the tip of Cape Cod. A few minutes later Breese crawled forward through the tiny passageway along the starboard side of the flying boat and handed Read a message from the Chatham Naval Air Station.

It read: "DELIGHTED WITH SUCESSFUL START, GOOD LUCK ALL THE WAY. ROOSEVELT." All three commanders logged the message.

Read had already taken quick readings with Byrd's instruments and got out an ordinary ledger book, alphabetized down one edge. On page A on

May 1 he had written: "Note Book — TransAtlantic Flight, May, 1919 — A.C. Read, USN — Commanding Officer and Navigator of NC-4." Page B listed the names of the crew. From May 3 to May 7 he had short comments on weather delays and accidents and on other pages he listed the matters he would record in flight — fuel and water supply, drift, visibility, speed, altitude, and engine operation. Engine vibration made Read's hand shake, but he recordedthe takeoff according to Greenwich Mean Time: "Took off at 2:02, Left Rock. 2:09, Clearing gradually at Montauk Pt. Sun came out."

Updrafts from Block Island and a northwest wind created turbulence and bumpy air, and Read crawled back to tell Rhoads, who looked slightly air sick, that the intercom wasn't working and he couldn't contact the pilots six feet behind his station. Rhoads crawled off to check the system. Read ordered Rodd to contact Towers and ask if the Four could increase speed as it was having trouble staying in formation in the bumpy air. Towers gave both the One and the Four the okay to proceed at their own speed but ordered them to remain within radio range. Read crawled forward and stuck his head up between Hinton's knees, startling the pilot. He ordered Hinton to take the Four down to 1500 feet, look for smoother air and increase the speed.[44]

When Bellinger, lagging behind on the right flank, saw the Four surge ahead, he ordered his pilots, Marc Mitscher and Lou Barrin, to speed up and the One took the lead. The Four was on the left of the Three about 400 yards out as the commanders tried to stabilize their V formation over Vineyard Haven Sound. As they flew over Martha's Vineyard, Read waved his arm in a circling motion to Hinton. Both pilots nodded. The lighter and faster Four had gotten ahead. Stone swung it in a wide western circle and came up on the Three's port side and slightly behind it. The planes started acting more as a unit and maintained a fairly accurate formation. From the air it looked like they were moving in slow motion over the water and land below, although they were actually going about 75 miles per hour. At 2,000 feet the craft had not slipped the bonds of earth. Trees, landmarks, boats and waves breaking on shore were easily visible. Two F-5L twin-engine flying boats, which had greeted the mission at Chatham, dipped their wings in a goodbye salute and turned back to base as the trio pointed north from Monomoy Point at 1:20 PM for the overseas jump to Halifax.

Hinton and Stone must have had a feeling akin to Louis Blériot's in July 1909 when the French aviator discovered himself out of sight of land for the first time in aviation history as he flew his monoplane across the English Channel. "Below me is the sea, the surface disturbed by the wind, which is now freshening. The motion of the waves beneath me is not pleasant. I drive on. 10 minutes have gone. I have passed the destroyer, and I turn my head to see whether I am proceeding in the right direction. I am amazed. There is nothing to be seen, neither the torpedo destroyer, nor France, nor England. I am alone, I can see nothing at all — rien du tout! For 10 minutes I am lost. It is a strange position to be alone, unguided, without compass, in the air over the middle of the Channel."[45]

Until Blériot's flight, pilots had guided themselves by landmarks on the ground or followed the iron compass — the railroad — from place to place. But suddenly, like Blériot, the Four was out over the ocean. Cape Cod was lost in the haze behind. They had to rely on the compass and the station ships ahead as they thundered out over the Atlantic. To the west, out of sight, were the coast of Maine and Casco and Penobscot bays, safe harbors. But ahead there were only the other planes and haze. And below? Below there was the great, gray depths of the Atlantic with its endless waves and white caps rolling toward an unseen shore. With all the radio and ship support they were alone. They had to keep the Four level and fly on, trusting the judgment of Commander Read in the bow.

Their next landfall was Cape Sable on the southern shore of Nova Scotia, 250 miles across open ocean, about three hours mostly over trackless water with only two destroyers to provide waypoints. There was still a slight haze and a light wind on the pilots' faces as they roared on. Read noticed that the Four was on a diverging course from the other planes and went back and tugged on Hinton's leg. Hinton explained he was trying to avoid bumpy air. Read replied that they had to stay on course. He later noted in his log: "Found pilot was steering a course of his own. I heaved to port to gain distance to north and pass near Elizabeth Island."[46]

This was a shakedown part of the mission for the Four because it had only been tested in the air for five hours before the launch. Every hour, Rhoads and Breese checked and logged the readings on their gauges. The Four cruised at about 1,500 rpm with 28 pounds of oil pressure and water at 120 degrees. There were separate gauges for each of the four engines in the aft compartment as well as on the pilot's dashboard. Much could go wrong. And at 1:50 PM it did. Rhoads noticed the rear pusher engine losing oil pressure. It was down to 10 pounds. He reported this to Breese. They shut down the engine and Breese crawled forward to notify Read. Read was signaling to Hinton and Stone to speed up, waving his arms with a forward motion, and was about to crawl back to speak to them about lagging when Breese tugged his pants leg.

The pusher engine was out, Breese explained. The oil pressure had been dropping and the spark had cut out during the past 10 minutes. The Four could fly on three engines, but the four-blade pusher propeller created drag when it wasn't turning so it slowed the craft down. Read crawled back and looked at the propeller. He asked where Rhoads was. Breese pointed aft to Rhoads, lying on the deck in the rear compartment. Air sick, Breeze said.

Read ordered Rodd to radio Towers and Bellinger. They would proceed on three engines. Dit-dah-dit-dah-dit, the message went out and both NC radio operators acknowledged it.

At 2:05 PM, lagging miles behind, the Four passed over the *McDermut*, the first station ship. The *McDermut* was spewing black and white smoke alternately and steaming in the direction of Sable Island. The other flying boats were almost out of sight in the haze. The Four pointed toward the second station ship, 50 miles further on. Forty-five minutes later halfway to the *Kimberly*, station ship two, steam and water blasted from the forward center engine of the Four over the pilots' heads and with the sickening sound of metal tearing apart, a connecting rod flew lazily end over end, looping into the sea below. Both center engines were gone.

The Four couldn't fly on two engines. Underpowered, they had to land. Read scrambled aft and yelled at Hinton and Stone to turn her into the wind and take her down. He continued back down the tunnel to radioman Rodd, saying to notify Towers they were landing at sea and to ask him to order the *McDermut* and the *Kimberly* to search. Both station ships and Harry Sadenwater, the radio operator on the One, received the distress call. Robert Lavender, aboard the Three, acknowledged the call and Towers, seeing the flash of wings as the Four turned to descend, ordered Read to broadcast his position as soon as the craft was down safely. He presumed that Read was heading to Chatham for repairs.

At the best of times the Four was cumbersome in the air. With two engines out it was primarily a question of trying to control the glide as far as possible and hitting the waves at the right angle. Both Hinton and Stone took the controls as they wrestled the beast around in a turn. Since the plane flew nose high even when landing, they couldn't see over the bow, so each looked over the side as the water rushed up. From the air the sea could be deceptive. What looked flat and calm from 500 feet could turn out to be four- to six-foot waves. It looked good, but they had no choice; they were going in.

At 100 feet Hinton and Stone idled the engines. The symphony of the wing-support wires changes. Breese and Rhoads strapped in. Rodd stopped sending and hastily finished reeling in his radio antenna so it wouldn't be torn off when they hit the water. He secured some radio tubes he was considering using. Read crawled forward and watched the water. White caps. Better get down. He ducked back into the hull as the plane sat smoothly down on the crest of a wave, slid forward, and crashed with a tremendous splash. The seas were running at 8 to 10 feet. A third wave sent water washing into the nose cockpit, over the pilots and even through the rear hatch. The Four porpoised from crest to crest as it slowed and, after bouncing the length of a football field, began sliding up and down the waves in a roller-coaster rhythm. But the boat hull was sound. No one was injured. Rhoads, wide awake now, manned a bilge pump in the aft compartment to send the collected water over the side. It appeared they were out of the race before they ever reached the starting point.[47]

Read shot a sextant position and called out a course heading for Chatham Naval Air Station about 80 miles distant at Cape Cod.[48]

5

Chatham, Massachusetts, Chatham Naval Air Station

[Aviators] have learned discipline through constant contact with two of the oldest statutes in the universe—the law of gravity and the law of self preservation. Ten feet off the ground these two laws supersede all others and there is little hope of their repeal.

—Walter Hinton[1]

May 8–13, 1919

On the water off Cape Cod, Hinton and Stone ran the two working engines at low revs and headed the Four into the waves to try to reduce the bumpy ride. While quite seaworthy, the Four wasn't designed for long voyages and offered an uncomfortable pitching, yawing, up-and-down experience that could sicken the most experienced salt. Rhoads and Breese donned telephone linesman harnesses and crawled up to work on the failed pusher engine. If they could fix it they could fly into Chatham on three engines.

A sodden Read stood up in the bow and shot a sun line with his sextant. They were 80 miles off Cape Cod. He had thought they were about 20.

Before reeling in his antenna wire Rodd had gotten off a distress call that was picked up by Lavender aboard the Three and two destroyers. The crew of the Three had seen a flash of sunlight on wings as the Four turned back and Towers presumed Read was either headed back for Chatham or would land near the *McDermut*. On the surface, Rodd discovered no one heard him on the low frequencies of the battery-powered emergency radio. He could hear the airwaves filled with radio-traffic babble among the destroyers as they searched, discussing where the Four was and how to go about finding her. Finally, he broke in and sent an SOS, even though the craft was in no real danger of sinking. Still no answer and the chatter of the search ship operators continued. Read was furious. The Four idled for over an hour just holding its headway in the waves without seeing any ships. Rodd still couldn't get a message through. Rhoads and Breese had hooked to the guy wires atop the Four and were still trying to fix the pusher engine. It was no go. They unhooked, scrambled down and advised Read the Four would never get off the water.

At 5 PM Read ordered Hinton and Stone to increase power on the still operational outboard engines and set course for Chatham Naval Air Station. Read figured if they were found by a destroyer enroute, fine; otherwise, with careful navigation, they should get to the air station by dawn Friday. On two engines the Four could do eight to ten miles an hour through the seas. For the first few hours it was a rough up-and-down ride. Rhoads, who joined the Navy as a coal passer, continued to be sick and several of the others had queasy stomachs from the wave action on the Four. Rhoads broke out his own home remedy for hangovers or seasickness that he had smuggled aboard — big cans of tomato juice and drinks. It seemed to work for him. He offered some to Rodd and Breese, but they weren't inclined to try it. Rhoads crawled forward and pulled at Hinton's leg. "How about you, Meester Hinton?" he said. Hinton took a couple of swigs to be polite.[2]

About 7:30 PM in the waning twilight, Read spotted the outline of a destroyer 10 miles to the north. He ordered Hinton and Stone to bring the Four about and head for the ship. But the unidentified ship turned and steamed away at high speed. They were alone again miles from land. The Four resumed its plodding course for Chatham. After the sun set the sea grew smoother. A full moon came up and the sky filled with stars. It was a beautiful night. Breese and Rhoads napped and stood watch in shifts in the rear. Stone and Hinton took turns at the controls as they chugged toward the safety of Cape Cod. Rodd tried various tubes in his collection, but finally gave up on the radio in disgust. Even Read catnapped for a few minutes. Stomach settled by the tomato juice, Rhoads investigated the sandwiches. They were ham, but fairly flavorless. He discovered the glass lining of the Thermos was broken and the coffee full of fragments. Rhoads threw it overboard.

Shortly after midnight the vigilant Read spotted a steamer's lights on the horizon. He ordered Hinton and Stone to give chase and the engines were revved up. The Four plunged forward, wallowing like a walrus. They got the Four up to 14 miles an hour, but they couldn't make enough speed to intercept the steamer. She disappeared over the horizon. The engines, strained by the extra stress of the chase, coughed, sputtered and died. The Four drifted northward. They were afloat in the Atlantic without power more than 30 miles from shore. Breese and Rhoads clambered out on the lower wings, careful not to step off the struts and risk plunging a foot through the canvas. They hoisted themselves up the engine nacelles and worked on them. Read, meanwhile, looked at the clear gauge for gas supply. It was empty. He ordered the pair to come back in. Rhoads reached up with a wrench and banged on the side of the gravity tank making a hollow clanking sound, unnecessarily confirming Read's assessment. Breese discovered that with the two center engines out, there was not enough wind to turn the small propeller that pumped gas up to the gravity feed wing tank. Rhoads pumped gas up by hand. After 10 minutes they got the starboard engine going and the crippled plane circled on the water like a wing-shot duck for a quarter-hour while Rhoads and Breese worked to get the port engine running. Try it, they finally shouted. Hinton threw the switch and the engine sputtered to life as it got gas. Read took a new sighting and ordered a course once again for Chatham. They plodded on again at 10 miles an hour through the early hours of morning.

As first light crept up behind them in the eastern Atlantic, they saw ahead the sweeping beam of Highland Light on Cape Cod. Read ordered Hinton and Stone to turn the Four south to follow the shore of the barrier island toward Chatham Naval Air Station and Pleasant Bay. Hinton said he could smell bacon frying for someone's breakfast as they paralleled the coast.[3] Rodd, an amazing radio technician who carried spare tubes in various pockets, booted up his radio again. He could still hear the airwaves crowded with traffic a hundred miles away as four destroyers scoured the Atlantic for them. The sea channel into the air station was twisting and rimmed with sandbars, so Read ordered a careful approach. While they were standing off the channel, the engines died again and the Four drifted. Two HS-2 flying boats came roaring down the channel to join the search and the Chatham pilots realized as they passed a few hundred feet overhead, that the Four was sitting right below them. The planes radioed Chatham that the lost Four had been found and requested a towboat. Chatham Naval Air Station, sitting on 36 acres on Nickerson's Neck, named for the farm there, came alive with excitement.[4]

A sea sled, a boat with an unusual concave hull that could attain speeds up to 42 miles an hour, raced out to take the Four in tow. Within a few minutes, the Four was safe at the Air Station moored to the 240-foot-long boat dock with all four engines silent.[5]

And the press had already coined a new nickname for this Nancy — the Lame Duck. Breese directed the air station mechanics as they swarmed over the craft. The crew was directed by chief machinist's mate Grover C. Farris, who summoned a local auto mechanic, George Goodspeed, from Bearse's Garage to help figure out the problems. Read went into the offices to see whether they could get replacement engines and parts if necessary or whether they were out of the race. Hinton, Stone and Rodd went to the mess to eat and then the barracks to sleep.[6]

On May 9 the harbor front at the Naval Air Station was a scene of controlled chaos as mechanics in coveralls swarmed over the NC-4 while Hinton and Stone, exhausted from the hours of taxiing through the night blackness at sea, slept the day away. A determined Putty Read with the support of the Air Station's commanding officer Phillip P. Eaton, organized and directed the repairs. Eaton, a Coast Guard officer, was aviator No. 60. He learned to fly at Pensacola in 1917 the same year Hinton became an instructor there. The mechanics removed the center engines within an hour. There was no high-compression Liberty engine available so they would have to make do with a low-compression substitute and replace it at Trepassey, where a 400-horsepower replacement engine was available.

Hoping to forestall Towers' and Bellinger's departure from Trepassey Bay without the Four, Read contacted mission control in Washington, headed by his old friend Lt. Commander Kenneth Whiting. Read, Whiting, Richardson and Hinton had all served on the *Seattle* together. Read wanted to report on the status of the Four and find out what happened to the other planes. Whiting called Read back:

> Whiting: "This is Whiting, Read. What was the trouble?"
> Read: "We lost all the oil from the engine."
> Whiting: "How did it get out?"
> Read: "I don't know as we've not found out yet."
> Whiting: "What's the arrangement of the vent pipes on the oil tanks? We used to have trouble with oil being siphoned out."
> Read: "We haven't been able to find any leak. We're getting ready to take one of the motors out and overhaul the other one. The other people are taking a nap. We were taxiing 14 hours."
> Whiting: "Have you got all the assistance you need?"
> Read: "Yes, they're doing everything for us here."
> Whiting: "There's nothing we can do for you here?"
> Read: "No, I don't think so. We will be here a couple of days and then join Towers. We will not need the destroyers if they've been recalled, as we'll go by way of the Maine coast."
> Whiting: "Will you go straight to Trepassey or refuel at Halifax?"
> Read: "We'll stop at Haifax to refuel."
> Whiting: "Do you want anything from Garden City [N.Y.]?"
> Read: "Haven't found that we need anything yet."

Whiting gave Read the bad news that the Department of the Navy had ordered Towers and Bellinger to proceed without the Four if they were able. For a week, more than 40 ships on station have been spread out across the Atlantic awaiting the flight and some newspapers had already criticized the cost of the mission, estimated at more than $1 million.[7]

Then Whiting transfered Read to his wife, Bess Burdine Read, who was waiting at the Navy office to get word on her husband. She and their six-month-old son were living with Read's aunt, Mrs. Albert Barker, widow of the one-time commander of the U.S. fleet, Admiral Albert Barker, so she had close and easy ties to get information from the Navy Department.

Bess Read, the vivacious, outgoing heiress to the Burdine's Department store fortune in Miami, learned of the transatlantic flight six months earlier aboard a train to New York when Putty casually informed her that the Navy was planning to make the great hop first. "He said he had a little secret and he didn't want me to tell anyone," she later recalled. She was dumbfounded, but excited at the prospect. "In his own words, as I remember them: 'Now, the Navy is getting ready to have a big flight across the ocean. It's never been successful before, and we are trying very hard to make this a great thing and a big success.'"[8]

At Chatham, with little chance of a quick getaway, Read tried to put the best face on things. He didn't let on that he had already talked to Whiting and knew the center puller engine on the Four that had thrown a connecting rod was junk, and that he had no idea when the pusher engine might be repaired. Read cabled Towers aboard the *Baltimore*, the mission mother ship in Halifax Harbor: "PROBABILITY GOOD ENGINE REPAIRS 48 HOURS. CAN YOU WAIT?"

A sailor from the radio room delivered the message to Towers' officer quarters. Towers glanced at it and didn't hesitate. He ordered the seaman to direct the radio operator to send back: "NAVY DEPARTMENT ORDERS EARLIEST FLIGHT CONTINUATION. SORRY."

Read didn't share that message with his crew and he didn't give up. All the servicemen at Chatham had gotten caught up in the excitement of touching history in the form of the NC-4. They would do anything to help get the Four off the water and on her way. Part of the problem was that, while willing, they had never worked on engines and systems as complicated as the Four's. It has been 24 hours since Read had had more than catnaps during the 80-mile voyage to Chatham, so the exhausted commander went to bed while Breese, Rhoads and the Chatham mechanics installed the new engine.

In 1919 weather forecasting was almost as much of a mystery to the military as it was to the general public. One British forecaster, who failed to predict disastrous storms and was vilified by the public for his ineptness, committed suicide. In this case of faulty weather prediction, an unforeseen storm moved in while Read slept, preventing the Four from continuing on to Halifax even if the engines were repaired. But reports on weather conditions telegraphed by ships from the Azores were equally bad and the Three and One were captives at Trepassey, awaiting good weather and the go signal.

By May 12 it had been raining steadily with gale force winds for two days. The storm sat over Cape Cod. Rodd had made friends with the Chatham radio operator, who was fascinated by the Four's new equipment. Rodd insisted that the Four be covered with balloon fabric to protect the radios from the downpour and, while continuing his testing, could hear Norfolk, barely audible on the direction finder. Each day he broadcasted on the continuous-wavelength set to Chatham station to test the signals on both the buzzer and the telephone.

Over the three days the mechanics also replacd the semi-rotary auxiliary gas pump with one of an older design because the new one simply didn't work and broke down under pressure. They also cleaned the carburetor jets because the gasoline joint seals continued to be eaten by the gas and bits of disintegrating rubber kept clogging the system.

When the connecting rod on the center puller engine broke, it carried away part of the forward main nacelle strut. Chatham mechanics bolted a wood strip to the damaged strut to brace it. And they replaced the towing ring, which broke when the sea sled hauled them the last mile into the station.

The repair crews continued to have problems and on the fifth day, May 13, as they tried to test the forward center engine, a starter broke because an inexperienced Chatham mechanic installed it wrong. Neither Breese nor Rhoads double checked it. Rumors circulated on the station that Assistant Secretary Roosevelt would withdraw the "Lame Duck" from the race to quash the newspaper criticism of ships standing by idly at sea while weather held the flying boats in port.

There were no spares for that model starter at Chatham, so Read called Whiting in Washington, who ordered an F5L flying boat to head north from Rockaway with two replacements. Because the F5L couldn't possibly reach the Cape before dark and the winding channels at Chatham were a danger to any landing, the commanding officer ordered a smaller HS-2 seaplane to fly south to Montauk Naval Air Station on Long Island to meet the Rockaway plane and ferry the part back. But the overeager HS-2 pilot hit a sandbar on takeoff from Chatham and crushed its bottom. So the Commander ordered out one of the two Goodyear blimps to make the trip south. The blimp was a slow but steady form of transportation that came down slowly enough to make night landings more practical. Less than half an hour after the B-18 blimp left, Montauk radioed Chatham that the Rockaway pilot was prepared to fly straight through and make a night landing at Chatham in the moonlight. Read was enthusiastic, knowing the part would get there in time that the Four might be able get off early the next day.

That night Read ordered all of his impatient crew along with Chatham mechanics into boats to fire flares and wave lanterns when the Rockaway pilot arrived after midnight to guide the twin-engine F-5L onto safe harbor waters.

Breese and Rhoads had discovered that while they came from opposite ends of the social scale, they were kindred spirits in something more than engine repairs — they both liked to drink and have a good time. By 11 PM when they rowed out to their station, Rhoads was comfortably but not noticeably drunk. They had been celebrating with their new Chatham friends the fact that with any luck they would catch the transatlantic expedition the next day by flying straight through to Trepassey.

May 14, 1919

As the roar of the engines from the arriving flying boat sounded over the harbor at 12:30 AM, Rhoads, with the exaggerated care of a person unsteady on his feet, stood up in the boat, aimed a flare pistol at the sky, and pulled the trigger. Nothing happened. Rhoads looked down the barrel and pulled the trigger again. The emergency flare fired past his face with a roar and a whoosh, scorching his cheek and leaving him temporarily blind with black powder burns on his face. He sat down, holding his face in his hands. The flying boat landed safely without any help from Rhoads. Breese rowed the boat back to the Four and helped the disabled mechanic into the rear compartment.

Hinton asked what was wrong with Rhoads an hour later, when he crawled back looking for Read. Breese explained the situation and Hinton, Stone and Rodd agreed to keep Smokey out of sight until after takeoff later that morning, because there was little question that Read would scrub him from the mission just like Howard, the mechanic who lost a hand. Rhoads went to sleep on a stack of supplies in the aft cabin and snored while Breese and the Chatham mechanics installed the spare starter on the forward puller engine.[9]

By sunup, the Four was ready to fly and while Hinton and Stone were idling their engines to check them, the B-18 blimp showed up from its overnight excursion to Montauk. Read was desperate to be off. He hadn't shared the news that the Three and the One would fly as soon as the weather cleared over the Azores and so he failed to notice Rhoads' absence or see him to note the sooty powder burned into his cheek.

At 8:10 AM the Four, following an escort boat to keep it clear of the sandbars, taxied down the channel to the cheers of the Chatham station sailors and gathered townspeople and the blasts of boat horns and was airborne. The puller propeller had an ominous wobble and the engines ran roughly as they circled the Cape at several hundred feet. Rodd already had his radio up and running, talking to his friend at the Naval Air Station using the skid fin

5. Chatham, Massachusetts, Chatham Naval Air Station

The crew of the Four get ready for takeoff at Rockaway Beach on Long Island (U.S. Navy Photograph).

antenna. Shaking off the water that had washed over him, Read looked to Hinton and Read for advice as they circled. Both shook their heads. Eight minutes later they glided back down the channel and landed. Breese, Read, Hinton and Stone looked at the forward propeller. It wasn't cracked; it just wobbled badly when revved to flying speed. Meanwhile Rhoads busied himself clearing an oil line that had already gotten clogged.

Read explained the situation at Trepassey to his pilots. If the weather cleared the expedition would leave without them. But Read had a plan for the Four. Once airborne they could cut the forward puller engine to idle speed and fly on three engines to Trepassey and replace the low compression engine there. They had a two-day window to reach Trepassey and get the Four ready to fly.

The storm that held the Three and One at Trepassey was moving east. Within 48 hours the Three and the One would probably get the go-ahead to fly to the Azores. The ships spread out across the Atlantic had been on station for a week. Some had been scattered by the weather, but only a few of them could hold their positions much longer. If the Four wasn't at Trepassey and ready to fly with the Three and One, her flight would be cancelled. Read noticed Rhoads hanging back behind the other crew members. In mid-briefing he asked, what was wrong with his face?

Rhoads answered sheepishly he burned it on the engine exhaust.

Read asked if he was all right and could fly. Rhoads confidently answered yes and was allowed to stay.

At 9:01 AM, having been escorted again to open water by a guide boat, the Four once again charged forward, water swirling over her decks and past the fuselage, drenching the crew despite the closed hatches. It was cold. Hinton had on two sets of heavy flannel underwear, a flannel shirt, a jersey, a regular aviator's uniform and a leather flying suit. He was still cold. They lifted off at 9:07 escorted by the HS-2 flying boat 1850–1916.

About a half hour later Rodd picked up a radio message from a Fire Island operator to the C-5, a Goodyear dirigible designed to be the Navy's ace in the hole in the race to put the first aircraft across the Atlantic. At its plodding 40–45-mph pace, the hydrogen balloon piloted by Lt. Emery Coil had a distinct advantage over the Nancies. It didn't crash-land if it had engine problems. It was motoring its way up the coast along the same route as the flying boats.

Shortly after 10:00 the Curtiss HS-2, falling behind because of its slower speed, dipped its wings in salute and turned to head south as the Four flew north at 90 miles per hour. In half an hour they were at 3,000 feet and at one point a strong tail wind pushed their air speed to 109 mph, faster than anyone expected the NCs to ever fly.

Hinton and Stone followed Read's directions as they curved northeast across the Gulf of Maine, south of the mouth of the Bay of Fundy where the tides of 30 feet were among the highest in the world. Read navigated them toward Seal Island off the southern tip of Nova Scotia.

The station ships whose radio operators were chewed out for clogging the airwaves when the Four was missing appeared in order on the horizon, First the *McDermut* at 9:56 AM EST (42° 14' N and 68° 38' W) turned and steamed northeast in the direction of the *Kimberly*, then the *Kimberly* steamed toward the *Delphy*, white smoke trailing from her stacks to help point the way. As the Four flew over, off-duty sailors waved and shouted. The *Delphy* (stationed at 44° 13' N and 64° W), like the rest of the transatlantic fleet, displayed its number painted in canvas stretched across the deck at the bow. Ship sirens whooped and screamed encouragement as the ships disappeared behind them. Shortly after flying over the *Delphy,* the new puller center engine, which had been idled down, began to splutter. Hinton and Stone looked at each other. Read crawled back to talk to Breese, who assured him that since the engine wasn't pulling much weight it would probably clear itself.

Rodd was having a field day, experimenting with different tubes and talking back and forth to various radio stations and the ships. His friend, the Chatham radio operator, informed him the C-5 passed overhead at 10:40 AM. A few minutes later Rodd received a call from Bar Harbor telling him to stand by for a rush message from Washington to be answered immediately. But the operator then sent a long weather report on 600 meters before switching to 1400 for the important message.

At 11:17 New York time, the dit-da-dit-da-dit of Morse code translated into a greeting from Assistant Navy Secretary Roosevelt in Washington via the Bar Harbor radio station in Maine. Roosevelt, borrowing a page from the storied life of his uncle Teddy, wanted to put his personal stamp on this adventure.[10]

Rodd's transcription of Roosevelt's message read:

WHAT IS YOUR POSITION? ALL KEENLY INTERESTED IN YOUR PROGRESS. GOOD LUCK. ROOSEVELT.

Rodd gave the message to Breese, who crawled forward and handed it to Read. Read read it and smiled, crawled back with Breese to the radio room, and dictated this response:

ROOSEVELT, WASHINGTON, THANK YOU FOR GOOD WISHES. NC-FOUR IS TWENTY MILES SOUTHWEST OF SEAL ISLAND MAKING EIGHTY-FIVE MILES PER HOUR. READ.

Rodd translated a message from Whiting asking for a report on total gas and supplies loaded at Chatham, got the details from Breese, and sent it. At 11:30 Bar Harbor forwarded a second message from the Navy Department in Washington:

TOOK THREE MINUTES FOR ROOSEVELT TO SEND DISPATCH TO NC-4 AND RECEIVE YOUR REPLY. THIS BEATS ALL KNOWN RECORDS.

Read smiled at the note and handed it up to Hinton and Stone at the controls. Inspired by the exchange, Rodd tried to send a message to his girlfriend. But the Marconi station at Bar Harbor, Maine, turned him down because management hadn't yet set charges for telegraph messages from seaplanes. Breese asked if Rodd could reach his wife in New York, but Rodd got the same answer from the Maine radio operator.

Read spotted the Sable Island light east of Nova Scotia's southern coast. Rodd picked up the mother ship *Baltimore* in Halifax Harbor and advised them at 12:15 PM that the Four would land there for just a few minutes. At 12:30 PM they got a radio message from the Barrington Passage Radio station: "You look good. Took a snap. Would like print?" Rodd radioed back: "Glad to have some." A short time later they spied the *Ludlow* standing off the coast toward Sable Island and Rodd radioed them that all was well with the flight, ignoring on Read's orders the spluttering center engine and the fact that the starboard engine was missing on several cylinders.

The air was rough and Hinton and Stone had trouble controlling the bouncing 10-ton Nancy. Rodd bade his friend at Bar Harbor "DN" goodbye and reeled in his 250-foot-long antenna wire as Hinton and Stone circled Halifax Harbor where the *Baltimore* was moored. The ship had been modified to carry 5,000 gallons of aviation gasoline in 6-by-20-foot tanks on deck. Eleven minutes later, at 1:09 PM, they glided in to a tumultuous welcome of horns, sirens and cheers. No one on board the Four could really hear them because they had been deafened by the engines despite the layers of handkerchiefs stuffed inside their flying helmets over their ears. A boat heaved to alongside the Four and fastened a towing harness; a few minutes later the Lame Duck was moored astern of the *Baltimore*.

While Breese and Rhoads checked out the engines, Read went aboard the *Baltimore*. He was handed weather reports from Trepassey and the Azores and copies of radio traffic from Towers to the *Melville* anchored at Ponta Del Gada, the Portuguese islands' capital. The Trepassey dispatch read: "Off shore storm from Cape Cod eastward has passed north, leaving light variable winds from Trepassey to Azores and the sea has subsided. Conditions therefore fair for a start this evening for the long leg of the flight, but the arrival of NC-4 probably will delay it until tomorrow when weather will be even more favorable between here and Azores." It appeared from the traffic between Towers and Ponta Del Gada that Towers planned to launch on May 15 or 16.

Read wrote this message, which Rodd radioed to Towers:

HAVE ARRIVED HALIFAX. EXPECT TO LEAVE WITHIN A FEW MINUTES.

A message came right back from Towers:

CONGRATULATIONS. WEATHER IMPROVING ON AZORES LEG. EXPECT TO LEAVE TOMORROW AM HOPE YOU ARE WITH US.

An hour later Rhoads delivered the bad news. Shreds of rubber gasket decomposed by the gasoline had again plugged the carburetor jets. And the forward center Olmstead propeller was cracked. There was no way the Four would reach Trepassey before May 15. Luckily a replacement prop that had been left behind by the One and Three was available. As Rhoads and Breese and the mechanics from the Baltimore switched propellers and cleaned out the carburetors and gas lines, they saw the cigar-shaped C-5 chugging slowly along like a tortoise east of Nova Scotia on its way to Trepassey. It looked like the dirigible might beat them in crossing the Atlantic.

Read fired off another radio message to Towers:

WILL ARRIVE TOMORROW. WAIT FOR ME. HAVE A VERY IMPORTANT SUGGESTION TO MAKE.

May 15, 1919, Halifax Harbor, Nova Scotia

Read was determined. He rousted the crew out before daybreak. As they worked on warming up the engines one of the starters broke. Another delay. And the Four crew still had to change that center forward engine once they got to Trepassey. The *Baltimore* had spare starters, but it took three hours to install one. Finally at 9:53 AM, the Four, convoyed by an HS-2 flying boat, the 1850–1916, got off the water at Halifax. At 10:16 the HS-2 turned back because it was unable to keep up with the Four. But within minutes the Four's wing engines started sputtering and coughing and oil pressure fell on the forward center engine. Read motioned his pilots to land. Stone and Hinton put it down off Musquodbolt Harbor in a moderate sea and Rhoads and Breese went to work cleaning jets and fuel lines.

They landed about 18 miles from Halifax. Rhoads found a piece of rubber in the gas lead to one engine and replaced a spark plug. At 12:45 PM they were off again. Hinton and Stone took the Four up to 3,000 feet. The sky was indescribably blue as they flew the 170-mile run from St. Cape Breton Island to St. Pierre off Newfoundland and they occasionally flew through fleecy lumps of small, white clouds. The air was as troubled as the tides in the Bay of Fundy and the Four, despite its size, bounced and skidded with both Hinton and Stone hanging onto their controls. The wind was behind them, pushing them along at speeds up to 109 miles an hour. Read crawled back and ordered a course change after St. Pierre so they would come into Trepassey from the south. The temperatures gradually were falling and when Read stuck his head out of his cockpit to take a drift measurement, an icy blast stung his face and hands, limiting his ability to get an accurate reading. Despite layers and layers of clothing, he was still cold even when he sat down in his manhole cockpit. The other crew members were also chilled through. Ice formed on the struts of the Four as they made the turn at St. Pierre. They flew out across Newfoundland's Avalon Peninsula to approach Trepassey into the wind from the northeast.

As the crew looked toward where St. John's would be 3,000 feet below, they saw a dirigible. It was the C-5 heading out across the Atlantic. But Breese noted that she was flying backwards and appeared out of control. So Read ordered Rodd to get on the radio and check. Breese crawled forward with the news. The C-5 broke her mooring ropes in gusts of wind up to 60 mph and was adrift and lost. No one was aboard. One of those watching the C-5 head out to sea from Signal Hill in St. John's was Hinton's friend and mentor, Lt. Commander Richard E. Byrd, who designed the bubble sextant for the NCs.

As a consolation prize Byrd, who hailed from a politically powerful Virginia family, had been secretly tapped to captain the C-5 to Europe utilizing the same ships at sea. Now the C-5 was lost forever and with it Byrd's chance at fame in the first Atlantic crossing. Read didn't say that he was secretly pleased to watch that bulbous threat to fame disappear over the eastern Atlantic. But the pleasure was short-lived. Rodd intercepted a message between the destroyers *Buchanan* and *Walker* that indicated they were moving to their stations on the line of flight to the Azores. Towers was preparing to leave without them.

A few minutes later Breese came forward with a message intercepted by Rodd from Towers to Washington:

WEATHER FAVORABLE. PREPARING FOR IMMEDIATE TAKE-OFF."

Read crawled back and urged Hinton and Stone to increase their speed. He estimated they were about an hour from Trepassey. He went back to the radio compartment and told Rodd to keep him informed of the launch progress. A few minutes later back in the commander's cockpit, Read received this note: "THE CREWS ARE ENTERING THEIR PLANES." A half-hour later Rhoads crawled forward with another note from Rodd: "THE PLANES ARE TAXIING INTO POSITION FOR TAKE-OFF."

Read crawled back, printed a note and gave it to Rodd, saying to send it to Trepassey immediately:

"COMING IN FOR A LANDING."

Rodd protested that they were 50 miles out, but Read said to send it anyway. The *Aroostook* confirmed their worst suspicions by warning the Four to watch for other aircraft on the water as they come in for a landing.

Giving up the charade, Read ordered Rodd to advise the *Aroostook* they would need a spare engine ready for immediate installation once the NC-4 was brought to its moorings.

Read returned to his command post, leaning out into the icy blast, watching for Cape Pine, the last landfall before Trepassey Bay. Ordering the pilots down to 500 feet, Read suddenly spied the blue bay glistening in the afternoon sun. The NC-3 was taxiing, leaving a white wake trail behind as it prepared to lift off for the Azores. But rather than lifting off, the flying boat, as it approached the bay entrance, slowed and started to wallow in the chop and then turned and headed back down the bay. The Three couldn't get off the water with its heavy load of fuel and equipment.

Stone and Hinton flew the Four over Mutton Bay and across the Powels Peninsula and at a minute before 7 PM (New York time) they land in Trepassey Harbor. A few minutes later the Four was tied up at her moorings next to the *Aroostook*. The trio of giant flying birds was reunited.

6

With the NC-1 and NC-3

"When you get it right mighty beasts float up into the sky. When you get it wrong people die."

— Roger Bacon[1]

May 8, 1919, to May 15, 1919

After the NC-4 turned south with a flash of sunlight on the yellow dope of its wings and disappeared east of Cape Cod, the pilots of the One had little time to dwell on its fate. The air was rough and the plane constantly tried to swerve to the right. Lt. Commander Mitscher and his co-pilot, Lt. Louis Barrin, both wrestled with the controls of the One all the way to Halifax.

The starboard wings taken from the cannibalized NC-2 were improperly rigged and there was no time to test them before the mission started. At 90 mph in turbulent air the best that can be said of the huge planes was that they were unwieldy. Gusts of wind buffeted the One and it rocked and yawed violently. Sometimes it took long minutes for the pilots to regain control, correct the altitude and get level again. The Three pulled steadily ahead and became a dot in the distance. When Bellinger recognized Seal Island he ordered the pilots to cut the corner and head for Cape Sable rather than fly over destroyer 3, the *Buchanan*, to the north. Bellinger then told Barrin and Mitscher to take the One up to 3,500 feet while looking for calmer air. Towers in the Three stayed low over the water and Bellinger lost sight of her against the dark background.

Night was falling as the Three arrived over Halifax. The bay was coated with silver in the waning light as the Three touched down at 7:58 PM. The One then appeared out of the twilight and started its glide into Halifax from 1,500 feet and touched down at 8:10 PM. Only after the pilots throttled down the engine's roar and the flying boats were under tow to their moorings could the crews hear the bells, whistles and sirens of Halifax, whose populace had turned out to greet them. Storekeepers and businesses closed their shops to let their employees join in the waterfront celebration.

Bellinger's hands and knees were bruised and sore from scuttling back and forth from the bow cockpit to the stern radio compartment. He met with the captain of the *Baltimore* as support mechanics checked out the plane.

Mitscher went to work on the problem of the heavy starboard wings. He poured ten and a half gallons of water in the port wingtip float to help the balance. The next day they would find out if it worked. Like the crew of the Four, the engineers discovered some of the new Olmstead propellers had cracked tips, and Towers ordered all the props replaced. But there were no replacement hubs for the props aboard the mother ship *Baltimore* and new ones from Rockaway would take days to arrive. The ever-present and resourceful Byrd, looking for his chance to take part, solved the dilemma by remembering spare propeller hubs were left at the Halifax Naval Air Station where he was commander when it was abandoned in January 1919. If they were still there, they could be retrieved in three hours. Byrd commandeered a fast boat and with a couple sailors made a quick trip to the old air station where he and Hinton once plotted to conquer the Atlantic. A search turned up the necessary hubs in a storage room.

With repairs made at Halifax, the One and Three made ready to hop to Trepassey on May 10. Richardson and McCulloch got three engines running on the Three, but the fourth wouldn't start and, after repeated tries, the electric starter on the Three stripped its gears with a nasty, ratcheting scream because the oil had grown thick as sludge in the cold temperatures. Meanwhile aboard the One, the pilots got only one engine running and taxied about the harbor with it, trying to start the others. Bellinger glanced up from his charts to see the craft headed directly for a large marker buoy. He turned, shouted, and waved at Barrin and Mitscher. Barrin, a one-time circus acrobat, cut the single running engine, hoisted himself out of the pilots' cockpit onto the hull, and scrambled over the nose of the Three, jumping into the bow cockpit with Bellinger. They both fended off the buoy by pushing against it with outstretched arms. The plane still hit the buoy, but wasn't damaged.

But when Barrin attempted to climb back to the pilots' cockpit the way he had come, over the hull, he slipped on the wet canvas and plunged a hand through it, severely spraining his wrist. With Barrin gingerly nursing his injured hand, he and Mitscher got the other three engines running. Meanwhile Engineer Clarence Kessler crawled forward with a message from Towers: "Proceed alone. We are still having engine trouble. Rhodes and chief botswain Moore are replacing a starter motor."

Excited to be on his own at last, Bellinger gave the order to take off. The One taxied across the bay and left the water at 8:49 AM, making a climbing turn as they passed out of the harbor. The One passed Cowboy Pond at 8:54 AM, its point of departure, and paralleled the coast north. The winds were variable and came primarily from the northwest against the port side of the craft. When Bellinger saw smoke from the first destroyer, there was so much of it he couldn't figure out where it was coming from. When he finally located the *Stevens* dead ahead, he turned and waved to the pilots and pointed at it with glee. For 45 minutes the oil pressure remained low from the cold, but pressure gradually rose as the oil heated up. Bellinger, experimenting with his navigation equipment and attempting to compensate for wind drift, ordered so many course changes that pilots Mitscher and Barrin wondered where he was headed. Between Gunyon Island and destroyer 1, the drift changed from eight degrees to 32 degrees in 22 minutes. Ensign C. J. McCarthy from the Bureau of Construction and Repair, who was on the first leg of the trip to compile data on any problems, made several unsettling discoveries. The drift indicator worked well when it was properly adjusted, but it had so many movable parts that need to be set that he got disgusted with it and put it aside. There was considerable lag in the compasses and the lateral inclinometer was sluggish and of not much use. The radio compass was useless because there was so much exposed ignition cable on the NCs that it created intolerable static. The good news in the rough air was that the 10 gallons of water in the left wingtip float solved the starboard wing heaviness. At the fourth destroyer, the *McKean,* Bellinger ordered the pilots to take the craft up to 2,500 feet to try to avoid wind gusts.

The air was so contrary when they arrived over Trepassey and the pilots had so much trouble setting the One down that Barrin remarked that he was sorry they didn't have an extra pontoon on top of the plane as it would have been easier to land on it. As the pilots taxied to their assigned buoy near the *Prairie,* they were again greeted with shouts and cheers from boats, ships and people on shore. Bellinger ordered the ensign jack and the mission pennant hoisted. After Barrin cut the engines, they coasted up to their mooring. Bellinger got his bow line through a buoy ring with some difficulty in the chop, but before he could make the end fast, the wind blew them backwards into a motor boat full of well wishers circling the stern. The crash broke an elevator horn on the tail's horizontal stabilizer, which would have to be fixed before they would fly again. Bellinger later said, "I didn't have a gun, so of course I didn't shoot anyone, but I felt like it." The engines were started again and the One secured to the buoy. Then Bellinger ordered Barrin to have the ship's doctor look at his wrist. The physician ordered it soaked in ice water and then taped. Mechanics from the *Prairie* and the *Aroostook* discovered that most of the radiator tubing braces cracked or broke during the turbulent flight and they repaired, renewed or replaced them.

As mechanics worked on the Three at Halifax Harbor, trying to get her ready to fly, the Cunard ship *Mauretania* arrived in port carrying two British aviators, John Alcock and Arthur Whitten Brown, who hoped to bridge the north Atlantic nonstop in a Vickers-Vimy bomber that had been converted for the air race prize. The contestants were all getting closer to the start.

When the Three was finally ready to leave Halifax at 8:15 AM it stayed aloft for only 30 minutes before oil pressure in the pusher engine dropped from a normal 35 pounds to 5 pounds. Towers ordered Richardson and McCulloch to take her down off the Nova Scotia coast. The culprit was an oil strainer with a mesh too fine for cold oil to flow through. While Rhodes and Moore were investigating that they found another crack in an Olmstead propeller — one of the new ones on the starboard engine. Towers ordered them to fly back to Halifax and the *Baltimore*. Lavender used the emergency radio to advise the *Baltimore* to have spares ready since the main radio's wind-driven generator made it useless on the water. They arrived back at Halifax at 10:30 AM.

The *Baltimore* was out of spares so an uncracked, used prop was reinstalled on the center tractor and the prop from that engine was put on the starboard tractor. The Three took off again for Trepassey at 11:40 AM.

Richardson and McCulloch spelled each at the controls in 20-minute shifts as the wind buffeted the giant craft as it flew across the mouth of the Gulf of St. Lawrence, making it slide sideways through the air and occasionally plunging down several hundred feet toward the gray surface below before the pilots could recover. The pilots kept the Three climbing, looking for smooth air, and finally they found it at 3,500 feet. But the icy cold at more than half a mile high, varying wind velocity, direction and height made it difficult for Towers to navigate. When it arrived over Trepassey the Three, like the One, had difficulty setting down in the narrow bay. Conflicting wind currents grabbed them and shook them first one way and then another. It took more than 40 minutes for the pilots to finally set her down on the water at 6:30 PM.

Mechanics from the *Aroostook* clambered aboard as soon as the Three was moored astern. They removed carburetors, checked fuel lines, and inspected bearings, nuts and bolts. A 50-mph wind whistled and screamed around the ships through the night, rocking the crafts, making the repair chores similar to changing a light fixture atop an unhappy horse. Both commanders stayed awake all night, worrying about their planes in the gale. At first light Bellinger and Towers checked their craft and were relieved to find them intact. Repairs continued throughout the day and the planes were refueled, ready for flight, but the weather reports predicted even worse.

May 11, Trepassey Bay, Newfoundland

May 11 dawned sunny at Trepassey, but the same storm warnings that locked the Four into Chatham held the Three and the One. The good news in the bad weather was it held the British flyers at St. John's, Newfoundland, 80 miles to the north.

The residents of the tiny hamlet of Trepassey, which once was a pirate's retreat and grew into a fishing village, were fascinated with their newfound friends. The harbor was full of ships larger than most had ever seen. Flying boats big and small were in the water and the air. There were a constant air of amazement over what might come next.

And while Towers, Bellinger, Richardson and Mitscher checked the wind and water aboard two single-engine Curtiss MF flying boats from the *Aroostook*, the crews of the ships fraternized with the townspeople and got up baseball games between ship crews. One captain paid a farmer a princely $75 to turn a field into a temporary diamond.

May 13, 14, and 15, Trepassey Bay, Newfoundland

Fog settled over the Avalon Peninsula on May 13, blanketing the landscape so even the small flying boats couldn't go up. That didn't stop the sailors from the *Prairie* from beating the sailors from the *Aroostook* 4–1 in a ghostly baseball game at Meadow Point during which the outfielders frequently lost sight of the batter. By May 14 the fog cleared and the sky brightened.

Thinking about the cracked Olmstead propellers and the hoped-for arrival of the Four, Towers decided to wait until the morrow for the *Edwards* to arrive. It carried sets of new Paragon propellers. Just before noon on May 15 Towers received word that the Four was down again off the coast of Nova Scotia. When the *Edwards* arrived with its replacement props, mechanics again swarmed over the two flying boats, substituting the older, reliable Paragons for the Olmsteads. Towers reluctantly decided to fly on without the Four. The ships at mid–Atlantic had now been on station for four days and were carrying only oil enough for a week at sea without refueling. One of the refueling tankers, the *Maumee*, had already had engine trouble and was floating dead in the water in mid-ocean while repairs were being made.

At 1 PM on May 15 the planes cast off from the mother ships and taxied around the harbor to warm up the oil in their engines. Crowds gathered on shore and sailors lined the rails of the ships in the harbor. A 25-mile-per-hour wind blew from the west across the harbor, but the day was clear. Six-foot swells ran out of the south, directly into the mouth of the inner harbor, meaning that if the flying boats didn't get off the water quickly they would have to abort before they crash into the waves coming at them through the harbor mouth.

Richardson and McCulloch taxied the Three to the far north end of the inner harbor with Barrin and Mitscher close behind them in the One. They turned the craft, revved up the giant Liberties, and charged back down the bay. The crowds cheered. Spray raked them as the crosswind pushed water into the cockpits. Towers turned his back to the bow of the flying boat, trying to protect himself and the pilots from the deluge. Halfway down the bay the Three was up on plane, but the two pilots couldn't get any more out of their engines. As they approached the opening to the outer harbor, Richardson cut the throttles and the Three dropped clumsily back into the chop. A support boat took them in tow to save the engines as they returned to the starting point. The One got off the water and circled the harbor several times and then landed and re-tied to the mooring buoy to wait for the mission leader. For two hours Towers tried to get off the water for the transatlantic flight and for two hours he failed. Finally he ordered the Three back to her moorings where they reduced the fuel load to 1,630 gallons. Towers, soaked to the skin and frozen, decided to abort the mission and returned to the mother ships to try again the next day with all three flying boats.

Then the Four appeared, swooping down from the northwest over the harbor like a giant pelican. It is 7:08 PM (New York time). The plane, with Hinton and Stone both at the controls, but Hinton in charge, circled the larger Mutton Bay three times while the pilots discussed a way to get her down in the tricky crosswinds. Hinton had noted the two taxiing flying boats, as did Read. The support crews aboard the ships waited anxiously as Hinton finally brought the Four in over Fanny's Pond. To avoid the crosswinds, Hinton flew so low that the Four passed with its unholy roar between the homes of George Curtis and Richard Devereaux before gently dipping down in the chop.[2]

From shore the Four almost looked like a submarine as the entire fuselage was submerged in spray and water and then, as it slows, the craft emerged and taxied for the *Aroostook*. It was Breese who solved the problem of why the two flying boats couldn't get off the water with 1,690 gallons of fuel on board, according to the gas gauges. The scion of a New York family, of Groton and an Ivy League education had formed his own reserve unit during the war that trained on their own on a private Long Island estate. Enamored with speed, the youths had mostly started with motorcycles and then took up aviation as an exciting challenge. None had been particularly trained as engineers. But Breese, who had been in charge of checking fuel consumption, had become something of an expert on the Liberty engines. He pointed out that on land, when the hull was level, the gas came up to the full mark at 1,600 gallons, but in the water the NCs tipped forward and the full mark was actually about an inch lower. That means every tank had one to five gallons of extra fuel for an additional 50 to 300 pounds of weight. Towers ordered the mechanics to reduce the gas load on each of the flying boats by 90 gallons, which would reduce their load by about 450 pounds.

While the mechanics were busy mounting a new engine on the Four to replace the low-powered one that got them to Trepassey from Chatham and installing the reliable Paragon propellers, Towers briefed the crews on the flight plan for the next day. Weather permitting, they would leave in the late afternoon so as to arrive over the Azores after daylight on May 18.[3]

Trepassey, which was certainly no vacation spot in 1919, had an ironically gloomy name. Trepassey derived from the French word *trepass*, meaning the dead or departed. The brig *Bonnee Lass* from Barbados sank off Trepasssey in bad weather with a cargo of molasses for St. John's and for several days bodies washed ashore in a place commonly called Purgatory. It was one of many vessels that foundered in the area. Several dozen homes and a Catholic church made up the village. There were no telephones. When the transatlantic mission was in port there were about 8,000 sailors in the harbor and the hamlet. Even St. John's, 140 km away over rough, narrow, twisting roads, only had about 10,000 residents in 1919. But it did boast electric streetcars on some main streets. St. John's had become famous as the projected jumping-off point for at least five competitors in the Great Atlantic Air Race for the *Daily Mail's* $50,000 prize. It had been chosen for a transatlantic flight base quite simply because it was the most easterly point in North America, not because of the rocky terrain or the forbidding weather.

Trepassey began buzzing with anticipation in early April when Bellinger and Stone, scouting Newfoundland for launch points, arrived on April 9. The pair had arrived at Trepassey by a circuitous route because pack ice had most of the Newfoundland harbors blocked. The destroyer *Barney*, captained by Bellinger's friend Reggie Kaufman, on its journey northward from Halifax, had to skirt ice so thick the ship couldn't plow through it all the way up the Newfoundland coast. Finally at Placentia Bay, the Barney anchored in the lee of an island. In the summer of 1918 on an early scouting mission Byrd had recommended this bay as a hopping-off point. But in April it was inaccessible, packed with ice. The night the *Barney* anchored there, the wind shifted and trapped them in the ice. Then the wind began pounding ice against the bow and anchor chain. Kaufman, concerned that the *Barney* might be holed and sink, tried to move the ship, but it was futile and dangerous to be moving in ice fields at night in unfamiliar waters so they gave it up. By the next morning the winds had pushed the ice away and Kaufman hastily put Stone and

Bellinger ashore in a boat and the *Barney* retreated through the ice fields to open ocean, seriously damaging one propeller and taking an ice pounding in the process. After a 20-hour wait Stone and Bellinger caught a train to St. John's and began interview local residents about the ice and weather.

"You could get any answer you wanted about the weather, depending on how you framed your question," Bellinger later reported. "Thus — 'It isn't raining, sleeting and snowing like this around here all the time is it?' Answer — 'Why no. I should say not.' 'It is raining, sleeting and snowing like this around here most of the time isn't it?' Answer — 'Yes, I would say it is.'"

In St. John's the two aviators transferred to a tipsy, narrow-gauge railway train that ran south to Trepassey. From examining charts in Washington, Bellinger had concluded that the bay might be the best jumping-off point. It was a long, slow journey. If the train went more than 20 miles per hour, the cars would rock and the sides would hit the ground and they would have to slow down. Since there were no rental accommodations, the conductor arranged to put the pair up with a farmer's family in Trepassey, and Stone and Bellinger slept together in a soft, narrow, double bed.

The pair had been told their mission was secret, but before they left Washington aboard the *Barney*, a reporter showed up to take Bellinger's picture. Bellinger asked him what he was talking about and the reporter informed him he knew all about the mission. It seemed Roosevelt had called a news conference and told the reporters everything after he instructed the Navy brass to keep the trip secret.

But after covering the ground in Trepassey, Bellinger and Stone had no illusions about the site. Bellinger noted it as "a dreary, windswept, fog-bound stretch. High hills fringe it about. From these hills, the winds which blow almost ceaselessly roll into the Bay and boiling and churning make flying conditions hard." Shortly thereafter the *Barney* anchored in the Reach and Stone and Bellinger were taken aboard from a fast motorboat and the *Barney* limped south back to Halifax and then Washington, D.C. The mission would start from Trepassey and briefly make the hamlet on the southern shore of Newfoundland famous.

In their official report Bellinger and Stone wrote to the Bureau of Aeronautics:

> Newfoundland and its surrounding waters represent the most unfavorable weather conditions for operations of seaplanes of any on the Atlantic Coast, and the harbors with surrounding hills are very unsatisfactory for making a getaway [takeoff] except when wind conditions are suitable. The harbors form a suitable anchorage for ships only under good weather conditions or during offshore winds not exceeding moderate force. Poor holding ground for anchorage is to be expected, due to rocky bottoms in most harbors.[4]

Because of the harrowing experience of the *Barney,* a group of naval aviators called on the director of naval aviation and suggested flying directly from Rockaway to Azores and refueling at sea. But this approach was rejected due to the difficulty of predicting wave conditions in mid–Atlantic, which turned out to be a prophetically smart decision.

May 16, 1919, Trepassey Bay, Newfoundland

Mechanics worked through the night on the Four, getting her ready to fly the Atlantic with the Three and One. In the early dawn of Friday, Richardson, Hinton, Mitscher, Stone and Barrin took a boat down the harbor to inspect the seas. They discovered white-capped rollers pushed by a west wind marching at them down the narrows. It would make it dangerous and difficult to get airborne if the seaplanes didn't get off the water in the inner harbor. Shortly after 1 PM (New York time) the winds died and the seas subsided into chop. Meanwhile the engineers continued to make tests on the new engines on the balky Four. Weather reports from the ships at sea flowing into Washington by radio were good and the mission's forecasters, Lt. Roswell F. Barratt and Willis Gregg of the U.S. Weather Bureau brought in a favorable report. The mission is a go. About 5 PM Newfoundland time, Towers formally assembled the three crews on the quarterdeck of the *Aroostook* and thanked its captain, James H. Tomb, for his hospitality and support. Tomb had made a bet with Towers — the *Aroostook,* which would steam east the day after the flight left, would get to the eventual goal in Plymouth, England, before the NCs. The NC men saluted the officer of the deck and the ship's ensign and then got in the waiting boats ready to take them to the planes.

Towers carefully stood atop his stool in the bow and waved a hand to Read and Bellinger and shouted, "Let's go." The eight engines of the Three and One barked into life, but the Four's were silent; they still wouldn't start. The One and Three throttled down to reduce the din.

"How long?" Towers demanded of Read. "Ready in 15 minutes, sir," Read shouted back. Breese, an inveterate tinkerer, who at one point experimented with seawater in set of batteries thus destroying them, tried one of his amateur remedies. He had discovered that if he hooked the 12-volt batteries into the 8-volt ignition system, he could get plenty of spark as long as he disconnected before the wires melt. The forward center Liberty coughed to life in a cloud of blue, oily smoke. The other 12-cylinder engines were also shocked to life with the jolt of extra electricity. The Four joined the Three and the One circling the harbor, warming their oil for the launch.

Towers waved his arm forward and down, the signal for takeoff, and got down off his stool. Richardson and McCulloch pulled the throttles wide open and sent the Three plunging toward the narrows, fighting the westerly crosswind with ailerons and rudders. The Four followed in its wake and the One brought up the rear.

Hinton, Stone and Read quickly realized that the Three was not going to make it into the air before it hit the chop of the outer harbor, and Read motioned Hinton to swing off to one side. Hinton swung to port then did something that other pilots had said couldn't be done: he rose into the crosswinds and popped the giant Four up over the steep surrounding hills at 5:37 PM.[5] The Four was no longer the spanking new craft of Rockaway. The hull was rough and dirty gray. The midsections of the wings were stained with oil from the engines and the tail was discolored by exhaust fumes. The Four circled across Powle's Point toward Mutton Bay as the crew craned for a view of the Three, still gripped by the water. Towers ordered Richardson to abort the effort and turn back for another try, and Bellinger in the One followed suit. They moved as far up the inner harbor as was practical. Again Richardson and McCulloch gave the Three all the gas they could and she plunged down the Bay toward open water with the One trailing. Again Towers ordered Richardson to abort as they approached the narrows with no hope of getting airborne. Towers ordered the Three back to the *Aroostook* where a tender came out to greet her. The problem was weight. Towers ordered anything expendable stripped off the craft and dumped into the launch. They tore up 50 lbs. of slatted flooring designed to keep the crew dry and off-load spare oil and radiator water. Lavender argued when Towers ordered the 26-lb emergency radio transmitter over the side. Towers tersely reminded Lavender of who was in command. It went. And last, Towers ordered the 160-pound Rhodes off the plane. Rhodes started to protest, saw the look in Towers' eyes, and quietly climbed into the support boat. His transatlantic adventure was over.

The Four circled for nearly 20 minutes while Towers stripped weight off his plane. Then Read ordered it back down and it landed in the bay and taxied back to the vicinity of the Three and One. Finally, with a wave of his arm, Towers directed them back to the north end of the harbor and the formation once again lunged down the bay toward the narrows. At 6:06 PM, after a run of one minute, the Three left the water, followed by the Four at 6:07 PM. The One ran down the harbor at 30 knots, still gripped by the surface. It couldn't make any more speed and water showered the entire crew with icy spray as it approached the wall of waves in the narrows. Bellinger wished that he had attempted a full-load takeoff while the Three was jettisoning equipment and crew. He was sweating as he notes the looming seas ahead. He put his hand on the bottom of the hull and felt the wooden boards working against the water pressure. Finally the One gained speed again, slowly,

slowly and got up on plane as it struck the first big wave. The Three propoised off the wave into the air and slammed down hard into a second wave. It porpoised up and down again then lightly kissed the cap of a third wave and lifted off. But at 10 feet altitude above the waves, there was no chance it could swing its 28,750 pound bulk above the surrounding hills and fall into formation to starboard and behind Towers' Three. So Barrin and Mitscher headed out through the shipping channel to the sea like some strange tugboat just above the waves.

Hundreds of villagers and fishermen from nearby ports and hundreds of sailors lining the decks of the *Prairie* and the *Aroostook* cheered as the One rose from the water, but their sounds were overpowered by the whistles, sirens, horns and bells of the ships and the dozens of small boats in the harbor, some of which had raced along parallel to the takeoff run of the NC-1.

The One headed east for Mistaken Point where the flying boats would leave the sight of land in this strange formation and head for the island of Corvo in the Azores, more than 1,300 miles away. The Four was at 600 feet and soaring and the Three was at 75 feet. Bellinger was overjoyed just to be in the air. The afternoon waned with the sun glinting from behind off the red, white and blue verticals of the tail and the yellow-doped wings. Despite Mitscher's water-in-the-float solution, the One kept yawing to starboard because of the larger surface of the wing taken from the Two, and it forced both pilots to keep their hands on the controls. Barrin's injured wrist gave him considerable pain as he steeled himself for the long, dark hours ahead in the uncharted night of the north Atlantic. They were off on their mission to be first to bridge the Atlantic. Wireless operators and radio operators flashed the news to the world. The NCs were flying the Atlantic.

7

May 16–17, 1919, Aboard the NC-4

"The highest art form of all is a human being in control of himself and his airplane in flight, urging the spirit of a machine to match his own."[1]

With the launch preparations of May 16 underway in Trepassey Harbor, Lt. Commander Richard E. Byrd, who had so desperately hoped to be part of the historic mission, left the inner harbor and drove up Signal Hill to have a good vantage point to watch his friends disappear into the twilight on their transatlantic voyage.

Byrd knew that his friend Hinton, a former enlisted man with little formal education, who had been elevated to a temporary lieutenancy, was at the controls of the Four because of Byrd's personal efforts on Hinton's behalf. Byrd had great confidence in his friend, as did Read, who had killed an attempt to get Hinton removed from the mission because a group of naval officers ambitious to get another of their own on the flight complained to Towers that Hinton was dangerous and a daredevil, even though the Ohioan had logged hundreds of hours in the NCs without an accident. Towers said Hinton's fate rested in Read's hands. Read said, simply, "I'm comfortable with Hinton. He doesn't take unnecessary chances."[2]

Hinton as a pilot was something of an oddity — only an elementary school education and from a poor Midwest farm background. Most of the aviators of the day were the sons of rich East Coast families or graduates of the service academies. Some were both. Rank and family background both played roles in the Navy hierarchy. When the Coast Guard's first aviator, Stone, who was higher ranking, deferred to Hinton, letting him take the left cockpit seat of the Four, it was an admission that Hinton was the better pilot. When the pair made the only test flight of the Four, Hinton said: "'Elmer, you've got my seat.' Whether Read had talked this over with him I don't know — I never asked. Stone said, 'You have the experience needed on a trip like this — that's your place [the pilot's seat].' Read was standing on the deck about midway between his cockpit and ours. I looked at him and he gave me a smile and nodded yes."[3]

After clearing Powell's Head, the three flying boats curved gracefully in the sky with the Three in the lead and the Four to its port at about 600 feet. The One — much lower — had climbed to about 100 feet. None of the overladen craft could get any higher without risking losing an engine. For about three minutes the watchers on the ground could see them spaced two miles apart, silhouetted against the horizon in still, bright sunlight before they disappeared from view.

The water below was smooth and the reflected glow of the sunset filled the sky. Icebergs looked like a fleet of sailing craft as they drifted south below. The air rushing by was cold. All of the crew were bundled in their cumbersome leather flying togs over their uniforms and long underwear.

Hinton and Stone saw the Three ahead, "rising and falling in the changing air as if on the slow, high waves of an invisible sea." All other sound was submerged in the roar of the engines. There was a sense of space — "open, illimitable, so vast that the pair feel shaken free from the earth, winging eastward in a new world whose laws are alien to what they have known before."[4]

The NC-4 airborne with its full crew on board (U.S. Navy Photograph).

By 7:17 PM local time, or 22:47 GMT, Rodd reeled out his 200-foot-long antenna with the lead fish on the end. A Marconi operator in Detroit before the war and before that on Great Lakes steamers, Rodd was a wizard with radios. He kept meticulous notes as he worked contacts with Cape Race, the destroyers and sea.

The pilots checked the instrument board — clocks, compass, oil and water gauges, altimeter, tachometer, inclinometer. Rodd was working his radio. Breese and Rhoads were in the rear compartment. Rhoads seemed to be asleep. The Four flew through a growing darkness. Hinton and Stone switched on their lights. The Three had disappeared.[5]

It was impossible to see straight ahead because it was as if they were riding the back of a whale, but they could see off to the side at a 45-degree angle and they could turn and look to the rear. The faster Four kept overtaking the Three in the loose formation and finally Read, concerned about the prospect of a midair collision, ordered the pilots to steer clear of the Three and forget the formation. The One, which Read had seen occasionally its blinking red, white and green lights, trailing behind, has also disappeared. They were alone in the night sky with more than 1,150 miles to go.

There was disorienting darkness then stars appeared. These and the "lines of the ocean where the stars cease" gave the pilots their only means of orientation. "The engines labor on." The dozen unmuffled, exhaust ports sent out flaming jets of unburned gas. "In the vastness and invisibility of the time and place those red tongues, each proclaiming the adequacy of its cylinder 850 times a minute, are reassuring." Oil pressure on each engine held steadily at the 30- to 40-pound marks and water temperature gauges showed needles in the comfort zone.

"Ahead a swift, narrow stem of flame runs up the sky, bursts into flower, and scatters shiny petals across the night. The star shell of the *Greer*, destroyer One marks the sky." In a minute gem-like lights gleamed below and the *Greer* radio operator told Rodd her number and gave him the Four's location. Rodd checked her off the chart and the Four flew on. Rodd heard Lavender testing the Three's radio system and established contact with him at 2300. He sent a message to Lavender asking him to tell McCulloch and Richardson to turn on their lights. No response. Eventually Lavender got through to tell Rodd that their lights, drenched by the three takeoff attempts, simply didn't work.

As the Four flew over station ship 3, the *Buchanan*, Rodd picks up a radio bearing on station ship 10, the *Crosby*, some 350 miles distant.

The plan was for the three planes to fly south of the line of destroyers. Each ship would shine a search light in an arc from horizontal to vertical in the direction of the prevailing wind. Each ship's number was displayed in electric lights eight feet high on the stern deck. Each would steam slowly in the direction of the next ship and as the next ship received radio word that the planes were approaching, it started to fire its white-green star shells to the northwest that exploded 4,000 feet in the air.

As the Four consumed fuel, they climbed to 1,000 feet and gleams of silver from the east reflected from wings and motors. It was the edge of the full moon, which in rising increased visibility tenfold. Hinton and Stone relaxed a little. Read ordered them higher to stay above a cloud layer.

Suddenly, almost an hour after they had abandoned the formation, an unlit shape loomed from above out of the night on the port side of the Four; both pilots instinctively veered right as Read motioned the same, a hard turn to starboard. It was the Three running without lights. Hinton and Stone accelerated. The Four surged ahead past the ghostly Three and Hinton, Stone and Read saw her no more.[6]

Near station ship 5, the *Boggs*, Rhoads decided to check the outboard engines. Read ordered Rodd to alert the ship that the mechanic was using the Aldis Lamp, usually used for signaling, to shine a bright light on the wings, tail and engines looking for oil, water or fuel leaks. He reported all was well.

Rodd picked up pieces of messages as 1,350 statute miles away east of the Azores, including one from the *George Washington* ordering a train be reserved for President Wilson, who was enroute to the peace talks at Versaille.[7]

So many radio operators aboard merchantmen crowded the airwaves trying to contact the planes and be part of the adventure that the Canadian operator at Cape Race rebuked them and told them to get off the air because they were interfering with radio communications among the flying boats and the support destroyers. "Listen to that limey jump on these fellows," Rodd radioed to Lavender aboard the Three and Lt. Harry Sadenwater on the One.[8]

The moon came up about 0030 GMT. "It is a huge thing, almost blood red, distorted and divided into three parts by the clouds fringing the horizon."[9] As it rose it shrank into a cold white disc, providing welcoming light to see gauges or the unlit Three if it got close.[10]

The Four rode through the night with Hinton and Stone spelling each other. The off-duty pilot took catnaps and Read occasionally crawled back through the compartments to check on his crew. Rodd stuck to his radios without a break. Read carefully navigated them from ship to ship, spotting some star shells 50 miles ahead only moments after passing a station ship. Ever the careful navigator, Read presumed each ship was on station and then shot a line for the next ship from that point. Rhoads scuttled back and forth between Read and Rodd carrying handwritten messages and each time he crawled past Stone in the narrow passageway, he gave the pilot a pat on the leg. Both pilots suffered from leg cramps periodically from the constant work with the rudder bar.

Beyond the *Crosby* on station 10 at 0545 GMT, the sky in the east began to pale. Fifteen minutes later Rodd reported he was getting radio bearings on signals from ships at stations 12 through 17. They passed over a merchant ship at 0645 as they approach one of the main Atlantic steamer lanes.[11]

As dawn weakly broke in the eastern sky, the Four, like the other flying boats, was in the vicinity of station ship 14, the *Cowell*. The crew's confidence was growing; they were more than halfway there. The pilots started eating a little, some nibbling on chocolate. Other crew members ate ham sandwiches and drank cold coffee from their Thermoses.

After flying over station ship 15, the *Maddox*, Read and the pilots spotted what looked like a black wall of storm ahead at 0745, but it turned out to be fog moving east, like the Four, toward the Azores. Visibility was reduced to almost zero, but they passed through it without incident and then picked up the dim shape of station ship 16, the *Hopewell*. Visibility continued to be poor.

Then they hit really bad weather — fog and rain and clouds. When they passed the *Stockton*, station ship 17, no one saw her. At 7:45 AM (local time), the weather got worse.[12]

The sun disappeared. Read was a ghostly figure with his head sticking out of the cockpit 10 feet ahead. He couldn't see the wing tips. He motioned Hinton and Stone to climb, looking for clear air. Read suddenly felt the wind increase against his face. He looked at the compass and it is spinning; a glimpse of sun confirmed they were in a steep, banking turn. The plane merged into a "gray blanket of moisture." It appeared the pilots had lost control of the wallowing Four. Read waved his arms then crawled back and jerked on Stone's leg, fearing the pilot had fallen asleep. He hadn't. Neither had Hinton. They were having extreme difficulty orienting the craft with no horizon. Finally the sun broke through again in a patch of blue. They regained control and the Four climbed out of the fog at 3,000 feet.

They flew over a white plateau of billowing vapor below that shrouded the ocean in mist. Soon clouds and fog appeared above them as well as below. Read ordered Rodd to check surface conditions ahead. Station ships 19, the *Dent*, and 20, the *Philip*, one of the specially rigged meteorological ships, reported poor weather conditions. But station ship 21, the *Waters*, reported 10 miles of visibility. After passing over the *Dent* and the *Philip*, Read signaled to Hinton and Stone to descend, looking for clear air beneath the fog. But the fog persisted. With Hinton and Stone flying at several hundred feet altitude, Read spotted what looked like a tidal rip through a break in the fog and then he saw a dim line of rocks. He had brought them directly to Flores, the westernmost island in the Azorean archipelago, a 55-square-mile dot in the middle of the Atlantic. They were over European soil as the nine remote volcanic islands, spread out over hundreds of miles of ocean, belonged to Portugal. The rugged, flower-laden terrain of Flores explained its name. Read ordered them to skirt the west coast as he calculated a course for Faial, some 152 miles east, southeast. Faial was a secondary target for the flying boats with the support ship *Columbia*, anchored at Horta Harbor on its south coast. The primary goal, Ponta Delgada, on the island of Sao Miguel, was still 307 miles distant.

The crew was jubilant, reassured. Rhoads checked the oil and gas supplies. There was plenty to make Ponta Delgada. Their elation was brief. Dense fog closes in around them again. They miss station ship 23, the *Gridley*. Ahead beyond Faial and between the Four and Ponta Delgada lay the island of Pico. It was named for its volcanic peak that thrusted 7,713 feet into the sky, almost a mile and half, a looming danger in anything but clear weather.

Read decided any port would look good and began calculating a course to find land again. Faial was another dot in the ocean at 67 square miles. Suddenly a hole opened in the fog and Stone and Read spotted the northern shore of Faial. The pilots banked to starboard, seeking Horta on the south coast. Rough air tumbling down the rugged coast made the Four pitch and yaw as Read signaled Hinton to land. The Four splashed down and taxied toward shore. A lone farmhouse emerges from the haze. This wasn't Horta Harbor, one of the best water sanctuaries between the continents. Read ordered them back up. They continued southwest along the coast. Between gusts of obliterating fog, Read caught a glimpse of the *Columbia* at anchor in Horta Harbor. Hinton swept down to the harbor and safety. They had been in the air for 15 hours and 13 minutes. The most difficult leg of the great crossing was complete. The *Columbia*'s whistles trumpeted the triumph. Small boats of local fishermen surrounded the Four as it taxied close to the mother ship, one of which run into the bow, punching a hole in the fuselage. Read was furious as the Four is taken in tow to its moorings. Rodd, who hadn't had a cigarette in 15 hours, scrambled out of his cubby in the rear of the Four so he could light up as they transferred to boats to go to the *Columbia*.[13]

8

May 16–17, 1919, Aboard the NC-1

"The air is an extremely dangerous, jealous and exacting mistress. Once under the spell most lovers are faithful to the end, which is not always old age."
— Winston Churchill[1]

The NC-1 finally broke free of the watery grasp of Trepassey Bay at 1841 GMT. P.N. L. Bellinger was wet but jubilant as the flying boat waddled ox-like down the channel toward Mistaken Point the last bit of land they would see in Newfoundland. They were so overladen they couldn't rise above the hills, but had to follow the channel out to sea. It was not a pretty exit, but they were on their way.

Mitscher was at the controls. It was cold. He was wearing two pairs of long woolen underwear, covered by a regulation forest-green uniform. Over that he wore a leather flying suit with a hood, fur-lined boots, and heavy, fleece-lined gloves with wide gauntlets. His favorite hunting knife was strapped to his hip and he wore goggles and the soft leather helmet with earphones.[2] The Three in the lead and the Four dropped down to form a ragged formation as they disappeared out over the sea, oblivious to the cheering, whistling and shouting they left behind on shore. All the pilots kept their heavily laden craft, which each weighed more than 14 tons near the surface.

It would be dangerous to try to force more altitude and pilots had learned from experience that an overloaded plane handled better near the surface. The ground effect of a cushion of air compressed between the wings of a low-flying plane and the ground was a scientific discovery yet to be discovered.

The only reason to gain altitude beyond 100 feet over the calm seas was the icebergs that were drifting south, freed from the frozen ice pack to the north by the coming spring. Sadenwater and Rodd on the Four were already in conversation, but there was no radio contact with the Three. A little over an hour later the One was still not high enough to fly over the *Greer*'s masts as it fired its star shells to the north and arced a floodlight into the wind direction, while steaming east. By the time they reached station ship 2, the *Aaron Ward*, they were high enough to fly over the icebergs sailing below, but the temperature drop made it even colder in the open cockpits.[3]

Bellinger could see the Four's lights ahead. They had turned on the white light on the upper wing and the red and green lights, showing the port and starboard struts at 2300 just as the One had. But there was no sign of the Three because it had no lights. Sadenwater sent a message forward that Rodd on the Four complained to Lavender about not being able to see the Three, and Lavender reported the Three's lights were out because the circuits were soaked during takeoff. Bellinger asked Sadenwater to find out what course the Three was steering. "150 magnetic" was the reply.

Bellinger presumed the Three was ahead somewhere. He knew that his craft, the One, was probably the least airworthy of the mission. It originally had been built to carry three engines and then a fourth was added. It had been wrecked in the storm at Rockaway and then the starboard wings were burned off in the hangar fire and the salvaged wings from the NC-2 were not quite the same size and had been rigged improperly.

But as the One approached station ship 5, the *Boggs*, Bellinger spotted a winking light almost dead ahead. Someone on the Three frantically waved a flashlight warning them off. Mitscher and Barin swerved abruptly away to avoid a rear-end collision. A few moments later Sadenwater crawled forward with a message from Towers: abandon formation flying.

The *Ward*, station ship 6, was 20 miles off her coordinates when word reached her that the mission had been launched. Commander Milton S. Davis raced back to his station. At 11:30 the *Ward* lookout reported "a strange reddish light off the starboard bow about 25 degrees." Commander Davis focused his powerful glass on the object and said to his aide it was like "looking at Mars through a faint haze."

A few moments later others spied the object and the stern watch signaled with an Aldis light that a craft four or five miles distant was "seemingly sailing straight into the moon." The crow's nest signalman shouted out, "NC-1." The *Ward* radio operator sent: "Destroyer *Ward*. Good Luck." Just before the hurrying One rode out of view, Sadenwater sent back: "Thanks."[4]

Throughout the night Sadenwater and Rodd kept up a periodic conversation between calls to Cape Race and the destroyers they were passing below. At 0221 GMT Sadenwater radioed "Cape Race Radio from NC-1.... All well here and we are in commercial radio communication. Good morning, Cape Race, from NC-1."[5]

The One continued to lag behind the Four and by the time the Four passed over the *Hopewell*, Bellinger was trying to make out the *Cowell*, two

When the NCs taxied to lift off from Trepassey Harbor they were so overladen with fuel that the fuselage appeared to be submerged. The NC-4 with Hinton at the controls lifted off first (U.S. Navy Photograph).

station ships behind. They then flew over the *Hopewell* and the *Stockton* without incident, although the *Stockton* was 15 miles north of where Bellinger calculated she should be. Because of the lowering visibility Bellinger couldn't calculate whether he was off course or the *Stockton*, station ship 17, was off station.

The One passed station ship 18, the *Craven*, without actually seeing it and before they got to station ship 19, the *Dent*, they hit heavy fog. Bellinger turned and looked back. He couldn't see the rear of the One or the wingtips. He could only see the engines 12 feet behind him.

Mitcher and Barin strained to see their instruments. The inclinometer, which indicated when they were flying on an even keel with a bubble like a carpenter's level, was sluggish, as the bubbles slid back and forth without coming to rest. The One yawed back and forth as the pilots overcorrect. Several times she slipped into spiral dives. Twice when they brought her out of a dive, they discovered they had turned 180 degrees and were headed back to Newfoundland. They carefully turned her around and put her back on course in the thick fog.

Bellinger finally ordered them to climb, to try to get above the fog, and at 2,500 feet they emerged into the sun, flying along over the clouds and fog below. They continued climbing slightly to stay above the cloudscape below.

The crew of the NC-4 on its U.S. publicity tour swarm over the craft making sure it is ready to fly the next day. The tour went as far west as Texas and up the Mississippi to St. Louis, but always stayed in close proximity to water in case of an emergency landing (Burns collection).

For two hours they flew on without seeing the ocean. Bellinger tried to shoot a sextant sunline, but the air was rough enough that he didn't trust the result. They were now at 3,200 feet. Bellinger ordered them down, hoping to find clear air under the cloud bank. Mitscher and Barin felt their way down through the swirling vapors. Finally, when their gauges told them they were 75 feet above the waves, they broke into the clear. All any of them could see was miles of dull gray ocean. They could see for half a mile through the patches of fog, but there was nothing to see.

Bellinger reckoned that they were somewhere in the vicinity of station 20, the *Philip*, or station 21, the *Waters*, but he had no idea where he was in relation to the two ships. If he was correct, they were near Corvo, the smallest and northernmost island in the Azorean chain or Flores. Both presented problems. Corvo had no safe harbor or support craft and Monte Gordo, a volcanic peak, stood 2,549 feet high. The highest point on Flores was Morro Grande, which is 3,090 feet high and it, too, didn't have a suitable safe haven. Both peaks represented danger in the fog.

At 11:40 Washington time, Sadenwater sent the message: "SOS, SOS, SOS, NC-1 lost in fog about position 20."[6]

Christiansen reported they had enough fuel for about two and a half more hours of flying, plenty to get them to Horta or Ponta Delgada, if Bellinger was correct about their location. Bellinger needed to know where they are.

But Sadenwater in the rear compartment, unlike Rodd, continued to have trouble with his radio direction finder. In the air with the engines running, it had an effective range of 10 miles and with the One flying at 90 miles an hour, even if they got a bearing on a transmitting ship they would be past it within a few minutes.

Bellinger's dilemma was to continue on, hoping to sight a ship or land, or to put the One down on what appeared to be long, oily rollers, shut down the engines, and get a radio bearing on their position. He consulted with Mitcher and Barin and they agreed. Put her down. Sadenwater sent out the message: landing in fog near the *Waters*, all ships begin sending radio bearing signals. At 1310 GMT the pilots touched down and discovered what appeared to be 10-foot seas were actually twice that high. The Three popped back up in the air after hitting the first crest, porpoised again after the second crest and then buried her nose in the bottom of the next wave. A 20-knot crosswind blew through the wave troughs. They would never be able to get off the water until the seas died down and wind conditions improved.[7] "That calm, smooth water was rough as hell," Bellinger later recalled.[8] The first voice that Bellinger heard was that of Engineer Machinist Mate C.I. Kesler: "What in hell are we landing here for?"[9]

Christiansen scrambled out onto the wings to check for damage and found the floats and wings intact. Sadenwater began sending signals. The One, which was nose heavy, turned head into the wind and started drifting backward at five to ten knots along the swells, where she alternated between teetering on a wave crest and skidding down the slope of a trough sideways, only to be picked up by the next 20-foot roller.

Bellinger ordered Christiansen and Kesler to rig a sea anchor. The anchor slowed their drift for a moment and then the cable broke. Mitscher made another sea anchor, designed to stabilize the flying boat, from a large bucket by punching holes in its bottom with a hunting knife. (He carried that knife with him for the rest of his life.) They fastened it to a manila line; it held and slowed the skidding One, but the seas were tearing at the wings and tail and within an hour the ailerons, elevators and one wingtip float were torn off. The One would never fly again.

Bellinger ordered them to don life preservers and as he spoke the right wingtip and float broke off and drifted away. Mitscher crawled out on the lower left wing to slit the fabric to allow water to flow through. He cut himself in the effort and Bellinger bandaged it. He said later he wondered if they were all going to be shark food as he could see dorsal fins circling the crippled craft.

Sadenwater sat over his radio key, sending emergency signals for four hours. There was no answer. He could hear the ships searching for them, just like Rodd did off Cape Cod, but they were too busy talking to listen for the One's signals.

Finally, about 1700, a destroyer acknowledged Sadenwater's call and asked for a series of Vs so they could pinpoint the One's location. Sadenwater sent them. Then silence. He didn't know if the signals had been received. The batteries died, but the crew had already rigged a canvas wind chute to aim the propeller blast at the small generator prop. Sadenwater transmitted for another 60 minutes then the wind chute came lose, blew into the generator prop, and broke its blades.

Christiansen installed a spare generator prop and they re-rig another wind chute. Sadenwater began sending again when they were hit by a heavy

The NC-3 was a wreck when Lt. Commander John Towers sailed it into Ponta del Gada Harbor in the Azores after completing a 200-mile odyssey through high winds and stormy seas (U.S. Navy Photograph).

cross sea and tipped to starboard. The One heeled over with both starboard wings under water. Everyone except Mitscher at the pilot controls and Sadenwater clambered carefully out on the port wing to make a counterweight to prevent the One from going belly-up.

Slowly the starboard wings came back out of the water, but in the hasty climb out to the wing someone kicked the last generator prop and broke it. There would be no more calls for help. Sadenwater joined the rest of the crew on the upper wings where three men perched on each, awaiting rescue.[10]

At 1740, the exhausted crew, who had been awake for more than 24 hours, spotted smoke from a ship stack. Mitcher and Barin started the engines and headed the One on an intercept course while the rest of the crew hung from the port wing to keep the ship balanced. Everyone was soaked. Some were seasick. Sandwiches were soggy. The ship disappeared in the fog. Had the One been seen?

A few minutes later they got their answer. The Greek freighter *Ionia* appeared out of the mist a few hundred yards off. The lookout had seen them.

For two hours they floated a hundred yards apart in the heaving seas before the *Ionia* could get the One in its lee and launch a lifeboat. The rescue was hazardous because one moment the two craft were alongside each other and one man could jump into the boat and the next moment the One was 20 feet below in a trough with the lifeboat riding above her. The rescues took almost an hour.

The *Ionia*, captained by B.E. Panas and headed from Hampton Roads, Virginia, to Gibraltar with a load of coal, had no radio. Panas agreed to put a tow line on the One and divert to Horta with his newfound passengers. Two hours later the tow line snapped and Panas ordered the *Ionia* to heave to and stand by the floating wreck.

At 0035 the destroyer *Gridley*, which had been station ship 23, appeared and asked the *Ionia* if she had seen an airplane. Panas advised them he had the crew of the One. After discussing whether to transfer the crew of the One to the *Gridley* in the heaving seas, the captains agreed Capt. Panas would take them to Horta and the *Gridley* would stand watch over the hulk of the One. The *Ionia* arrived at Horta at 1230 GMT on May 18 and the One's crew was reunited with the crew of the Four aboard the *Columbia*.[11]

9

May 16–20, 1919, Aboard the NC-3

"This plane may remind of you of some things you used to know: that life is in the moment, joy matters more than money, the world is a beautiful place and that dreams really, truly are possible."
— Lane Wallace[1]

When Dick McCulloch piloted the NC-3 east of Mistaken Point, Newfoundland, the last bit of land they saw until they reached the Azores some 1,350 miles away, the craft was in a soaked state of disarray. Two attempts to get off the water drenched all of the crew and particularly Commander John Henry Towers, who bore the brunt of the deluge in the forward cockpit with his back to the spray.

They called their leader "Smiling Jack" in a typical Navy reversal. Jack Towers rarely smiled. He was a tremendously focused and determined individual who didn't look for friends among his men, but earned their deep respect for his ability to lead.[2]

But the ship was also in disarray because they were trying to sort themselves out after tearing up 50 pounds of decking designed to keep their feet dry and dumped it into a support launch and off-loaded spare tools, oil and radiator water. They inadvertently also sent back a five-gallon can of drinking water. Towers also, without hesitation, had ordered Lavender to pull out the CG-1104 emergency radio transmitter that weighed 26 pounds and told the reserve engineer, Ensign Braxton Rhodes, who weighed 185 pounds, he wasn't going. Rhodes was not the biggest man on board; Richardson weighed 243 pounds, but he outranked Rhodes and was the flagship pilot. "I'm sorry, boy," Towers said, as Rhodes reluctantly got in the launch. Lavender vehemently protested leaving the radio and Towers gave him that look and said, "I am the commander of this mission." The radio went in the launch.[3]

While the sea was smooth off Mistaken Point, McCulloch, who had been called back from the Naval Reserve for this mission by his friend Towers, found the air rough. The Three rose and fell as though it was breasting 50-foot waves and then sliding down the troughs only to rise up the next. They were climbing at a rate of 50 feet per minute.[4] Both pilots remained at the controls.[5]

Lavender reported they had no lights. McCulloch already knew because the dashboard lights didn't work. The circuits were soaked in the three take-off runs. Towers looked astern, checking to see if the Four and the One were in formation. They had been told to fly between 400 yards and three miles from the lead craft in V formation. He had difficulty making out the flying boats astern in the haze.[6]

As the Three flew over the *Aaron Ward*, station ship 2 at 11:25PM, the ship's crew lined the deck and cheered. The NC-3 crew could already see another star shell fired to the east from station ship 3, the *Buchanan*. Meanwhile Lavender was having trouble reeling out his 250-foot antenna. It kept tangling and locking. It was only after they flew over the *Buchanan* that he finally got it deployed. At 11:30 McCulloch spotted a passenger steamer going west, brilliantly illuminated, and Towers saw a second steamer.

At 12:03 AM the moon rose and McCulloch viewed it as "a great assistance" while Richardson complained that it was red as fire and, due to the clouds and fog banks, gave them a skewed horizon and blinded the pilots, who had been using a flashlight to see their gauges. Other thin clouds appeared, obscuring the surface and making the magnesium flares, designed to check drift, useless unless the craft dropped down within 50 feet of the surface, which Towers was not going to risk that at night. He ordered McCulloch and Richardson to hold the Three at 1,000 feet and they spotted station ships 4 and 5 — the *Upshur* and the *Boggs*. But they got a scare near the *Boggs* when both pilots and Towers saw the NC-1 suddenly loom up behind them out of the fog at about 2,000 feet. Boatswain Moore frantically waved them off with a flashlight from the rear cockpit and the One veered away. A short while later the Three found itself buffeted by the slipstream of the faster Four and Towers told Lavender to radio both flying boats and tell them to abandon the formation as too dangerous.

The Three noted the star bursts from station ship 6, the *Ward*. But after they saw a star shell burst from the *Palmer*, station ship 7, a heavy overcast obscured their view at 1,000 feet and the pilots asked Towers' permission to rise above the approaching fog bank so they could use the moon and stars as reference points. Towers gave them permission to take the Three up and noted the star shells of station ship 8, the *Walker*, but soon realized that the flying boat lacked the speed to get above the fog bank and ordered her back down to 1,000 feet where the air was clear but so turbulent they had to go back up.

At 2,000 feet it was better and they passed over station ship 9, the

Thatcher, at 4:10 AM and broke into the clear with the now pale disk of the moon in the eastern sky. It was beautiful above the clouds, "like sailing over a sea of snow." Occasionally, through a rift in the clouds, they could see the One and Four below, each on one side. The star shells were exploding above the clouds so it was easy to stay on course. The engines were running beautifully, 48 cylinders "spitting short purplish flames with a roar."[7]

From time to time Moore crawled up to pass Towers details of radio messages and the fuel and oil supply.

At station ship 10, the *Crosby*, at 4:45 PM, the clouds thickened again and Towers ordered the bird up until it got in the clear at 3,500 feet. Over station ship 11, the *Kalk*, Towers realized the Three was going to pass north of the destroyer rather than on the prescribed course south of the ship, but he didn't order the pilots to alter course. He figured he was on course and the *Kalk* was out of position, but must have seen the Three. He decided to let them deal with it. Just as they were abreast of the *Kalk*, it fired a star shell that burst just under the flying boat. Richardson and McCulloch both looked daggers at Towers.[8]

They were eight hours out of Trepassey, flying into a misty dawn that didn't break, but appeared gradually in shades of lighter gray. They passed over the *Meredith*, station ship 12, safely, but 13, the *Bush*, and 14, the *Cowell*, were hidden by high, thick cloud masses. Lavender called ahead for "weather reports, star shells and radio compass signals."[9]

By daybreak they were at 4,000 feet in cold, clear air with an "impressive and beautiful" view below; no destroyers were visible, just a sea of billowy white.

Twice star shells breached the cloud layer and exploded before them, fired by the invisible destroyers. After sunrise Towers ordered McCulloch and Richardson to plunge 2,000 feet through the clouds to 500 feet, looking for clear air. Instead of finding the *Maddox*, station ship 15, they ran into heavy rain squalls. Tower couldn't navigate effectively as the pilots tried to fly around the worst of the storms, sometimes making 180-degree turns to avoid the dark masses. One of the pilots spotted the vague shape of a vessel to the southwest and alerted Towers on the intercom. Towers put his glass on it and it was painted the war colors of destroyers. He presumed it was the *Maddox* and that it was at its post. He orders a 20-degree turn to the south in order to pass within sight of station ship 16, the *Hopewell*, and later over the *Stockton* at 17. It was an almost fatal error, as the Three was heading southeast now, well away from the line of destroyers.

Lavender transmitted their position every half-hour, but unbeknownst to the Three crew, the radio ground wire broke shortly after they passed the *Stockton*'s position. Lavender could hear radio transmissions, but nothing he sent went out.

Both pilots had stayed at the controls and Richardson, who had been working round the clock during the last two weeks of preparations at Rockaway, was exhausted. Suddenly he passed out and slumped to one side, asleep at the wheel. McCulloch shouted in the intercom to Towers and he crawled back, shook Richardson awake, and handed him the prescribed treatment of the day — a strychnine pill. It jolted the embarrassed Richardson to an upright position and he rejoined McCulloch at the controls. Later Towers gave him a second tiny dose of the lethal poison. (Richardson later wrote: "I cannot describe the mental agony this condition caused, fully realizing the seriousness of my condition and the responsibility resting on me, yet in spite of that unable to control my physical condition.")[10]

They flew into rain. McCulloch hunched close to the tiny windshield and gained some protection. The taller Richardson, whose head stuck up above the windshield, and Towers, in the open front cockpit, were getting hit by the raindrops which were stinging pellets, hitting at more than 80 miles an hour. For six hours, they flew through rain, half-expecting the water missiles to break the propeller blades, and when the rain stopped, they ran into fog so thick that they couldn't see ten feet ahead of the Three. They sideslipped once, but the pilots recovered. They were working together — Richardson watching the wingtips and working the ailerons "to keep the plane in trim" and McCulloch holding the plane on course with the rudder and elevators.[11]

Towers told McCulloch and Richardson he didn't know whether they were north or south of the *Stockton*, so he ordered a course change of 10 degrees northward, hoping on a parallel course to spot station ship 18, the *Craven*. The clouds were piled so high they couldn't get above them and visibility was less than 300 feet. They presumed they were near the Azore Islands, but they were lost and they feared that if they continued they would fly into Mount Pico's 7,315-foot bulk in the fog. A lull in the storm gave Towers a chance to shoot a quick position on the sun with his sextant as the craft rocked back and forth, sending the bubble on Byrd's artificial horizon device darting back and forth. The reading said if they continued on the current 90-degree heading they would fly right into Pico. Near Pico is Faial and Horta Harbor, an emergency landing spot, where the backup cruiser *Columbia* is at anchor. Towers distrusted the equipment, discounted the reading, and calculated they should turn north 60 degrees, as they were about 50 miles southwest of Faial. Moore crawled forward and handed Towers a note — two hours of fuel left. At 11 AM Towers made a decision, crawled back, and passed McCulloch a note: they should land and try to ascertain their position from the water. Richardson and McCulloch agreed. From 500 feet the waves looked fairly calm through the haze, but it was low-lying fog that gave an appearance of smooth water. Instead, the waves were running 10 to 20 feet high. The Three changed course

9. May 16–20, 1919, Aboard the NC-3

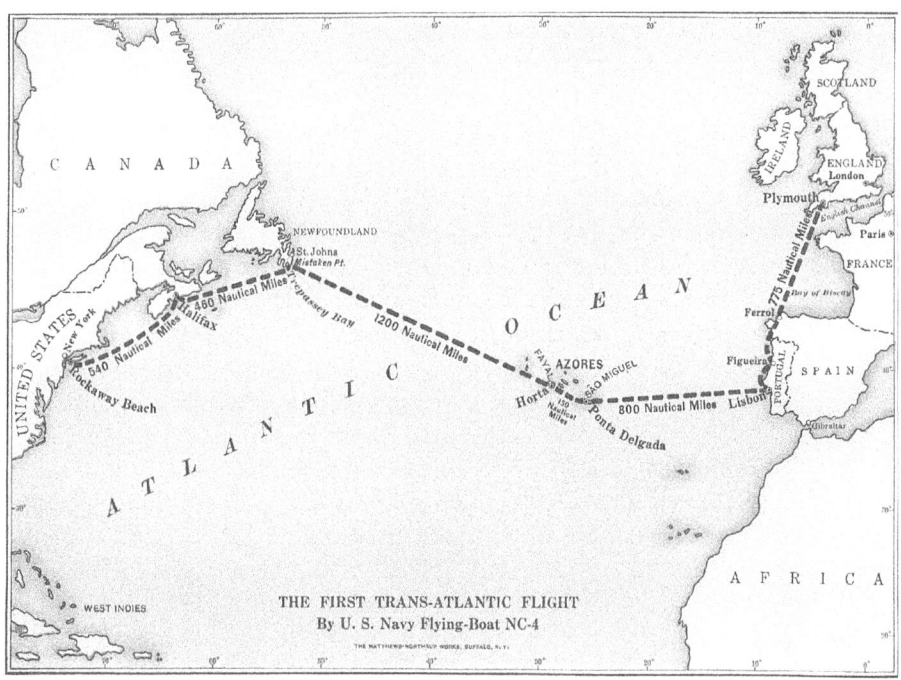

A map of the route of the NC-4 was published in a promotional book produced by the Department of Education, Curtiss Aeroplane and Motor Corporation in 1919 after the successful flight. It was called *The Flight Across the Atlantic*. The 88-page volume that belonged to Hinton was chopped up to use photographs and maps over the years when Hinton was interviewed by writers (Burns collection).

and descended into the wind. The Three touched down on the first wave smoothly, but smashed the second one head on with such force and speed that water sluiced through the craft, soaking everyone, and the center engine supports bent like a bow-legged cowboy, rendering the motor useless. The hull was damaged above the water line and there was a leak under the cockpit. Water sloshed forward and backward in the bottom of the hull. The crew plucked wet jelly sandwiches out of the bilge. There were five chocolate almond bars and six tins of emergency rations. They discovered they had ditched the five-gallon drum of drinking water at Trepassey. Radiator water was not a substitute. It was coffee brown with rust and engine oil for flavoring. It was 1:00 PM. The Three would never get off the water without the center engine. They needed help.

Towers got a fix on the sun and Lavender, checking his equipment, found the broken ground wire and got a radio bearing on the *Columbia*. They calculated they were about 34 miles southwest of the ship in Horta Harbor. The crew tried to relax while Lavender began sending distress signals: Dot-dot-dot, dash-dash-dash, dot-dot-dot. There was no response. Lavender could hear radio traffic, but the ship radio operators were using a different wavelength. The Three was operating at 425 meters. There was no emergency radio because it was aboard the *Aroostook*, already sailing for Plymouth, the mission's final destination.

Three hours later, Lavender learned by listening to destroyer radio traffic that the search for the Three was 400 miles to the west between the *Hopewell*, station ship 16, and the *Craven*, station ship 18. He sent Moore forward with a note and the bad news. Towers figured they were southeast of Flores and nearest to station ship 23, the *Gridley*. It would be an accident if they were found.

Running the port engine to generate wind for the radio propeller so Lavender could send his SOS caused the Three to rear and "plunge ... heavily into the approaching seas," so Towers ordered McCulloch to shut it down. The Three turned and sailed backward as Towers set course for the shipping lane between Faial and San Miguel to the northeast.[12]

Towers believed they would die. He didn't tell the crew, but he secured his log book inside his uniform. It would explain what happened in case his body was eventually recovered. At 8:00 PM Towers set two-hour watches for each crew member and assigned them duties. Bolts and wires were tightened and everything secured. He took the Very pistol, emergency flare gun, in case any ship or boat was spotted. They raised the American flag upside down as a distress signal and deployed two canvas-bucket sea anchors on a cable to stabilize the craft. Towers estimated the wind as gale force between 65 and 70 miles per hour.

They drifted at up to 15 mph and the pilots used the controls to steer off the wind by up to four points without turning sideways to the rollers that could swamp them. They drifted through the overcast all day and the winds and rain picked up during the night and pounded the crippled craft and its occupants. When Towers was off watch he was awakened several times to take readings on the stars and moon through cloud holes. He discovered the boat was sailing east rather than north. If they missed San Miguel in the Azores the next landfall would be Europe or North Africa. Towers knew the craft and crew couldn't last that long.

A heavy storm came out of the north-northwest with dawn on May 18. Driving rain, winds of 45 to 50 miles an hour, and 30-foot swells pounded the Three. The lower port wing ribs broke, the tail went under, and the elevators snapped off. Moore and Richardson crawled slowly out on the wings and punched holes through the canvas to let pooled water drain. They also cut away the broken wing and the control housing that was banging against the hull.

9. May 16–20, 1919, Aboard the NC-3

The men took turns pumping water out of the hull. In a vain attempt to calm the seas, Towers ordered oil poured over the side, but it blew away too fast to be much use. A heavy sea at 9:00 AM took the port pontoon and Towers ordered the men to take turns as human counterbalances on the starboard wing, strapped to the plane with Moore's telephone linesman's harness. Towers dropped pieces of broken wing rib overboard to check drift and calculate their speed. Both bucket sea anchors tore away and they deployed the big sea anchor which the ocean ripped to pieces. Next they tried torn wing fabric, which also was torn free. Finally they took the antenna wire, doubled it up, and used that to secure a smaller section of wing fabric.

At midday the lower elevator disintegrated and threatened the hull until it was torn free. A half-hour later, at 12:37, Pico's summit was spotted to the northwest. By Towers' calculation they were 45 miles southeast. He ordered Lavender to rig his radio again and the pilots started the port engine to give it power. Lavender transmitted their position. No response. Nothing. The running engine spun the flying boat around and it almost flipped over in the cross sea.

The welcome sight of Pico, land beckoning to them, made some crew members think they should head for it. Towers said, no, as the 60 mph wind shifted and was coming from the northwest, blowing them away from the island. If they used the last of the fuel and didn't reach land they would surely be lost. Each time there was a lull in the blow, Richardson and Mitscher used the engines to crab toward the islands. As night fell the winds continued and the flying boat surfed down some of the 30-foot waves at 20 miles per hour. No one discussed their chances. The moon rose again after midnight. Towers could get good fixes on their position, but that didn't help anything. Men not on watch tried to sleep. Men on watch smoked soggy cigarettes and let cold water spray keep them awake.

Towers took his turn on the wing, working to tighten bolts and guy wires that were constantly coming loose. Off watch, he crawled under the pilots' seat and tried to rest, but was bounced back and forth in the plunging craft and was finally flooded out with the water nearly two feet deep in the hull. Crew members pumped bilge round the clock. One crew member had to lie on his side in the water under the gas tanks in order to keep debris out of the suction hose. They changed positions frequently to allow that man to try to get warm. Hands were swollen from exposure to seawater and the phosphorescence of the white caps played tricks on their minds. Some thought it was searchlights from rescue ships. Richardson awakened from a break to see what he believed was a sea snake paralleling their course, only to realize it was the glow on the radio antenna wire trailing in the sea.

Gradually the pilots learned to control the craft's stability in spite of the changing winds and waves. It meant they didn't have to keep a man lashed to the starboard wing for balance and risk him falling asleep and disappearing overboard. They tackled each wave individually, head on, square to the crest as soon as they could see it.

At dawn on May 19, the winds and seas slightly moderate. It was clearer. Towers ordered Richardson and McCulloch to steer a course toward San Miguel, but a squall forced them to detour south for two hours. They slowly worked their way back northward at six knots. Towers was confident they were on course to reach the Azorean capital of Ponta del Gada at 9:30 PM after he shot a longitude line from the sun.

Three quarters of an hour later, Moore in the aft cockpit, which was near the prow of this strange backward-sailing craft, sang out: land ahead. It was San Miguel, the largest island in the Azorean archipeligo. Towers figured if the wind held direction and they could head three points more to the north, they would make landfall. Everyone was jubilant. Land was 44 miles away by Towers' reckoning. There was hope.

Towers crawled back down in the hull and retrieved his uniform hat, which had been floating in the bilge for two days, an unnecessary accoutrement. The pumping took on a different spirit and the crew discussed what they would like to eat first—they all agreed: bacon and eggs. Towers got his camera out of a waterproof pouch and, as the Three bobbed and splashed in the rough seas, snapped pictures of the crew.

The crew took down the distressed American flag signal, hoisted it upright, and mounted the flagship pennant. Lavender transmitted again. Again without success, but he picked up radio signals as far away as the *Baltimore*, still in Halifax Harbor in Nova Scotia.

Rain squalls hit the revived Three crew as it worked slowly to within seven miles of the coast and then Towers ordered them to parallel the shore on a course to their original destination—Ponta del Gada. They could see trees, vineyards, a sugar factory and houses on shore as the day passes. At 4:12 PM, as they near the harbor entrance, Lavender reported they had been spotted from shore. The *Harding* dashed out of the harbor toward them, stacks smoking, spray flying, coming to the rescue.

Not to be denied his triumph of seasmanship, Towers grabbed the Aldis signal lamp and warned them off, but asked them to stand ready to render assistance. The ship's radio operator replied: "It's a miracle! It's a miracle!" The *Harding* passed so close to the Three that her wake sent new waves crashing into the wrecked flying boat. Moore and McCulloch scrambled out on the wings to create balance and just then a big wave dislodged the starboard pontoon. The plane almost sunk before the pontoon and the wire dragging it were cut free.

9. May 16–20, 1919, Aboard the NC-3

Commander J. H. Towers, U. S. N., and his crew after their terrible battle with the sea off the Azores

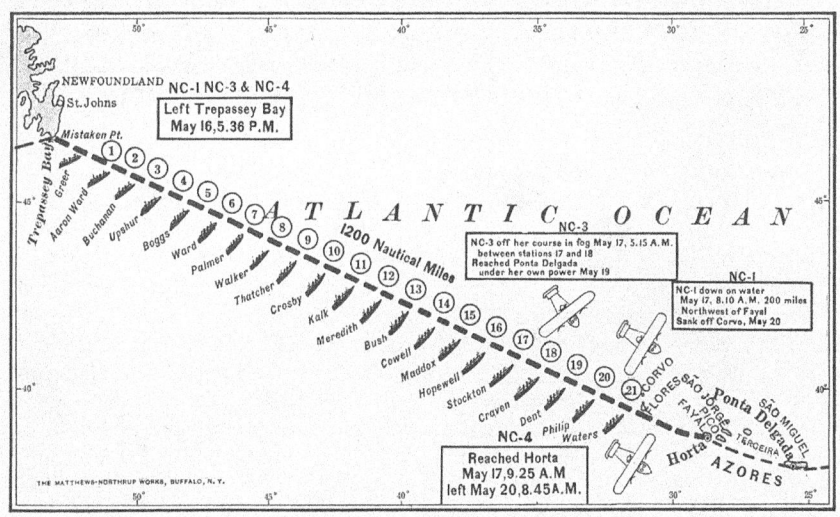

Third Leg, U. S. Navy Flying Boats NC-3, NC-1 and NC-4 from Trepassey Bay to Azores.
(Time given is New York Standard)

Map of the route of the Nancies Trepassey to the Azores, from the 1919 promotional book that Curtisss published, under a photograph of J. H. Towers and his crew.

Richardson started the center pusher engine as Lavender climbed out of the aft cockpit without using the safety tunnel. A yell from Towers saved Lavender from death in the spinning prop. The Three, wing fabric in tatters, pieces missing fore and aft, crabbed in under the eastern end of the Ponta del Gada breakwater to discover bedlam in the harbor.

Boats were flying about like water bugs. Boom, boom, boom, boom, the Portuguese fort fired a 21-gun salute; rockets arced into the sky as two whale boats from the *Melville* were carefully positioned under the Three's wings so it couldn't capsize. The island residents had been waiting more than two days to greet the transatlantic flyers. The NC-4 was still stuck at Horta. The NC-3 was first into port as she reached her mooring at 6:30 PM GMT. The derelict NC-1, chased by the destroyer *Fairfax,* was finally rammed and sunk to avoid danger to shipping. The Four had been locked in at Horta by the same weather the Three just sailed through. The Navy brass were going to take no chance of flying the Four to Ponta del Gada in bad weather. She was the last hope for a successful completion of the transatlantic crossing to Lisbon.

Towers and the crew members were haggard, dirty, and unsteady on their feet. They were assisted into the admiral's launch and out on shore near Admiralty House, where cheering citizens, local dignitaries, and the Commander of Naval Operations in the Azores, Admiral Richard H. Jackson, greeted them. Before the dazed fliers could clean up, eat, or sleep, they stood through the accolades of the Portuguese officials and listened to the cheers of the crowds.

Towers' telegram to his wife Lily in Washington, D.C., is terse: "MRS. TOWERS, 1715 19TH STREET. SAFE AND WELL.—JACK."[13]

10

Brits Fly for Honor: March 28, 1919–May 18, 1919

> *"There is beauty as well as mystery about the Atlantic, defying logic and rational reasoning. The rescues are particularly noteworthy.... What chance was there of finding a tiny aircraft in the vast Atlantic?*
>
> — David Beaty, "The Water Jump"

Harry George Hawker could have been the prototype for the film version of *Crocodile Dundee*. The Aussie ran away from home when he was 12 and became one of the land down under's top auto racers and mechanics before deciding to switch to the new field of aviation. Small, wiry with unusually long arms, and curly receding hair, he could barely read, but loved a good prank and a colorful story.

Australia in 1911 was not the place where aviation was popular, so he headed to England to try his luck and quickly became one of that nation's top pilots with his fearless willingness to take flimsy aircraft aloft.

When Hawker and navigator Navy Lt. Com. Kenneth L. MacKenzie-Grieve, the heart of the Sopwith expedition, arrived in Newfoundland aboard the steamer *Digby* on March 28, they faced lousy weather and the physical problem of getting a heavily loaded airplane off a runway they couldn't even see because it was buried in snow. The advance parties probed snowdrifts with long poles in order to find a suitable airfield and realized that Newfoundland weather in the spring was almost always bad.

The single engine Sopwith, specially modified for the Atlantic bid, supposedly could fly 3,000 miles on the amount of gas it could carry, more than enough for the ocean jump. In test flights in England, it had already flown more than 1,800 miles as the aviators munched on sandwiches made by Hawker's wife, Muriel.[1] But at 6,150 pounds, fully loaded, Sopwith engineers weren't that confident. So they modified the *Atlantic* so the undercarriage can be dropped once Hawker, the Aussie expatriate, was airborne, which could create a problem in landing in Ireland, but could be dealt with later.

The British lauded the NC crews for their accomplishment and the flyers met with the nation's dignitaries. Prince Edward, who later abdicated the throne, is in the center standing next to Lt. Commander Read. Hinton is the second man from left. The second man from the right is a young Winston Churchill (Burns collection).

With that reduced weight, an increase in speed of seven mph, and a favorable tail wind, they hopefully would reach their destination 2,000 miles distant — Fermoy, Ireland.

Hawker had survived testing hundreds of new craft throughout World War I. He had walked or crawled away from dozens of mishaps in the air and on the ground. He was so banged up from his exploits that he was rejected for service because of a bad back. A number of Hawker's renowned pranks at his home base, the Brooklands Aerodrome, centered around a semi-tame brown bear kept in the shed there. Tom Sopwith brought the animal from America.

Hawker was a man who whistled while he worked and had long fingers that twitched noticeably. Most felt that was from his previous air accident injuries. When things went badly, he could be sharp and irritable while he tried to solve mechanical problems. At night his wife, Muriel, read to him, first the aviation and auto publications and then teenage adventure stories.

On this tranatlantic adventure, Hawker planned to crash again in Ireland, but safely. The belly landing was considered the lesser threat than sitting down in the ocean. But the engineers had taken that possibility into account, too. They designed the aft part of the fuselage into a small, detachable, two-man boat and provided rubberized suits that MacKenzie-Grieve and Hawker could don while awaiting rescue.

Hawker and Grieve, "a phlegmatic Scotsman," were competing for the *London Daily Mail* prize, a princely $50,000 in U.S. dollars, in the spring of 1919. Sopwith hoped to win worldwide recognition in commercial aviation markets for a version of the plane it intended to sell to the public as the Sopwith *Transport*.

The *Atlantic* is powered by a 12-cylinder, 360-horsepower Rolls-Royce engine, which Hawker in his unabashed Australian machismo had proclaimed "the finest in the world." The plane was 31 feet, 6 inches long, with a wing span of 46 feet, 6 inches. It had a cruising speed of 105 mph, burned 15 gallons of gas per hour and fully loaded could reach a maximum altitude of 13,000 feet.

But the first problem the Hawker team encountered was the cold, snowy, rainy spring weather and Arctic ice. "Newfoundland is ruled by weather; it is part of the language. Weather sayings are taught to the children."[2]

St. John's harbor was sealed by an ice pack when they arrived off the coast, so the *Digby* sailed southward and westward around the island to the shelter of Placentia Bay. There, Hawker, Grieve and their two giant crates and a number of smaller cases were transferred to the *Portia*, a smaller vessel which could take them ashore.

Grieve, 39, joined the British Navy when he was 14 — a family tradition. During the war he served as navigation officer aboard the seaplane tender *Campania* and got interested in flying.[3] He was loaned to the Royal Air Force when the Sopwith Company asked for him to work with Hawker.

From Placentia Bay the entourage, including a Rolls-Royce engineer and a Jury's Imperial Pictures movie cameraman on hand to record the event for history, moved slowly by narrow gauge rail across the island to St. John's, where the crates were unloaded and teams of horses and men were hired to muscle the heavy crates six miles over soft, muddy roads to a snow-covered, L-shaped field that wrapped around a hill near the Mt. Pearl Naval Observatory. It was not much of an airfield, but "the very best place available."[4] The advance team, headed by Capt. Montague Fenn, had already built a couple sheds, one 55 by 50 feet and 30 feet high, to house the Sopwith. They faced St. John's Harbor and the ocean on a slight decline at one end of the snow-covered field. The workmen spread heavy stone in front of the larger shed to aid in pushing the plane in and out.

On April 7 snow fell all day and this was followed by 12 hours of rain turning the Mount Pearl Aerodrome site into a mud bath. Workers dug trenches to drain the water out of the shed.

Hawker and Grieve moved into the best hostelry in St. John's, the Cochrane, which Hawker, with his perverse sense of humor, called "The Cockroach." The place was immaculate and well cared for by three sisters. The Cochrane boosted potted palms in the main dining room, Persian rugs, a billiard room and uniformed maids. It was presided over by the three spinster sisters-in-law of the owner William Drayton, a local merchant. The three — Kitty, Minnie and Agnes — helped run the hotel and packed sandwiches and drinks for the airmen each morning as they left for their airfield on the chance they might start their flight.

On the afternoon of April 10 Hawker made his first test flight with Grieve. On take off at 4:30 PM, he hit a bump and it nearly sent the *Atlantic* into a grove of trees as he got it airborne. Hawker ascended to 3,500 feet and circled over St. John's and Conception Bay doing high-speed tests over 100 mph for an hour. When word spread of the plane overhead, crowds gathered on the streets of St. John's and the Newfoundland Parliament recessed so the lawmakers could get a look at this phenomenon.

On Hawker's return to Mount Pearl, the *Atlantic*'s wheels sunk through the frozen surface crust of mud when the plane landed and it nearly tipped over. The tests had burned out the wireless and the rudder was slightly bent on the rough takeoff.[5]

That same day the air race competition arrived in the form of Frederick Phillips Raynham and C.W.F. Morgan with a Martinsyde biplane dubbed the *Raymor* from their surnames.

Raynham and Hawker knew each other well. Raynham was the manager of the Sopwith flying school at Hendon Aerodome near London when Hawker arrived in England and applied for a job as a mechanic in 1912. The brash Hawker persuaded Raynham to teach him to fly. Some folks regarded Freddie Raynham as the best test pilot in Europe. He was the first pilot to pull a plane out of a spinning nose dive with the engine running and live to talk about it. He earned his pilot's certificate in May 1911 before he was 18. Slight and clean shaven, the son of a Suffolk farmer, Raynham decided to become a pilot after seeing Frenchman Louis Blériot's first Channel-crossing craft on display in London.

But within seven weeks after soloing, Hawker, the student, beat his boss in a duration competition by keeping a Sopwith-Wright biplane in the air for 8 hours and 23 minutes and winning the equivalent of $2,500.[6] It was to be the first of many close finishes between the pair — all seeming to favor Hawker.

The Martinsyde entry had a 41-foot wingspan and was 26 feet long.

Powered by a single Rolls-Royce 285-horsepower engine, its builders claimed a cruising speed of 100 mph. Raynham and Morgan and their support crew also moved into the Cochrane, making it the unofficial headquarters of the Great Atlantic Air Race. It created a cozy, little British colony of daredevils, mechanics and pranksters surrounded by reporters clamoring for news. Practical jokes were imported to St. John's for a new cast of hapless victims. Raynham was also viewed as top notch at such stunts. Pools of water appeared mysteriously in the depressions in old leather chairs in the sitting room, soaking reporters invited to seat themselves for a press conference. A bucket of water artfully placed on a door doused a newsman summoned to a room for an interview. Garbage cans tumbled down St. John's hilly streets, perhaps nudged by the bumper of a borrowed car, piloted by Raynham.

Within a week of its arrival, the Martinsyde *Raymor* was ready to fly.

The crews spent so much time spying on each other's activities and tests while the weather remained windy, cold, and impossible to fly in that eventually the two teams strike a gentleman's agreement to advise the other two hours before a plane's pilot intends to make his bid for fame and fortune.[7]

Both pilots were betting that they could allow the U.S. mission to reach the Azores and still be able to beat them across. On the evening of May 16, they got word that the NCs were off from Trepassey, 70 miles to the south over winding roads. On Saturday evening (May 17), they got an erroneous report that all three had safely arrived in the Azores. It was now or never for the Brits. They had to fly on Sunday for the glory of the British Empire or risk being also-rans. At first both entries considered following the Yankees' route to the Azores, but reports from ships at sea of clearing weather to the north changed their minds. Both planned to strike the Irish coast at Fermoy and continue on to England.

"Tell old tinsides I will see him at Brooklands," Hawker said before takeoff. Grieve told the ground crew he would see them in London.

It took until 5:42 GMT (3:40 Newfoundland time) to get the *Atlantic* warmed up and ready. The wind was 20 miles per hour east-northeast, which meant Hawker would have to run diagonally across the field, skirt the hill and avoid a deep drainage ditch at the foot of it. Then he had to clear a fence and some trees at the end of his run. He had never taken the *Atlantic* up during the tests in Newfoundland or England with more than a three-quarter load of fuel.

Grieve sat beside but slightly behind Hawker. Thin with sunken cheeks and a big nose, he rarely said much. After he was chosen as navigator, he took flying lessons for six days and graduated, but he did not claim to be an aviator. He had pinned a sprig of Scottish heather to his lapel and carried a handkerchief from his sweetheart.

There were only a couple hundred spectators at the Mount Pearl field as they made ready because it was a longish six-mile hike from town.

The Sopwith rocked back and forth over the rough, uneven ground, gaining speed. It missed the drainage ditch by inches and the fence and the trees at the end of the runway by feet. The spectators cheered. They were off.

Hawker climbed the *Atlantic* to 2,000 feet, passing over Raynham's camp at Quidi Vidi Lake where mechanics were frantically putting the last touches on readying the Martinsyde craft. There were a thousand spectators watching there and they waved and cheered as Hawker and Grieve passed overhead, blowing goodbye kisses. Once the *Atlantic* achieved some altitude, Hawker throttled down and the plane started a steady climb in bright, clear air. After they passed the coast, Hawker pulled the lever and the 450 pound undercarriage dropped away into the sea. It was later found and recovered by a cod fisherman. The air speed indicator jumped up the predicted 7 mph. They were on their way. The lookout at St. John's Signal Hill — where a stone tower commemorates explorer John Cabot's arrival in America and where Marconi got his first transatlantic Morse code message — reported the craft out of sight a few minutes later.

A half-hour after Hawker flew over Quidi Vidi Lake, the *Raymor* was wheeled into position with Agnes Dooley's sandwiches, letters from Newfoundland officials to British royalty, and 350 gallons of fuel. There were handshakes all around and Raynham and his navigator Capt. C.W. Fairfax Morgan climbed aboard.

Morgan, who claimed to be a descendent of the pirate Sir Henry Morgan, had become the darling of the media. A young reporter for the *St. John's Evening News*, Joey Smallwood loved Fax Morgan's tales of his war exploits and helped the Martinsyde team locate their flying field on the flats north of the lake.

Morgan had a cork leg from war injuries suffered as a pilot in the Royal Naval Flying Service where he earned the Croix de Guerre and the Distinguished Service Order for shooting down German planes.

He told Smallwood his views of the rubber suits and boat that Hawker and Grieve took along as safety precautions: "I'm afraid those lifesaving gadgets are of little use. For myself, I have decided that I may as well take one deep breath if we strike the sea. We will be a very small speck in a big ocean out there."[8]

The wind was from the wrong direction for Raynham and Morgan to get a heavily loaded plane off the field at Quidi Vidi. It was behind the *Raymor*. In a head wind with a light fuel load, the Martinsyde craft could get aloft in 111 feet. Now it rumbled and shook at one hundred, two hundred, three hundred yards, finally hit a hump and lurched into the air. The spectators cheered as it shakily rose to 50, 75, and then 100 feet. Suddenly the Rolls engine stalled and the *Raymor* crashed back to earth, buckling the undercarriage. It rolled to the end of the runway and tipped forward on its nose. Raynham climbed out with a bloody nose. Morgan was hurt worse. He was looking over the side when the plane crashed and he struck his head. Two men lifted him out and supported him as he staggered away. He was taken to a nearby home where he fainted. The Atlantic bid was over for Raynham and Morgan. The Martinsyde was out. The injured Morgan never flew again.

Hawker and Grieve were unaware of their friends' fate. Their radio only had a range of 25 miles and they were already beyond reach.

They had their own problems to face. Ten minutes into the flight they reached the spring fog bank that often cloaked Newfoundland's coast. Grieve had already taken a drift reading and Hawker flew up through gray blanket to a cruising altitude about 10,000 feet with an air speed of 105 mph. Grieve held up a note in front of Hawker with a course heading. Hawker nodded and pointed the *Atlantic* east. By 10 PM GMT, the blue of daylight sky darkened to purple, and the clouds below lost color and became dull, patchy and gray, with only occasional glimpses of the ocean below. There were no more shiny glints on the plane edges from the setting sun behind them.[9]

A quarter-hour later, weather conditions deteriorated. They saw heavy clouds ahead and the sky around them became thick and hazy. The *Atlantic* pushed ahead, the engine ticking over smoothly, much of the noise funneled past the cockpit by a long exhaust pipe. It was bitterly cold. When Grieve took off his gloves to write and hold up course directions, his fingers turned numb. Occasionally they hit bumpy air and bits of rain that pelt like hailstones. At 11:00 GMT, while still climbing slightly, Hawker checked the temperature gauge. It was much higher than it should have been. He opened the radiator shutters to allow the cold blast to play over the unit, but the temperature didn't drop significantly.

Heavier and thicker clouds had completely obscured the ocean as they pushed on. Grieve held up a note directing Hawker to divert a little to the north to take advantage of the winds. The clouds confronting them now were too mountainous to climb over. Climbing risked the radiator boiling over and would use precious fuel. Hawker diverted around the cloud ranges, making it difficult for Grieve to get a star shot to keep them on course.

A little later, the moon rose, offering some brightness. The water temperature had risen from 168 degrees to 176 degrees Fahrenheit, 36 degrees below the boiling point. The engine ran smoothly on, but Hawker remained worried. Deciding that it was rust, solder or bits of debris clogging a filter,

Hawker signaled Grieve that he was going to try to shake it loose. He shut off the engine and dived the *Atlantic*. One thousand, two thousand, three thousand feet they fell in silence, the only noise the wind whipping through the struts and wires. Hawker pushed the starter and the Rolls roared back to life. The temperature was down somewhat. It appeared to have worked. Hawker pointed the craft up again to get over the clouds, but an hour later, at 12:30 PM GMT, the temperature was back at 175 degrees. They were now 800 miles out from Newfoundland. They could still turn back and reach the safety of land. The *Atlantic* ground crew piled wood for a huge bonfire after the plane left in case it had to return at night. Big, threatening clouds loomed around them now, forcing them to dodge on their eastward course. They made the decision to push on.

Hawker nosedived the Sopwith again, but this time when he restarted the Rolls engine and began to climb, the temperature jumped to hover near the boiling point. He dived the *Atlantic* a second time and it got worse. Radiator water started to boil away and froze around the cap in the chill air.

The radiator and engine held 19 gallons of water, but once it started boiling it would not take long for Rolls to run dry and seize. Hawker climbed the *Atlantic* to 12,000 feet once more and throttled her down close to the stall point. The top wing edge was covered with ice from water blown out of the radiator and steam spouted from a tiny hole in the middle of the radiator cap. The temperature gauge hovered just a little below 212 degrees.

With the moon well up at 12,000 feet, they were above most of the clouds for a time and Grieve got a navigational shot on stars to the north so they knew roughly where they were. They were north of the main steamer lanes. They were past the point of no return. At 6:00 AM, they confronted a solid, towering range of black clouds, peaking out at 15,000 feet or higher — too high for the *Atlantic* to climb over. But Hawker tried and more boiling water shot out of the radiator. That was out. He tried flying through the black range, but the craft was buffeted and banged about. Hawker shut off the engine again to try to shake the blockage loose and the craft glided silently down — 11,000, then 10,000, then 9,000, then 8,000, down to about 6,000 feet. The threatening blackness still surrounded them so they descended to 5,000, then 4,000, then 3,000, then 2,000 and finally 1,000 feet where it was brighter and they saw the first signs of the sunrise.

Grieve's calculations showed they were now in the steamer lanes. But they had a new problem. Hawker couldn't restart the engine. He got no response when he opened up the throttle. He shouted to Grieve to hand-pump gas, and the navigator bent forward toward the tank right in front of him and pumped furiously. Nothing happened.

The ocean was rushing up to meet them as they continued their downward glide to 500, 400, 300, 200 and 100 feet. Hawker could see the sea clearly. Grieve couldn't because he was hunched forward pumping, pumping. The ocean was rough with angry 12-foot waves. Hawker whacked Grieve on the back and yelled for him to take cover before they hit. He feared his navigator would crush his head on the gas tank when they struck. Hawker pressed the starter button again. They were at 50, 40 and 30 feet. Grieve braced himself for the crash. At 10 feet, the engine turned over, Hawker punched the throttle and the *Atlantic* flattened out, skimming over the waves, almost touching the water, and then climbed slowly, up, up, to over 1,000 feet.

Hawker told Grieve he didn't think Ireland was possible. They had enough gas, but could probably only get an hour or two more out of the engine before the water ran dry and the pistons locked up. It was a few minutes after 6 AM GMT. They decided to look for a ship to the south in the steamer lanes.

They zig-zagged southeast and southwest across the shipping lanes for two hours, dodging around clouds and rain squalls that steadily worsened. There was also fog at the lower altitude. Suddenly a ship hull loomed out of the mist, heading east on a course toward England. Hawker shouted with joy. Grieve was silent.

Hawker circled the ship with Grieve, firing the Very flare pistol three times. Sailors appeared on deck, then Hawker flew along her course and set the *Atlantic* smoothly down in big waves about two miles ahead. The *Atlantic* rode high with its partially empty gas tanks, although waves started tearing apart the main planes of the wings and occasionally crested right over the plane.

Hawker and Grieve donned their rubber life-saving suits, detached their little boat, and waited. Water sloshed around their ankles in the bottom of the cockpit. Their bid to be first was finished. They would be lucky to be saved.

The ship, a tramp steamer, the *Mary* out of Denmark, hampered by the storm, stood off about 200 yards. Three crewmen launched a lifeboat on a line, but in the worsening seas, it took the rescue craft 90 minutes to cover that distance and toss them a line, whereupon the crew on deck hauled both boats in. It was 8:30 PM GMT at sea on Monday, May 18, and 9:30 AM in Fermoy, Ireland, and Hook, England (Hawker's home), and the rest of Great Britain, where anxious thousands awaited news of the flight.

There was no radio on board the *Mary*. Until they could make landfall or see another ship with a radio, the aviators had simply disappeared into the great, gray ocean. It was small solace that the Danish master, Capt. Adolph Duhn, who spoke good English, told them if the rescue had been delayed another hour, both men would probably had drowned, as the storm worsened and developed gale-force winds. Duhn ordered the *Mary* to heave to and ride it out. She made small progress in a northerly direction away from the shipping route, away from the possibility of seeing a ship with a radio. It was impossible to save the *Atlantic*. It drifted away in the storm, largely submerged. The NC-4 riding out the weather at Horta was now the only plane in the race to be first.[10]

11

British Bombers Compete: May 13–26, 1919

"The danger? But danger is one of the attractions of flight."
—Jean Conneau[1]

British Royal Air Force officers Capt. John Alcock and Lt. Arthur Whitten Brown jounced along the rutted road back to St. John's, the provincial capital, in a rented Buick. They were frustrated and unhappy because they had driven an hour and a half south to Ferryland on the Avalon Peninsula to check out a possible site to launch their Atlantic bid and win the $50,000 *Daily Mail* prize. It proved unusable.

As they navigated the tricky roads late on that May 18 afternoon, a motorist, who recognized them, shouted out the news, "Hawker's away."

"And Raynham?" Brown asks

"Smashed before he could get it off the ground," came the response.

If Hawker and Grieve succeed that would probably solve Alcock and Brown's problems. They could forget about renting a pasture and they could leave the Vimy in England where it was still being readied for shipping.

Alcock was a cheerful sort "with ginger colored hair and a loud laugh, whose infectious enthusiasm makes him popular."[2] His navigator Brown, better known as Teddie, walked with a limp from a war injury and used a cane. He was an American who was born in Manchester, England, and raised there by his parents. He gave up his U.S. citizenship to join the British Army before America joined the war. The pair returned to the Cochrane where the tight-knit collection of anxious English airmen and their crews await word on the success of Hawker and Grieve's flight.

Because of the lack of suitable airfields, a fourth entry, their Handley Page bomber and its crew, had to locate 60 miles to the north of St. John's on an isolated field at Harbour Grace.

When Alcock and Brown arrived back at the Cochrane, they found Raynham with his head swathed in bandages. All night long the airmen at the

Cochrane waited for word of Hawker's arrival to flash by radio across the Atlantic. Thousands gathered in the morning at Brooklands, the former racetrack turned airodrome near London where Hawker proposed to land. False reports of sightings of Hawker's craft were sent out, but never confirmed. By the afternoon, everyone acknowledged that Hawker must be down at sea.

Admiral Mark Kerr at Harbour Grace and Alcock and Brown were weeks away from having their craft — both multi-engine bombers — ready to make the jump.

In fact, Alcock and Brown were just arriving, rattling across Newfoundland on that narrow gauge railway, on May 13, the day the first NCs arrived at Trepassey, but their Vickers Vimy bomber was still in England. The *Digby* had better luck with the ice that day and steamed into St. John's harbor to offload several huge crates containing Admiral Kerr's four-engine Handley Page V/1500 bomber. It had to be towed, tugged and hauled over rutted roads to the Harbour Grace field.

Alcock and Brown arrived in St. John's in the middle of the night, motored to the Cochrane, and had to sweet-talk the Dooley sisters into allowing them to stay there. Brown reported to his fiancée they spent their evenings playing cards or visiting theaters and observed that the chief occupation in the city "appeared to be the drying of very dead cod ... and [you] could recognize those areas with your eyes shut."[3]

With the failure of the Martinsyde and Sopwith missions, the last hope for the British expeditions to be first across the Atlantic rested on the chance the NC-4, weathered in at Horta on the island of Faial in the Azores, would fail.

While first reports indicated that all three NCs had arrived in Portugal, the British teams at the Cochrane learned that only the Four made it. And while it was not competing for the *Daily Mail* prize, it was sitting in a good position to claim the honor of first across.

The Navy was taking no chances that might risk failure. While 50-knot winds whistled outside Horta Harbor and heavy 14-foot swells rolled around the end of the breakwater on Sunday, May 19, the NC-4 stayed right there in the lee of the supply ship *Columbia*. Read expressed that thought in a letter to his wife, Bess. "We are the last hope and can't afford to take chances with the plane." He worried about sightseers running into the Four or a piece of driftwood striking the hull.[4] In fact, a curious sailor shortly after their Saturday arrival while refueling the Four punched the red button in the navigator's cockpit in the bow and sent flares whooshing across the harbor, which could have ended of the mission if spilled gas had been floating in the harbor.

The Four's arrival at Horta had been unexpected and she had taxied well into the harbor before lookouts aboard the *Columbia* sounded the alarm and then bedlam broke out. The *Columbia* signaled "Welcome to the Azores." Small boats set out from shore and came alongside the Four, with their Portuguese occupants tossing flowers at the flying boat. A motorboat was sent to guide Hinton and Stone to a mooring and then take them to the *Columbia*. The two pilots stood aside on the wing and let their superior officer, Read, board the boat first. When they arrived at the *Columbia* crewmen applauded as the crew was piped aboard, a singular honor for a Lieutenant Commander.

They were served coffee and a hot meal, and crew and officers kept popping in and out of the wardroom to see the fliers and get close to history in the making. An hour later the Mayor of Horta arrived with a delegation to welcome them to European soil. Each crew member was given a bottle of wine and a bouquet. None of the Americans spoke Portuguese, so none of them understood a word other than a reference to President Wilson.[5] The ceremony and celebration dragged on while the fliers fought exhaustion to stay awake. At one point Stone leaned against a pillar, fast asleep. In early evening the officer of the day brought word that Bellinger and his crew had been rescued by the *Gridley*.

The notoriously unreliable weather prediction was that the storm would lift in 48 hours. Sunday afternoon the *Ionia* appears at Horta out of the fog and Bellinger and his crew and the crew of the Four were reunited aboard the *Columbia*. The talk at dinner was about the missing Three and what happened to Towers and his crew. Several station ships were searching for the Three in the area they believed it went down. During the meal word came from the radio room that Hawker was airborne for England and Raynham crashed on takeoff. It meant that if Hawker was successful, he would be first across.

Monday again dawned gray and rainy. There would be no flying that day and no need since Hawker, now long overdue was obviously lost at sea.

News came that afternoon of the Three's arrival in Ponta del Gada without any mention of the flying boat's condition, so Read altered plans to fly directly from Horta to Lisbon in order to jump to Ponta del Gada so the flying boats could make the final hop together.

By Tuesday afternoon the weather changed and the seas flattened at the center cluster of volcanic mountaintops that made up the Azores. At noon they were safe enough for takeoff and at 12:39 GMT, Hinton gunned his engines and bounced the Four across Horta harbor and into the air, heading for the capital of the Azores.

Rodd put out his radio antenna and talked to the *Melville* while the insouciant Breese shaved with coffee-colored hot water drawn from the engines.[6] The 176-mile flight was completed without incident and Hinton circled the red-tiled roofs on pink, white, blue, yellow and brown houses at 2:20 PM GMT and green checkerboard fields[7] before landing behind the mile-long artificial breakwater at Ponta del Gada on the island of Sao Miguel. It appeared a majority of its 250,000 citizens turned out to provide another tumultuous welcome and celebration. When the engines were shut off, there was bedlam with piers and seawalls jammed with people and ships blasting their steam whistles.

A haggard Towers was aboard the first launch to reach the Four. He told Read: "I got here first, Putty, but you made it the way we had planned." He assumed, like most of the Navy hierarchy, that as commander of the NC division, which had been commissioned in Navy tradition like sailing ships, that he would transfer his flag and crew to the Four and finish the flight to Lisbon. Read, on learning the fate of the NC-3, said he presumed that Towers would move to the Four as Division Commander. "In the affirmative," Towers replied.[8]

Towers and the NC-4 crew were ferried ashore where they met Admiral Jackson at the landing, then cars took them to the governor's palace, where Read and Towers appeared on a balcony to a cheering crowd in the streets outside.

But there was trouble brewing. Admiral Richard E. Jackson, Commander of the U.S. forces in the Azores, without specific authority in the matter, radioed the Commander of Naval Operations in Paris at the peace talks, recommending Towers accompany the Four on the final leg of its crossing. He sent a copy to Washington. Towers separately informed the Navy Department in Washington that he intended to transfer his flag to the NC-4 and continue his command of the mission on its way to Lisbon.

Admiral Benson replied, "I will in no way interfere with this expedition except to render assistance," leaving the decision up to Navy Secretary Josephus Daniels.[9]

Towers had already had McCulloch talk to Hinton and Stone about the handling characteristics of the Four and put his personal flag aboard. It was a dark day for Stone and Hinton. They were out of the race by Navy protocol. A service friend offered to rent a car and give them a tour of San Miguel to help them forget their woes, so they accepted and left. They saw pictures of themselves plastered on walls and Azoreans gathered round them in the small communities to see the strangers from America who arrived by air.

While they were absent, Admiral Jackson got a message from Washington on May 20: "For Commander Towers. Your Navy Secretary Thinks Best Commander Read proceed in command of NC Four. You remain Ponta Delgada await further orders."[10]

It was a violation of Navy tradition and protocol, and Admiral Jackson and Admiral Harry S. Knapp in London, who saw the radio traffic, protested. But whether he was motivated by the thought of making Read, the small man's hero or whether he just wanted to show an overreaching Franklin Roosevelt who was boss, the Carolina newspaper publisher remained unmoved. The wily politician, who hoped to use the crossing to gain greater Naval air appropriations, reiterated his stand to Knapp with this message: "While secretary recognizes full merit Commander Towers services for which he should be rewarded, in justice to all concerned, does not approve his sailing in NC Four."[11]

A furious Towers ordered his flag removed from the Four in a huff and stalked off, absenting himself from the various official celebrations. It tainted the atmosphere of the celebrations organized by Azorean officials. Sympathetic Admirals C. P. Plunkett and Jackson made the *Stockton* available to Towers and he sailed for Portugal to be on hand in Lisbon to supposedly coordinate the celebrations when the Four arrived. Lavender and Sadenwater were ordered to return to the U.S. to report to the Bureau of Navigation and Bostswain Moore was put in charge of the parts of the Three aboard the *Melville*, which sailed for New York. The rest of the crews of the One and Three also boarded the *Stockton* to sail to Lisbon and then Plymouth to recover their personal effects stored aboard the *Aroostook*.

Ironically it was the *Stockton* that Towers missed at station 17 when he got lost in the fog. And it was aboard the *Stockton* where the only loss of life occurred among the entrants in the bid to be first. A machinist mate, James Welch, was fatally injured and two other men were seriously burned when a turbo-generator exploded.[12]

Without the pressure of an imminent British flight, the Four remained in Ponta del Gada awaiting good weather. Read, Hinton, Stone and the rest of Four crew toured the island by day seeing neat farms, goat carts and ox carts. Read was escorted by a French official who spoke not a word of English, and he got in a round of golf. By night they were feted in a series of lavish parties.

The Four was still at Ponta del Gada late on May 23 when Towers arrived in Lisbon and the print media picked up on the story of his ill-tempered behavior and speculated on a rift between Read and Towers. Some thought Read might have made a direct appeal to Daniels or that Byrd had intervened on his friend Hinton's behalf, but there was no evidence to support those theories.

In Lisbon, great crowds gathered on May 21 at the harbor on the Tagus River where the Four was expected to land. Some residents held their positions until well after dark, hoping to see the giant seaplane arrive.[13]

The weather at the Azores continued to hold the Four in place. Strong northwest winds on May 25 with clearing weather and occasional squalls caused Naval officials to move the Four to anchorage further inside the breakwater. All night searchlights were played on the craft and a steam launch circled as precautions to keep curious boaters away from seeking souvenirs or colliding with the Four.

Newspapers in Europe and the U.S. were filled with accounts of the race. Hawker, 31, and Grieve, 28, had been missing for six days and had been given up for lost; a search by British warships called off.

Finally on May 27, nineteen days late, the crew of the Four boarded an hour before sunrise only to find one balky engine. Breese and Rhoads set to work to repair it. At 10:18 AM Hinton taxied the Four into the swells and turned to windward. The Four roared across the water and jounced heavily into the air. Clearing the breakwater by only a few feet, it circled the harbor and headed for the European mainland. Sailors lined the ship rails in the harbor and soldiers and citizens lined the piers as steam whistles shrieked approval as the Four disappeared in the eastern sky. The weather was almost perfect with a few clouds in the sky and a slight northwest wind. Forecasters predicted the fliers might encounter cloudy weather and possible rain squalls midway on the course, which was marked by 14 destroyers deployed along the route.

Rodd reeled out his trailing antenna and sent Read's message to Admiral Jackson: "We seem to be on our way. Many thanks for your hospitality."

Ten minutes later Jackson's wireless operator sent the message to Lisbon: "They've started." On that news the *Rochester* fired its signal gun, its sound echoing across the hills of Lisbon. *New York Times* reporter Walter Duranty was on hand to record the citizens streaming toward the waterfront from cafes, stores and homes as though the Four would arrive at any minute. By noon there was a solid mass of people around the "great bronze statue" of King Joseph X on Black Horse Square, where a crew from the *Rochester* had set up a bulletin board and posted news of the Four's progress that was sent by flag wagging from the ship to a sailor on the seawall.

The Four passed directly over the first station ship at 11:13 AM, which surprised Read, making his calculations in the bow, because by his reckoning they were seven or eight degrees south of the proper course. About 25 minutes later the Four — making about 80 miles an hour — reported she had passed station ship 2, but instead of being over her they saw her 15 miles to the north. The third station ship was nowhere to be seen. Read ordered Rodd to get a radio fix on station ship 4. Rodd reported back that Read was 30 degrees south of the true course. He checked those figures and found he was 45 degrees south. They were headed for Africa, not Portugal. Then Read noticed the compass was off its gimbals. Read reset it and re-calculated their position. They sighted station 4 on schedule and reported passing the next 10 ships as they progressed along the chain of destroyers. When the Four passed over the *McDougal* at 7:16 PM GMT (3:16 PM New York Time), the *Rochester* by prearrangement sounded its whistle and siren and was joined by all the other ships decked out in red, white and blue bunting in the port of Lisbon. The faithful watchers knew that the Four would be over Lisbon in an hour. The sun was a red ball sinking in the west as the Four made landfall at Cabo da Roca, the westernmost point of the continent, and sought the mouth of the Tagus at Punta da Laje. Night had fallen, streetlights were coming on, and Navy artist Henry Reuterdahl remarked to *Times* correspondent Duranty that the scene looked like a Broadway stage setting prepared for a happy ending.[14]

A lookout aboard the *Shawmut* called out, "There she is!" The Four was a black speck coming upriver, the roar of its engines rushing ahead. The *Shawmut* turned its searchlights into the 30-knot wind as whistles, sirens, and church bells drowned out the sound of the Four flying at about 1,500 feet. Abreast the Tower of Belem, she began a long, steady landing and touched down at 8:01 PM GM (9:01 PM Lisbon time).

The *Rochester* fired a 21-gun salute as a motor launch raced out to meet the Four and lead her to a buoy. Read missed the thrown line and said, "Try again. I slipped."

Read was alarmed by the launches, fishing boats and sailboats circling the Four, waving and cheering, and shouted to the *Shawmut* crews: "Don't let those fellows come too close. If they foul her, there'll be damage done."[15]

Read advised the sailors standing night watch as he left in the *Rochester* launch, "If they come too near, hit them lightly over the head; that will keep them away."

On the quarterdeck of the *Rochester,* Read saluted an illuminated flag at the stern and asked permission to come aboard. Permission was granted and Towers rushed up to shake Read's hand. The Marine band struck up the "Star Spangled Banner" and officers and men froze to attention.

The *Times* man Duranty in the hyperbolic style of the era, called it "a wonderful picture." In the foreground was the little group who had done what no man had ever done before, standing stiffly at salute in the dazzling brightness of a searchlight. Beyond them were rows of naval and military officers in uniform, and a dark mass of civilians splashed with the color of women's dresses.

"On the left was the witchery of colored lights gleaming amid the bright-hued flags, and in the center and on the right background were sailors' faces — grave and reverent in homage to their country's national hymn — rising tier upon tier until lost in the darkness overhead."[16]

12

Lisbon and Beyond

"There is a sense of exhilaration in flying through the free air, an intensity of enjoyment.... The view of the ordinary traveler is inadequate as that of an ant crawling over a magnificent rug."
— Wilbur Wright[1]

"We are safely on the other side of the pond," Lt. Commander Albert Cushing Read cabled to the *Melville* at Ponta del Gada after the Portuguese dignitaries presented the crews of the three flying boats with that country's Order of Tower and Sword and the celebration aboard the *Shawmut* had died down.

For Read, Towers, and Bellinger, that moment marked the beginning of a short-lived celebrity status. Within 20 years the first flight was only a footnote in the chronicles of famed aviation achievements and sometimes not even that.

For Hinton, the unlettered son of an Ohio farmer with a knack for things mechanical, including flying, the flight and its aftermath signaled a dramatic change in his life. Most of the senior officers on the Nancies go on to distinguished military careers and the flight was only a line in their resumes of command. Hinton, who had been promoted to officer status only because of those extraordinary flying skills, realized that as a junior officer with no formal education, his Navy career was limited. He had witnessed his commanders being lionized in the media and how they profited by selling their personal accounts. He loved flying and had discovered the excitement of adventure. Aviation was his future. It was a way up and a way out. The somewhat awkward-looking 31-year-old man, who was generously described by the press as tall, broad-shouldered, strapping and handsome, was bemused by the public and media attention and accolades, the lavish Portuguese balls and celebrations — all for simply flying an airplane, something he was naturally good at. It was a lovely new world and he became entranced with staying in it. And the press loved Hinton, a plain-spoken son of the Midwest, who modestly understated his role and was quoted as saying the crews were only doing

12. Lisbon and Beyond

When the NC-4 finally arrived in Lisbon it was too dark for cameras of the era to shoot good pictures. The next day the Four crew re-enacted the arrival on the Tagus River so it could be recorded for history (U.S. Navy photograph).

a job. "Our four 400-horsepower Liberty engines hummed monotonously," he recalled. "The destroyers were passed as regularly as railway stations.... Luck was with us. The fog split open and we saw the northern tip of Faial Island."[2]

With the first transatlantic flight accomplished, the Navy publicity machine with Secretary Daniels' encouragement and approval went into action. Noted military artists stationed along the route produced paintings and sketches that were released to the press. Photographers and reporters were given special access. Postcards were printed. Newsreel cameramen stationed along the route had captured each stage of the journey from takeoff at Rockaway to touchdown at Lisbon. Well, not quite touch down at Lisbon. Camera film wasn't technologically capable of capturing good images in the dark in 1919, so after official partying at lavish settings in Lisbon, Read and the crew re-staged the arrival for the reporters and the military cameramen, who were preparing a newsreel to be released to theaters.

After two days of partying and celebration, at 5:24 AM on May 30, the Four roared across the Tagus and took to the air over Lisbon. Photographers and reporters had been alerted. People poured into the streets for a final look. Hinton took the Four toward the sea and made a wide turn and came back in for a brief landing near the *Shawmut*. Launches filled with cameramen paralleled the landing. When the Four had come to rest one called out: "That's fine, Commander, now how about doing it once more — just to be on the safe side?" Read reportedly responded, "Not on your life," and gave Hinton orders to take her up on a course along the coast for Plymouth, England.[3]

It is speculative to say whether Secretary Daniels was more motivated by the fact that Army Brigadier General Billy Mitchell months earlier had bragged to naval brass that navies and armies were obsolete and the future belonged to a separate "air force or by the need for additional Congressional appropriations if a distinctively Naval brand of air power was to grow." But Daniels knew Mitchell had friends in Congress and he was determined to emphasize the flight as more than a naval victory and one that belonged to the entire United States.

Newspapers from New York to the Rocky Mountains trumpeted the achievement in editorials and cartoons. Some speculated that it would not be long before posh seaplanes would be bridging the Atlantic commercially.

A half-century later, Richard K. Smith, of the Smithsonian, who wrote

Three artists were assigned to the NC mission and did a number of paintings depicting the flight of the three flying boats. Also movie crews were assign to shoot footage at the various stopping points along the route (Burns collection).

12. Lisbon and Beyond

The NC-4 refuels at the support ship *Shawmut* on the Tagus River in Lisbon Harbor before taking off on the last leg of the flight to Plymouth, England (International Film Service).

the definitive biography of the flight, quoted the distinguished editor of *The Aeroplane*, the world's leading English language aviation weekly, to put the accomplishment in perspective. C.G. Grey prophetically foreshadowed Charles Lindbergh, Amelia Earhart and other daring aviators when he wrote in his June 1919 issue:

> There is pure poetic justice in the victory being won by the Americans. After all, the first people to fly were the Wright brothers in 1903, on a machine of their own build with an engine of their own make. The first flights off and onto water were made by Glenn Curtiss in 1911, also in a machine and engine of his own production. And the first flying boat was designed and built by Glenn Curtiss in 1913, again with a home-made engine. Who therefore has a better right to be first across the Atlantic than an American crew on an American flying boat with American engines? We may regret our own failure, but we cannot grudge America her brilliant success.
>
> And now what next? The Atlantic has been crossed by air. We have lost the honour of being first across.
>
> There seems to be but a modified glory to be had in being the first to do a non-stop flight. So long as one can get from one place to another in any given vehicle, it matters little whether one stops for a drink along the way.

After the first non-stop journey we shall begin to introduce an illimitable series of minor classes in the competition. We shall have the "first one man flight," then we shall have the "first flight with one engine," "the first flight with two engines" ... "the first flight with one passenger," "the first flight with ten passengers," "the first flight with a woman passenger," and so forth and so on, *ad infinitum.*

One swallow does not make a summer and one trans-Atlantic flight does not make a commercial air service. We are still far from that regular service of aircraft across the Atlantic.... Such a service will come in due time, either by airship or aeroplane, probably by the former at first.

When it comes it will depend for its success upon perfect organization and not upon slap-dash gallantry. So like the first crossing of the Atlantic it may fall to the skill and organizing power of America. If so, as in the present matter, honour be to whom honour is due."[4]

But Grey was almost alone in Great Britain in that opinion on the day he penned those words. The British press largely ignored the NC-4's arrival at Lisbon and instead engaged in paroxysms of celebration over the fact that Hawker and Grieve had been found alive. They trumpeted that fact and the news that the pair were traveling by rail to London to the cheers of thousands of Brits lined up at cities, villages and hamlets along the way.

From Lisbon, after clearing the mainland at 5:55 AM, the Four headed north in largely favorable weather with occasional small rain squalls. Rodd let out his trailing antenna wire and sent a message from Read to the *Shawmut* at 6:12 AM. "FOR AMERICAN MINISTER. REQUEST YOU EXPRESS TO ALL HEARTFELT APPRECIATION OF COMMANDING OFFICER AND CREW OF NC-FOUR FOR WONDERFUL WELCOME. READ."

All four engines ran smoothly as the Four skirted the coast about 10 miles offshore. Originally no station ships were scheduled along the coast, but a careful Admiral Plunkett ordered five from European waters into positions along the route. At 6:25 AM a message was broadcast: "TRANSATLANTIC SEAPLANE FLIGHT NOW IN PROGRESS. SHIPS ARE REQUESTED TO RESTRICT USE OF RADIO APPARATUS TO AVOID INTERFERENCE WITH SEAPLANES."

However, Rodd reported it did not have much effect, as Spanish and Portuguese ships were chattering back and forth about the flight. The Four passed over the *Conner* on schedule at 6:33 AM (GMT). Rodd got weather reports from the *Conner*, *Rathburne* and *Woolsey* with difficulty because they hadn't been alerted to tune to the right frequency. He sent a message to the *Shawmut* at 6:48 AM to advise the station ships to listen on 425 meters. At 7:05 AM a plume of spray started leaking from the port engine of the plane.

Read thought about sending Rhoads out on the wing to determine if it was water, oil or gas, but decided it was too risky. With a "fair-sized swell" running, Read ordered the co-pilots to head for smoother water near shore. Rodd sent this message to the *Rathburne*: "WE MAY HAVE TO LAND. STICK

12. Lisbon and Beyond

close on 425 meters for my buzzer modulated set if I send the word 'landing.'"

Two minutes later he sent: "We have gas leak on port motor and may land soon." The *Rathburne* operator acknowledged the message.

Read spotted the wide mouth of the Mondego River near at Figuera, Portugal, as they approached shore and ordered Hinton to land. Rodd, sensing the descent, retrieved his trailing antenna and sent on his emergency radio: "landing, landing, sending on emergency antenna."

The Four sat down at 7:21 am and taxied toward the city. Read advised Rodd where they were. A half-hour later the Four ran aground on one of the many sandbars that dotted the river mouth. By revving the engines, they were able to slide off, but it was obvious they would have to wait for high tide before attempting a takeoff.

Meanwhile, a frustrated Rodd kept trying to break into the radio chatter about the Four not showing up on schedule over the *Rathburne*. It was 8:43 before he got an opening and called again only to hear a destroyer broadcasting: "Proceeding to assistance of NC-four."

A *Shawmut* operator, figuring out the situation, again warned ships to listen for messages rather than broadcast, but the chatter resumed and it was 9:18 am before Rodd was able to admonish the *Rathburne* operator to listen in the future and not transmit. He sends: "In mondego river. Must wait high tide at two GMT. Seaplane O.K. Cannot make Plymouth tonight. Request destroyers keep stations. What is best port to north to land within three hundred miles. Request report situation Comfran and Plymouth. Read."

Meanwhile, a crowd, many of whom had never seen a seaplane before, gathered on the southern shore of the Mondego at Figueira and the captain of the port and other officials were rowed out in a boat to greet the North American aviators and invited them, in a mixture of Portuguese and French, to lunch. The port captain explained at great length in largely incomprehensible language that high tide wouldn't occur until 2 pm. They provided boats to aid in mooring the Four to the river bank. Read Breese, Hinton, and Stone went ashore and met the town's mayor, who offered them free use of the city. Two destroyers arrived off shore and while the local residents warned that a small boat couldn't get through the riptide at the mouth at that stage of the tide, Captain Symington of the *Rathburne* appeared in just such a craft through the surf to check on the Four. Rhoads discovered the engine problem was a radiator water leak not a gasoline leak and he poured in a mixture designed to clog the hole while the motor is running.

At 1:14 pm, after consulting with Captain Symington, Read had Rodd semaphore to the *Rathburne* a request to have the nearest destroyer proceed

The NC-4 taxiing on the Tagus at Lisbon.

to Ferrol Harbor in Spain to anchor and serve as a tender for the Four that night since they couldn't reach Plymouth before dark.

Four minutes later the Four was airborne again and Rodd again was frustrated in his efforts to raise the *Woolsey*, whose operator was busy talking to another destroyer. It wasn't until the Four flew right over the ship at 2:20 PM that she acknowledged them. The weather was good for the most part, but they occasionally changed course to avoid small squalls. At 2:51 Rodd learned that the destroyer *Tarbell* would arrive off Ferrol Harbor at 3:30 PM to make a smoke marker. The Four passed over the *Yarnall* at 3:10 PM and at 4:15 they were advised the *Harding* would serve as their tender in the harbor for the night. Off Cape Finsterre the pilots caught a strong tail wind and arrived over Ferrol 15 minutes ahead of their estimates. The city, surrounded by high hills, had a beautiful harbor, but troubled air.

The Four circled over thousands of townspeople who had converged on the docks and the seawalls to see the transatlantic fliers, then spiraled down for a landing inside the harbor on the south shore of the Bay of Biscay at 4:47 PM. Fifteen minutes later the *Harding* arrived to take up its tender duties. Spanish officials made courtesy calls and offered assistance; the crew was fed and bunked aboard the ship for the night.

12. Lisbon and Beyond

Despite an unfavorable weather forecast, the Four taxied out and took to the air at 6:27 AM on May 31. With Hinton and Stone at the controls, it climbed rapidly and Rodd let out his trailing antenna six minutes later. The *Harding* relayed their departure to the *Mahan*, the next destroyer in a direct line to Brest on the French coast. For the first 40 minutes they were pelted by rain and squalls and thick weather caused them to change course frequently. Read finally ordered Hinton and Stone to stick to the course he charted in spite of the turbulence. The visibility deteriorated as they passed the *Mahan* at 7:43 and got worse as they flew on over the Bay of Biscay and they failed to see station ships 3, 4, and 5, the *Gridley*, *Dupont* and *Biddle*.

Read directed the pilots to edge to starboard of the course to make sure they didn't miss the northwestern corner of France at Ushant. He eventually spotted Ras Point south of Brest and ordered the pilots to circle the harbor before continuing across the channel to Plymouth. They were flying so low Rodd couldn't use the trailing antenna. At 11:15 AM Read directed Rodd to send this message to the Commander in France: "Greetings from the NC-Four. I am sorry we cannot stop. Read." About a half-hour later they got a reply: "To NC-Four, congratulations on your magnificent feats. Sorry you cannot stop and let us enterain you. Good luck. Halstead."

The Four ran into an increasing head wind as they left France. Just after noon they got a radio message from the *Stockton* in the English Channel saying visibility was seven miles and sun was shining. Rodd told them the Four was surrounded by fog and so low he couldn't let out the 250-foot-long radio antenna.

They passed somewhere to the east of the *Stockton* at 12:41. Rodd looked out the hatch and saw a merchant vessel, but couldn't raise her on the radio, speculating later that the operator was probably on deck watching them fly over.

Rodd, fearing they might miss Plymouth in the fog, asked Read to have Hinton and Stone take the Four up to 400 feet so he could let out the antenna and get a compass signal from a shore station. They climbed, but the fog became so dense they were forced to descend again. Then the fog thinned and Read spotted land at 1:15. They climbed again to 1,500 feet and Rodd put out his trailing antenna. Read had brought them right to Plymouth. In the fog they never saw three British F-2A seaplanes which had been sent out to greet them and escort them in. Those planes trailed behind the Four as it arrived over the hills of Plymouth.

Once again whistles, sirens and bells created a roar. The Four circled eastward over the citadel and at 1:26 PM, Hinton spiraled the Four down into a west wind behind the breakwater. They quickly taxied to a mooring buoy in an area known as the Cattewater west of Mount Batten to avoid the small craft in the harbor and the crowds rushing the shore. After showering aboard the *Rochester*, the crew was barged to the stone jetty on the waterfront where a monument marked the *Mayflower*'s departure. There they were greeted by the Plymouth mayor, dressed in a long, fur-trimmed crimson robe and a cocked hat and surrounded by three mace bearers and the town clerk in a shoulder-length wig. "The job was finished," Read later wrote.[5]

But the celebrations continued. Read and the crew were driven through Plymouth streets packed with people cheering them and a large crowd waited outside the Grand Hotel while they dined with local officials to cheer them again.

The next day at Paddington station in London, American sailors, soldiers and Marines packed the platforms, hoisted Read and his men onto their shoulders, and carried them out into the streets. Harry Hawker tried to get through the press to congratulate them, but couldn't get near them. The servicemen insisted on pushing the car carrying the Four crew from the station to a luncheon at the Aero Club.

They spent two days in London and then answered a summons to France from President Woodrow Wilson, who was in Paris ironing out the details of the peace treaty. They also met British Prime Minister David Lloyd George, Georges Clemenceau of France, and Vittorio Emanuele Orlando of Italy. They returned to London the same day for a round of parties and celebrations, which included meeting Winston Churchill and the future king of England, Prince Edward. On June 9 the officers received the Air Force Cross and Rhoads, as an enlisted man, got the Air Force Medal.

The Four crew and the remaining members of the Three and One crews returned to Paris for a week's leave before reporting to Brest in mid–June for transport back to the U.S. aboard a ship. Breese, always noted for his partying, had returned to Paris and was holed up in a hotel. Towers sent him a telegram telling him if he didn't make the ship he would be charged as absent from duty without leave and promised to reprimand Breese when they next met.

While the NC crews were in Brest waiting for the U.S.S. *Zeppelin* to sail, they learned that John Alcock and Arthur Whitten Brown had completed the first nonstop flight in 16 hours and 12 minutes from Lester's field in Newfoundland to a June 15 crash landing in a bog near the Marconi radio station in Clifden, Ireland. The media on both sides of the Atlantic went wild with banner headlines. The Americans were impressed with the daring of the deed and the British finally had something to crow about — the first nonstop flight.

Read put the feat in perspective in a quote for the *New York Times*. "While there is nothing which will add much information to the art of aviation as a result of the flight, it was a wonderfully nervy thing to attempt and a magnificent achievement. I have much admiration for the men who attempted the great feat in the face of such odds."[6]

12. Lisbon and Beyond

The *Zeppelin* sailed into New York Harbor past the Statue of Liberty on June 27 to more clamor and a tumultuous welcome. It was accompanied by the C-4 Navy dirigible as an escort and the sub-chaser *Herresshoff*, which circled in the channel "until the silver, cloud-like bulk of the C-4 against the somber sky revealed the *Zeppelin* approaching." "One plane flew within 100 feet of the *Zeppelin*'s deck to drop 12 invitations to dinner the next Wednesday at the Hotel Commodore for the aviators from the American Flying Club. The sub-chaser carried the wives of six of the aviators — Towers, Read, Hinton, Bellinger, Breese and Richardson — and the children of two — Margaret Richardson, 8, and Frances Breese, 3."

Breese's wife was worried that her sometimes errant husband wasn't on board because it had been reported he had missed the ship. She asked an *Evening World* reporter recently out of the Navy to wig-wag signal the sub-chaser. He sent: "If Lt. Breese is on board have him stand on the rail." A tall man climbed up on the rail and waved to the women lined up alongside Bess Read, braving the rain in their Sunday finery — hats with feathers, cloaks and high-heeled shoes — aboard the *Herresshoff*.

The New York World described the scene:

> Plodding slowly up the harbor under a lowering sky, which spat frequent dashes of rain, with a fleet of small craft on her flanks and astern and flying boats buzzin ahead, behind and over her, the transport, *Zeppelin* brought home yesterday the crews of the Navy's NC planes, six of whom were the first men in history to cross the Atlantic by the air route. Rain cut down the greeting fleet from 35 planes and two dirigibles to 10 planes, five of which made only a brief stay over the harbor, and one blimp. It denied observers massed on points of vantage ashore the pleasure of more than the haziest glimpse of the ship's great bulk as it slid ghost-like through the mist to Pier 4 at Hoboken.

A few minutes after 4:00 PM the *Zeppelin* was tied to the pier. American flags draped the upper levels of the pier and while the ship's band played "Hail, Hail, the Gang's All Here," "How Dry I Am" and "Can You Tame Wild Women," Towers marched his men up the gangplank to stand at attention. Towers, Richardson and McCulloch represented the Three while the whole crews of the Four and One were there with Read's men in a place of honor at the right of the line. All of them wore their Portuguese Order of the Tower and Sword and the insignia of the British Royal Air Force Cross. A cacophony of noise rose from the crowd on the two decks of the dock, from the street and from the area as whistles and bells of boats sounded in approval. *The World* reporter claimed to note a slight quiver on Commander Read's lips when he was greeted officially by Admiral James H. Glennon, Daniels' representative.

In a bittersweet note, Chief Machinist's Mate Harry Howard had arrived

Home again. The crew of the NC-4 sail into New York Harbor aboard the *Zeppelin*, a transport ship. Hinton is in the middle with his hands on the rail standing next to Lt. Commander Albert Cushing Read with his hands in his slicker pockets (International Film Service).

an hour early for the occasion. Howard had lost his right hand to a Four propeller in the final days of preparation and was replaced by Smokey Rhoads. All six Four fliers expressed regret to Howard that he hadn't shared in the adventure.

Read reportedly turned to the newspaper men and said: "Well, I went over in a seaplane and came back in a *Zeppelin*. That's some round trip.... Now I must go and see the best woman in the world; and as to my future plans they will depend on the United States Navy and Mrs. Read."

He continued, "Good Lord, men, there is so little I can say just now. This is a wonderful reception. They showed us a whale of a time in England and it seems as though it isn't over yet. I regret more than I can tell you, that only one of the NCs got across. It is too bad that the entire fleet was not successful." All of the mission aviators were then loaded into cars and escorted to the Hotel Commodore where they stayed while in the city.

The disassembled Four was supposed to be shipped to Anacostia Naval Air Station outside Washington, D.C., because it was felt that better publicity for Navy aviation could be achieved there when the craft was put back together.[7]

But everyone wanted a piece of the action. *The New York World* editor telegraphed Daniels on June 21 making a plea for the Four to be re-assembled in that city and put on display in Central Park for a week. "Actually hundreds of thousands would see it and it would be a fine thing for the Navy. Who knows but that more than one future admiral might find his youthful self-determination by gazing upon it. If it should be considered desirable it could be floated upon the lake in the park, but either on the lake or properly roped off in one of the park's large wide open spaces it would be one inspiring spectacle. Not one person in a hundred thousand really knows what the immortal ship really looks like."[8]

The Four was put on display in Central Park. Souvenir hunters walked off with more than a quarter of the plane's structure. It had to be refitted for

The NC-4 on display in Central Park in New York City after the successful Atlantic crossing. Souvenir collectors stripped so much fabric and so many parts off the craft that it had to be re-furbished before it could fly again (U.S. Navy photograph).

the east coast promotional tour. Hinton's admirers in Van Wert invited their favorite son to return to his hometown the help celebrate Victory Day on September 3, 1919, but Hinton telegraphed back, explaining that he couldn't get away because he was helping with preparations for the NC-4 promotional flight around the nation to spur interest in naval aviation.

That didn't stop the Van Wert locals, who then sent telegrams to Ohio's U.S. Senators, Warren G. Harding and Atlee Pomerene, and Ohio congressman Charles J. Thompson, asking them to intervene with the War Department to try to have Hinton detailed to Van Wert for that day that coincided with the opening of the county fair. However, their pleas weren't successful and Hinton never went.[9]

Hinton (right) poses with his friend Eugene Saylor "Smokey" Rhoads as they start the NC-4 publicity tour of U.S. cities (Burns collection).

The Minnesota State Fair organizers made a similar bid to get the Four, pulling what political strings its organizers could, but they got a rejection from FDR, advising that the cost of shipping the Four to the Midwest would be prohibitive.

The nation's newspapers helped promote the tour:

> WORLD HERO TO RECRUIT FOR THE NAVY
> Commander Read and His NC-4 to Tour Coast
> Nothing is impossible in recruiting. In one strata, submarines scout for men and from high up above the clouds, a sea-plane will scatter the news that the Navy is open to live wires.
>
> On September 22nd, Commander Read will start and fly in a non-stop flight from Atlantic City to Portland, Maine. On the way back the first landing will be made at Boston, with a short stop at Providence before the actual tour commences for the Florida Coast.
>
> It will give the people of the South a chance to see the smallest officer in the Aviation Service handling the Navy's biggest plane, which achieved the first Trans-Atlantic flight.
>
> The above drawing of the NC-4 in action was made on board the plane by Lieutenant Commander Henry Reuterdahl, right after the final finish at Plymouth, England.[10]

The drawing showed the Four in flight with whirling propellers overhead and one flyer walking on the wing.

Before the national tour left New York, someone had the idea to pose members of the Ziegfeld Follies on the aircraft's wings and the resulting picture got wide play in the press.

Everywhere the Four went, from a stop in Boston in late September and early October to its final destination at Pensacola before flying back to Rockaway for dismantling, the crew was greeted by cheering crowds. On a return visit to New York, on display at the Batttery, the Four again was ravaged by souvenir hunters and sunk at her berth. The Navy outfitted her again and moved her out of reach of the fans.

In early October the Four landed twice for repairs enroute to Philadelphia, where it was displayed at the Vine Street Pier. The Four with Read in command and Hinton at the controls toured more than 30 cities across the Northeast and South, including Philadelphia, New Orleans, St. Louis, and Washington, D.C., where Secretary Daniels spoke at a recruiting rally. It got as far west as Galveston, Texas, but mechanical problems caused Read to abort a plan to continue on to Houston on December 18, 1919. On their flight back, mechanical problems again forced the Four down. It landed in the Gulf of Mexico and was missing for hours before the crew managed to repair it and get it back in the air to fly to Mobile, Alabama.

The NC-4 ended its aerial career on January 3, 1920, when it was flown

The NC-4 on its national publicity tour. This was probably shot in St. Louis.

from Pensacola back to Rockaway. Its tender, USS *Isabel* was relieved of its support duty on January 4, 1920, and sailed back to Philadelphia.[11]

After the tour the Navy faced a problem of what to do with the giant, historic aircraft. Displaying it at the Smithsonian would be expensive. Housing for the machine there was estimated to cost $65,000 because a roof would have to be built over a 16,000-square-foot court large enough to accommodate the flying boat. The Naval Academy estimated it would cost it $35,000 to house the craft.[12]

Eventually the Four was disassembled and parts stored in several locations. It was decades before a Smithsonian official, Paul Garber, a curator who at age 10 had witnessed the first Wright brothers military flight, tracked the parts down and arranged for the Four to be rebuilt. It was Garber's efforts that led to the establishment of the National Air & Space Museum as part of the Smithsonian and the Museum's facility for preservation and storage in Suitland, Maryland, was named in his memory.

13

Ballooning into Canada

"If all else fails, immortality can always be assured by spectacular error."
— John Kenneth Galbraith[1]

A dog barked. All three men heard it. The night sky was moonless and starless. The balloonists could see no lights below the wicker basket that swung back and forth in the wind. But a dog barked and that meant civilization. For several hours they had been flying over forest, somewhere in Canada, somewhere north of Lake Ontario. But they didn't know that. The last place they identified on earth was a small town called Wells on the Hudson River in upstate New York. They couldn't find it on their charts.

All 15 bags of sand ballast were gone, tossed overboard to keep U.S. Naval Balloon A-5598 in the air. It was only a matter of time before enough hydrogen escaped from the bag overhead and they would be forced to land.[2]

A dog below meant shelter and people. The bark spelled hope to the three Navy lieutenants who last communicated with people on the ground when they had hovered in that dead calm over Wells 10 hours earlier and used a megaphone to ask a farmer and his wife, who were milking a cow in their barnyard, what town they were near.

That was before they got caught in gale-force winds that hurled the balloon north-northwest at 40 to 60 miles an hour. It had been an eerily quiet first balloon ride for Lt. Walter Hinton. None of the three men were really dressed for the weather. They had packed only enough sandwiches and snacks for a lunch around midnight, three messenger pigeons to send back to the base at Far Rockaway on Long Island east of New York City, and a railway map of the eastern U.S.

You don't hear any air noise when you are riding the wind. In fact, you don't feel the wind and if you lit a match it wouldn't blow out because it would be traveling at the same speed as the air. But you do hear sounds like people talking, dogs barking, or wolves howling thousands of feet below. It was an odd feeling for Hinton, who was accustomed to the un-muffled roar

A Navy balloon like the A-5598 that Hinton and his companions flew in to the far reaches of Hudson Bay. The wrecked balloon was found decades later by Indians (U.S. Navy photograph).

of giant Liberty motors on multi-engine planes firing so close overhead that he would stuff handkerchiefs inside his flying helmet to try to block the noise.

The phone call starting the balloon mission came from the dirigible office at Rockaway Air Station about 10:30 AM on December 13, 1920. "How would you like to make a free balloon flight today?" Lt. Louis Kloor asked Hinton, who was sitting in his spartan office in the multi-engine seaplane hangar. "Fine," said Hinton, who had never ridden in a balloon. "All right, the orders are signed, the aerologist reports ideal weather conditions.... Be at the officers' quarters at 11 o'clock for early luncheon," Kloor told Hinton. They were accompanied by Air Station Gunnery Officer Lt. Stephen A. Farrell, a 26-year naval veteran.[3]

The "Join the Navy" promotional tour of the United States by the first transatlantic flyer, the NC-4 that was ordered by Navy Secretary Josephus Daniels, had ended more than a year earlier and Hinton had spent the following months at Rockaway Naval Air Station as a Senior Squadron Commander testing planes and instructing pilots on multi-engine aircraft in a shrinking peace-time Navy. He had been promoted to officer rank in 1917 to instruct college graduates how to fly and to lieutenant in 1919 to pilot that giant flying boat across the Atlantic. He knew it would not be long before he might be dropped back to the enlisted ranks in the diminished service.

But Hinton was a different man than the 20-year-old from the great Black Swamp in rural western Ohio who had joined the Navy to see the world 14 years earlier. A headlined celebrity who hobnobbed with the glitterati of New York, he gave talks before private clubs and was lauded and praised. On January 16, 1920, when Prohibition went into effect with its ban on the sale or transport of booze, Hinton had helped his mentor and friend Jake Muller load the Friars Club liquor supply into cars and ferry it off to secure locations for the members before the clock tolled midnight

Hinton and his wife, Sally Adline, were drifting apart. She wanted a career naval officer, a home with security. She felt out of her element in the social swirl that surrounded her now famous husband.[4] Hinton wanted adventure and excitement. He had become a living example of that World War I tune: "How you going to keep him down on the farm once he's seen Paree?" Muller, a prominent New York businessman, member of the Friar's Club, and owner of auto dealerships and real estate, took a shine to Hinton's unpretentious charm at one of the pilot's New York talks and squired him around the city. When Kloor suggested Hinton might like to join him in attempting to set a distance record and learn how to fly a balloon, Hinton jumped at the chance and put in his application, which was approved on December 9. They had been waiting for a strong wind from the southeast so they could achieve maximum distance and perhaps set a record for a free balloon flight.

In those early days of balloon-flight experimentation, the idea was to see where the winds would take you rather than pick a specific designation. The plan was to free-fly for 12 hours and then land.

A cook packed six ham sandwiches, three apples, and two Thermos bottles of coffee for the trio. Hinton put a couple candy bars in a pocket. They stopped by the pigeon coop and picked up the carrier birds in a small cage to be released with messages or in case of accident.

Sailors brought the balloon out of the hangar and attached the basket to the load ring while the crew put aboard 21 bags of sand ballast, each weighing 35 lbs. An officer secured the instruments to the shrouds; they lifted off at 1 PM and quickly climbed to 1,000 and then 2,000 feet, drifting over Brooklyn and New York as a light wind from the southeast floated them northwest. Lt. Farrell did most of the navigating. Hinton helped by dropping bits of paper, watching on the Statiscope, dropping sand ballast when ordered. As they passed over the Brooklyn Navy Yard, they released a pigeon and it circled down and headed for Rockaway. They crossed the Hudson at about 97th Street and flew directly over Palisades Park then cleared the city, sliding through the air at 14 or 15 miles per hour.

Flying over New Jersey towns, Lt. Farrell asked if he could send a message to a friend in Westfield. Kloor agreed and they dropped a note attached to a sandbag, but it fell in a marsh. Farrell tried again and that message fell in a vacant field. As a gunnery officer, Farrell was interested in calculating positions and drift and they repeatedly checked those.

Hinton was enthusiastic about the flight, remarking it wasn't a great thrill, but it was fine to be able to move so slowly and peacefully over the land. A little before dusk they passed over a town that has a sign that read, "Central Valley, New York." They figured they were west of the Hudson, 40 to 50 miles north of New York City, but couldn't locate Central Valley on their charts of New York, New Jersey, Pennsylvania and Connecticut. The small railroad map Farrell had in his grip didn't show Central Valley either.

They floated along after dark, noticing a few house lights here and there, when suddenly they began to bump into the sides of hills and trees. That startled Hinton and Farrell, but Kloor, a ballooning veteran, thought little of it. The other two convinced Kloor to put out the drag rope so they could hear it when it hit trees. For a short time they passed over hills and then dropped down in a valley, saw lights, and called out. "Hello. Hello below. What place is this?"

Some boys with a lantern heard them and ran up and answered, "Wells." "Wells, New York?" Kloor asked. "Yes," they said.

"How far west are we of Albany?" Kloor asks. That stumped the youths whose life experience apparently was limited to the small town. After talking it over the youths decided they were being gamed and one said, "How the hell do we know?" and they ran off into the darkness.

The balloon drifted on and the drag rope appeared to get fouled in a stream, but was hung up on a tree. When Hinton and Farrell pulled on the line, it lowered the balloon toward the water rather than coming free. They pulled a lot of it in before it came loose and Kloor threw out some ballast. The balloon now was quite near a farmhouse where a man and his wife were doing chores. "Hello there!" the trio called. The farmer looked at his wife and said, "Did you hear that?" The fliers called out again. "Hello there!" The rural couple looked startled and glanced up at the giant hydrogen bag 100 feet above them.

The farmer confirmed they were at Wells, New York. He had no idea how far they were from Albany, but said they were near the headwaters of the Hudson River and the stream emptied into the Hudson. The men thanked the farmer, said goodnight, and sailed off into the dark. They figured it was about 9 PM.

An hour later they were pelted by heavy rain and lost sight of the ground. The rain showered down off the balloon into the basket. Hinton suggested rigging the basket cover as a tent to ward off the downpour. The men huddled under the cover and even with the drag rope deployed, they struck an occasional tree. At one point when Hinton was serving as lookout, he reported they were passing over water, but the clouds closed and the others couldn't confirm it.

The men dropped more ballast and ascended to 3,000 feet in search of an air current that would carry them further. At that level they were hit with a blast of storm air and the balloon bounced around. They couuld smell hydrogen gas leaking from the mouth of the balloon in the gusty air.

They sailed along smoothly for awhile and then saw the dark mass of forested slopes of the Adirondack Mountains ahead of them, with the wind whistling through the trees. The basket smashed against a large tree trunk, knocking all three men down. The force of the blow blew the balloon over and freed it from the basket weight; it bounded into the air. Branches cracked and broke as they swung like a pendulum from one tree to another. Finally, after striking a third tree, they were able to throw over half a bag of sand and the balloon shot up to 6,000 feet, with the bag now shifted in the netting so the basket rode along behind. They were afraid to attempt to land for fear they would be killed when the basket crashed down alongside the balloon bag. They passed over several small towns but it was close to midnight and no one was on the streets. They shouted, but no one answered. One person stood in a door, but didn't respond to Kloor's megaphone calls. The rain turned to snow during the night and when they again hit a tree, the jolt knocked a pile of snow off the top of the balloon and it leapt upward to 5,000

An artist's fanciful conception of the ill-fated flight of Balloon A-5598 that appeared in some newspapers. The craft never dragged its line on a house (Burns collection).

feet. After that, they spotted a few isolated lights, but saw nothing else that looked like a town or a city. At one point they saw a highway and a house, but they were traveling at about 45 miles an hour in the wind gusts, with the basket trailing along behind the bag, and decided it was too risky to land. They planned to wait until dawn when they could alight in daylight. All three men were soaked in their flying suits.

Without knowing it, they passed over Lake Erie and when December 14 dawned about 8:30 AM, they looked for signs of civilization — such as a house, a railroad, a highway, or any sign that might indicate the presence of living beings — but each time they came below the second layer of clouds, there were only trees, brush and snow to greet them, with nothing but forests ahead.[5] They concluded wrongly that they must be in the Catskills or Adirondacks in northwestern New York and watched for a small town so they could land. But hour after hour they drifted on at the wind's whim, seeing only trees. They had hoped to land near a railroad or town where they could obtain transport for the balloon back to Rockaway, but decided they would land at the first sign of civilization. While all three wore electrified flying suits, they were all soaked and cold.

By 10 AM they pitched over their last bag of ballast to maintain altitude and so they pulled in the 240-foot-long drag rope — designed to slow the balloon's progress and let the crew know when they were near the ground. Hinton cut the line into pieces five to eight feet long and as they appeared about to collide with a tree, they tossed over a piece and the balloon hurdled up over the branches only to face another tree and repeat the process.

Occasionally they saw large snow-covered rocks and one or another member of the crew called out that it was a house only to discover it was a large boulder.

When the drag rope was gone, they threw out their seats and then pulled up the rug from the floor of the basket and over it went. They dropped over two valises. Finally the two empty Thermos jugs were tossed with the realization that the next time they settled it would probably be their last.

Drifting along a mile above the forest, the three heard the dog bark and again saw what they thought was a house. The bark was distinct and repeated. They guessed it was about 1:45 PM. Only Kloor had a watch, but it stopped during the rainstorm. All three men shouted. Kloor gripped the valve cord and said, "Where there is dogs there must be men." Hinton and Farrell agreed. Kloor valved gas to descend slowly, knowing they had no more ballast to throw over to slow their fall. It took them about 18 minutes to descend. Kloor told Hinton and Farrell to bend their knees when they hit and climb up into the load ring if necessary.

As they dropped below the second layer of clouds at 1,200 feet, they spotted a stream off to the southwest. They figured that was their best chance at civilization. They took a compass bearing, then dropped it on the floor of the basket. Kloor ordered Farrell to take the lining they had stripped from the inside of the basket and throw it over as he and Hinton climbed up on the edge of the basket. Kloor wrapped the rip cord around his arm. The rip panel, a long fabric strip cemented to one side of the bag, could be torn off in an emergency, allowing all the gas to escape. Hinton wrapped the valve cord around his arm and hand. Kloor said, "Now" and Hinton held the valve open while Kloor pulled out the rip panel.

The balloon dropped like a stone, hit a tree then the ground, bounded into the air, and stopped against another tree with the bag draped over a big evergreen and the basket sitting on the ground. They discussed releasing another homing pigeon to inform Rockaway, but they had no message to send other than that they were lost in the woods and didn't know where. They decided to walk to the stream where Kloor thought he had seen a shack, although the others had missed it. They assumed that was where the dogs were barking.

So Kloor took the cage with two birds and a compass, Hinton carried his flying suit, a compass, and a flashlight, and Farrell carried his grip; they set out, hoping to reach shelter before dark. Hinton led the way, breaking trail through dense brush for the next several hours. It was tough fighting through the bushes and small trees and when darkness fell they still hadn't reached the stream. Farrell was exhausted, and he and Kloor decided to make camp and start a fire. Hinton felt they were near the stream and pushed on several hundred yards along a moose trail across a swale. He had only gone a couple hundred yards when Kloor and Farrell shouted for him to return with the knife so they could create shavings to start the fire. Hinton returned and then set off again and got about 100 yards when the others shouted for him to return and bring his matches. Hinton set his heavy flying suit by the trail and trotted back to the camp. It got much colder as night fell. They had no way of knowing how cold it was, but the temperatures dropped to 30 below.

Hinton walked until twilight and felt he was near the stream, but decided to return before he got lost in the dark. Farrell and Kloor had failed to get a fire started and Hinton moved them to a better campsite he had found. Along the way he had collected dead grass and put it into his pocket to dry. It was only then he realized that he had left his flying suit by the trail earlier. They searched for it, but they couldn't find it in the dark along the several confusing paths through the swale. Hinton got Kloor and Farrell to gather dry or rotten wood to make a fire and having no tools to chop it, they broke what they could with their hands. All three men pitched in to break down a dead sapling. It took considerable work to gather enough wood. Hinton started a fire and climbed the tallest tree he could find to see if he could see any lights or signs of people. He saw nothing. After 15 minutes he gave up. Hinton and Farrell tried to sleep, but couldn't; it was so cold. Kloor slept soundly. The sleepless aeronauts joked about their predicament, but they knew they were in trouble. They wondered aloud who would get their jobs back at Rockaway if they didn't survive. The cold was intense. The wind had shifted and now blew steadily from the west.

Farrell kidded Hinton that the pilot had spent 1,200 hours in heavier-

An artist's rendering of the three balloonists leaving their crashed craft near Hudson Bay, carrying homing pigeons and gear (Burns collection).

than-air craft, including flying the Atlantic without a mishap, only to have one the first time he went up in a balloon. During the night they heard howls which they took to be dogs, but were probably timber wolves. They were encouraged because they expected sooner or later to come out in some farmer's backyard, possibly in upstate New York. They had no idea they were closer to Hudson Bay, halfway to the North Pole.

Neither did the folks back at Rockaway, who had begun to worry. Commander Damon E. Cummings, the officer in charge, who had been on leave when the flight began, alerted the New York State Troopers, the New York State Rangers, the Army Airplane service, the Navy Recruiting Service and the media to help search the wilds of the Adirondack mountains in case Balloon 5598 had landed during the night.

Cummings also asked for help through the Navy Department from the Canadian government in case they had flown through the night and on into Canada, but Canadian officials didn't show much interest. While the U.S. media quickly got excited by the story of a missing transatlantic flyer possibly in the wilds of upstate New York or in a sparsely populated part of Ontario, the Canadian press showed no interest.

At the cold, gray dawn on December 15, the three men decided to veer more southeast and reached the stream banks after about half an hour. They followed the current downriver on the theory that it would flow into a larger stream where there might be people. They camped along the bank and celebrated by killing one of their carrier pigeons and cooking it. Kloor dressed the bird and Hinton broiled it on the end of a stick. Then Kloor carefully divided the small bird into three parts. Farrell and Hinton each took one half of the breast and Kloor the rest of the carcass. Kloor decided he had more than his share so he gave each of the others a wing. They ate their meager portions and sucked the bones for scraps of meat.

They walked along the stream bank until about 11 AM when they crossed over to find a better trail. Three times that day they stopped to rest and build fires. That night they tried to build a windbreak to give them shelter, but the wind shifted and the windbreak offered little protection from the cold. They realized they were in a ticklish situation and they talked about what their friends and folks at the station would think about them being lost or "bumped off," as Farrell put it.

Farrell recounted a Rockaway legend that every time the station got a new commanding officer, someone got killed or died and the station had recently gotten a new officer in charge, Commander Cummings.

Kloor again slept soundly while Hinton and Farrell, unable to rest in the cold, tended the fire. All three men ate some of the moss that moose had been eating and found it dry and unpalatable.

On Thursday, December 16, they set out again at daybreak with hopes of reaching the river where they thought they had seen a house. At 11 AM Farrell stopped and said he couldn't go on. He was exhausted so they halted, built a fire, and rested for an hour. But the older Farrell was losing hope. Hinton and Kloor heard him praying aloud, asking God to help them find the way. They started marching again at 12 PM and within the next half hour Farrell, who had been drinking water out of moose tracks, fainted and fell three times. He urged the others to leave him and said that he would follow their tracks later and catch up. Hinton and Kloor discussed taking the knife away from Farrell after the gunnery officer suggested that he was such a burden that he should kill himself. Hinton, in a bit of gallows humor, designed to keep Farrell moving, said that if Farrell killed himself, Kloor and Hinton would cook and eat him. That horrified Farrell, who was disoriented, confused and thirsty, and kept drinking water from "moose holes." Farrell gave Hinton $94 he was carrying and said, "You keep it. If anyone gets through you will. I can go no further." Hinton managed to get Farrell up after his last fall and moved him a few yards down the trail to a place where they built a fire while Farrell was unconscious. When Farrell revived, Kloor told him, "There is nobody going to follow tracks." Hinton convinced Farrell to strip off the bulky flying suit which made it difficult to walk and let Hinton carry it for him. Hinton rolled it up and carried it over his shoulder with the legs tied together under his arm while Farrell followed along, dressed in his long underwear.

The airmen did not cover much distance that day because of heavy brush that forced them to repeatedly detour away from the stream and then back to the creek again. They stopped twice to build fires and rest. At about 3:30 PM they chose a place to camp where they found fire wood and they killed and ate their last pigeon. Again Kloor slept soundly and Farrell and Hinton shivered, awake all night in the cold. At about 1 AM on Friday, December 17, Farrell noted the Big Dipper and the North Star were almost directly overhead. He pointed this out to Hinton. They both realized they were much further north than they had thought. They checked with the compass and concluded they were at about 55 degrees North. When dawn broke, they explained their situation to Kloor.

Farrell was continuously thirsty and made frequent detours to the creek to drink on December 17. On one of these trips he discovered that the ice was thick enough to carry his weight. He shouted to Hinton and Kloor, who had gone on ahead, that the ice was safe and all three of them moved onto the creek ice where walking was much easier and picked up their pace. As they neared the mouth of the creek, Hinton hung back with Farrell while Kloor crossed a grassy swale to the river. "We are saved," Kloor shouted. "I see sleigh tracks here." The snow on the river was only three inches deep and the tracks were fresh.

A half-hour later, the three reached a place where the river broadened to about two miles across and Hinton spied a figure traveling on the ice near the other bank. Hinton called out to Kloor and Farrell and all three shouted, but the man ignored them and picked up his pace. When the figure disappeared behind an island, Kloor and Hinton determined to catch him. Kloor followed the man around the island while Hinton raced ahead to cut him off and Farrell lagged behind. The pair trapped the man between them. He turned out to be an Indian trapper named Tom Marks who spoke no English and was wary of the three strange white men with their soft pilots' helmets. "We promised him the blue sky if he would take us to civilization," Farrell said, but the trapper couldn't understand them. He did understand when Kloor offered him a cigarette and Hinton gave him one of Farrell's dollars, but the only words the trio could comprehend were "Hudson Bay."

As soon as they released the Indian he hurried off refusing to wait for the pilots. Kloor, who was in better shape than Hinton or Farrell, tried to keep the trapper in sight. Thus the rag-tag procession reached a portage and Kloor told Hinton to stay there and wait for Farrell to catch up while he went on ahead to find the settlement. Hinton gave Kloor $10 of Farrell's money and told him to make shelter arrangements. Farrell struggled up about 20 minutes later and Hinton led him along a fairly good trail toward the settlement, which turned out to be Moose Factory, Ontario, on the shore of James Bay. About a quarter-mile from their goal, a dogsled team run by Indian women came out to greet them with hot tea and bread, but with civilization in sight Farrell and Hinton pressed on to the hut of the Indian they had seen on the trail, where they could sit down.

The post manager, a Mr. Gaudet, came and got them from the hut and took them to the post store. Gaudet explained there was no way to communicate with the outside world except by Indian runner. Their choice was to wait until the spring thaw, when they could canoe out, or walk out on snowshoes with dogsleds carrying supplies. Hinton, who had witnessed his superior officers sell their stories of the NC transatlantic flights to the newspapers during that mission, suggested the three of them not talk to the press until they could arrange to sell the story of their rescue.

The three sat down and wrote letters to their wives and friends detailing their harrowing experiences, but noting they were not for publication. Gaudet started a runner ahead on the 250-mile journey south to Mattice on the rail line with the letters and the news that the aviators who had been given up for lost were alive.

Back in New York, the press had moved on to other stories and morale among Rockaway sailors and officers was low as sailors worried about what had happened to their friends. Finally on December 20 — three days after Hinton and his comrades had been rescued — the Associated Press agreed to push the Canadian part of their service to carry a story to arouse interest there. Having concluded that the fliers were probably down in an inaccessible part of Ontario, Commander Cummings sent A. W. Evans to Ottawa to see if he could spark Canadian interest in the search. The trip was paid for voluntarily by the officers and men at Rockaway with the understanding they couldn't expect reimbursement.

Evans arrived in Ottawa at noon on December 22 and convinced reporters from the Ottawa, Toronto, Montreal and Quebec newspapers and the Canadian Press Association to publicize the search for the balloonists. He met that afternoon with officials of the Canadian government, who notified all railway branches in the vicinity of Ottawa and some telegraph stations to send messengers into the lumber camps to ask if they had seen the balloon.

On December 23, the Canadian weather reports for December 13, were analyzed and compared with a projected flight path from Wells. R. F. Stupart, director of the Meteorological Service in Toronto, concluded that with the 50-mile-per-hour gale blowing, the balloon would have crossed the St. Lawrence River at midnight and been east of Moose Factory at 8 AM on December 14, heading on a westerly course out over James Bay. "This would bring the balloon to a point north of any inhabited country, even beyond the furthest railroad north, which is the Canadian Pacific Railway," Lt. Evans reported.

Other Canadian officials informed Lt. Evans that if the balloonists landed and were rescued by lumbermen or Indians, it might be several months before news of their safety could reach the public. The Canadian Air Board notified a dozen lumber companies to alert their camps throughout the area. Lt. Evans concluded his report: "Assuming that the balloon landed on December 14 the occupants would have to get assistance from some source to live for any period in the territory where a landing might have been effected as they were without firearms and had very little food."

The three fliers stayed at the Moose Factory post store for 12 days, practicing walking on snowshoes and gaining strength, while the Indian women prepared and made duffels, moccasins, snowshoes and other necessary clothing for the next leg of the journey south. The coats were made from Hudson Bay blankets and each man wore two pairs of socks and moccasins that laced up their legs to keep out the snow. When the newspaper world learned that the men had been rescued, New York newspaper editors dispatched reporters north by rail to Mattice, each hoping to get the first interview with the fliers and the details of the adventure.

On Tuesday, December 28, an Indian runner left Moose Factory carrying a telegram from Lt. Kloor to the Naval Department and letters to the fliers' families and friends. That same day the trio left with two Indian guides, two six-dog teams, and provisions for 12 days of travel. One sled was fitted so that a person could ride in it if necessary, but the snow was waist deep and deeper, so they divided the loads and walked. No one rode. None of the three were experienced snowshoers and it was hard going for the airmen, particularly in the morning when the dogs were fresh. The sailors had to run to keep up.

The Indian guides had hitched a female in heat as the lead dog and occasionally the dogs would fight and they would beat them apart with axe handles. If a dog passed out from exhaustion an Indian would sling it over a shoulder and march on; when it revived he dropped it and it would follow them into camp. Kloor and Hinton and the Indians took turns driving the dog teams, breaking trail ahead of the sleds, and sounding the ice for weak spots.

The Indian runner reached Mattice after five days on January 2, 1921, where officials there sent Kloor's Western Union telegram to his commanding officer:

DRIVEN BY STORM MONDAY DECEMBER THIRTEENTH WEST BY NORTH TO LOWER HUDSON BAY. FORCED TO LAND AT 2:00 P.M. IN DENSE FOREST

The dog sled team that Hinton and his companions used to get back to civilization. All of the men suffered from what the Canadian Indians called "mal de racquet," which was sore muscles from walking on snowshoes. Hinton is the tall figure at the left (Burns collection).

TUESDAY DECEMBER 14TH ABOUT TWENTY MILES NORTH BY EAST OF MOOSE FACTORY, ONTARIO, LATITUDE FIFTY ONE-FIFTY LONGITUTDE EIGHTY ONE. LOST IN FOREST FOR FOUR DAYS. CREW SAFE AT HUDSON BAY COMPANY POST, MOOSE FACTORY, ONTARIO, CANADA. FIRST AVAILABLE MEANS OF TRANSPORTATION TO RAILROAD BY DOGSLED WHICH WILL TAKE ABOUT NINE DAYS LEAVING HERE ON OR ABOUT MONDAY, DECEMBER TWENTY-SEVENTH. DIRECT PAYMASTER TO WIRE FOUR HUNDRED DOLLARS FROM OUR ACCOUNTS PAYABLE AT COCHRANE, ONTARIO, FOR NECESSARY TRANSPORTATION AND SUBSISTENCE. NOTIFY NEXT OF KIN.

The telegram was received by the officer of the day at 11:10 PM and he telephoned Lt. Commander A.H. Douglas, who ordered him to forward it to the Commandant of the Third Naval District, to Operations, to the families of the balloonists and to the press.

The trip from Moose Factory to Mattice was as grueling for the fliers as the four days they spent lost in the wilderness. All three suffered from what the Indians called "mal d'racquete," severe leg muscle pains and strains from walking on snowshoes. They couldn't stop to rest during the day because their muscles would tighten up and they wouldn't be able to start again. Farrell rubbed Hinton's calves with some liniment the Indians provided, but it didn't appear to do much good. Hinton tried drinking some of it, but that didn't help either.

On the seventh day, they struck a faint track that a dog team had made several days before and followed that, with Hinton and Kloor breaking trail and the Indians driving the teams. They traveled six to seven hours a day and then would take two hours to pitch camp, cut wood and get ready for the Arctic night. All three men helped to set up a stove, cut brush for the floor of the tent and unhook the dog teams while the Indians made beds for the dogs, removed ice balls from the dogs feet, cooked the food and scraped the sleigh runners free of ice to prepare for the next day's travel. Each man slept on three blankets and under two.

They were in for a shock when they approached Mattice. The press had bannered the story of the lost transatlantic flyer being found alive when the Navy released the news. Hinton's wife had released his letter to the *New York World* and it contained references to Farrell considering suicide and Hinton's suggestion they might eat him. Two railroad-car loads of reporters and movie cameramen had rushed to the railhead to be first with the story of the rescue.

About five miles from Mattice, the Kloor party was greeted by sleds carrying movie cameramen, who insisted on shooting pictures. One reporter was injured when, in his rush to get there first, he stepped in front of a lead dog and it promptly bit him on the backside.

The reporters offered Hinton and Kloor a ride to the post which they accepted, and the group arrived in Mattice about 3:30 PM on January 11, the fifteenth day of their ordeal, to be greeted by dozens more movie cameramen, reporters, telegrams and mail. After a few pictures Kloor and Hinton were escorted to the private railroad car of E. B. Way, head of the Canadian National Railway, that had been set aside for them and they reviewed the telegrams, several of which were from Navy Secretary Josephus Daniels' office ordering them not to talk to the press until after they had reported to the Department. Then they would be allowed to speak freely.

Meanwhile Farrell had ridden and walked the final miles with the Indian guides on a heavy sledge. They took the gunnery officer to the home of B.P. Williamson, a Hudson Bay Company clerk, down a hill and over a rise from the village. The cameramen and reporters found Farrell there and gave him cigarettes and prodded him to tell his tale. At first the dog-tired, frost-bitten Farrell referred them to Kloor for comment, but eventually started answering questions when he learned that Hinton's letter to his wife had been published.

The reporters read him an excerpt from Hinton's letter: "Mr. Farrell fell from exhaustion several times. Wanted us to cut his throat and take his body for food, and asked us to go on and let him die, but we decided to stick and die together. I was the only one that did not express such feelings and kept them cheered up," Hinton wrote.

Farrell's "face paled, then flushed. A heavy-set man, more than 40 years old with streaks of gray in his hair, he sprang from his chair shouting:

'He has double crossed me. I wrote a letter to Frank Bent, Commander of Contracts in New York, and I wrote on the bottom if it "Not to be published." I did that because Hinton asked me to. He wanted me to because he and Kloor were writing a story, and they said if none of us talked they could sell the story and we could make our expenses....'"

"Did you offer to commit suicide or ask the others to cut your throat?" the reporters asked.

"That is absolutely untrue. It is silly and absurd, I was not ready to die, and we all meant to fight our way through," Farrell replied.

"Did Hinton carry your flying suit?" the reporters asked.

"He carried it some at the last, but more to keep himself warm than anything else. He wrapped it around him like a blanket. I helped Hinton more than he helped me; he was the weakest. I even slept on the outside and let him keep nearer the fire and I bundled up to him to keep him warm," Farrell said.

When Kloor and Hinton realized that Farrell had been taken elsewhere at Mattice, Hinton volunteered to go get him and convey Daniels' orders not to talk to the press. It was a bad mistake. By this time the distraught Farrell was furious with Hinton and Kloor and irrational and embarrassed. He

13. *Ballooning into Canada* 147

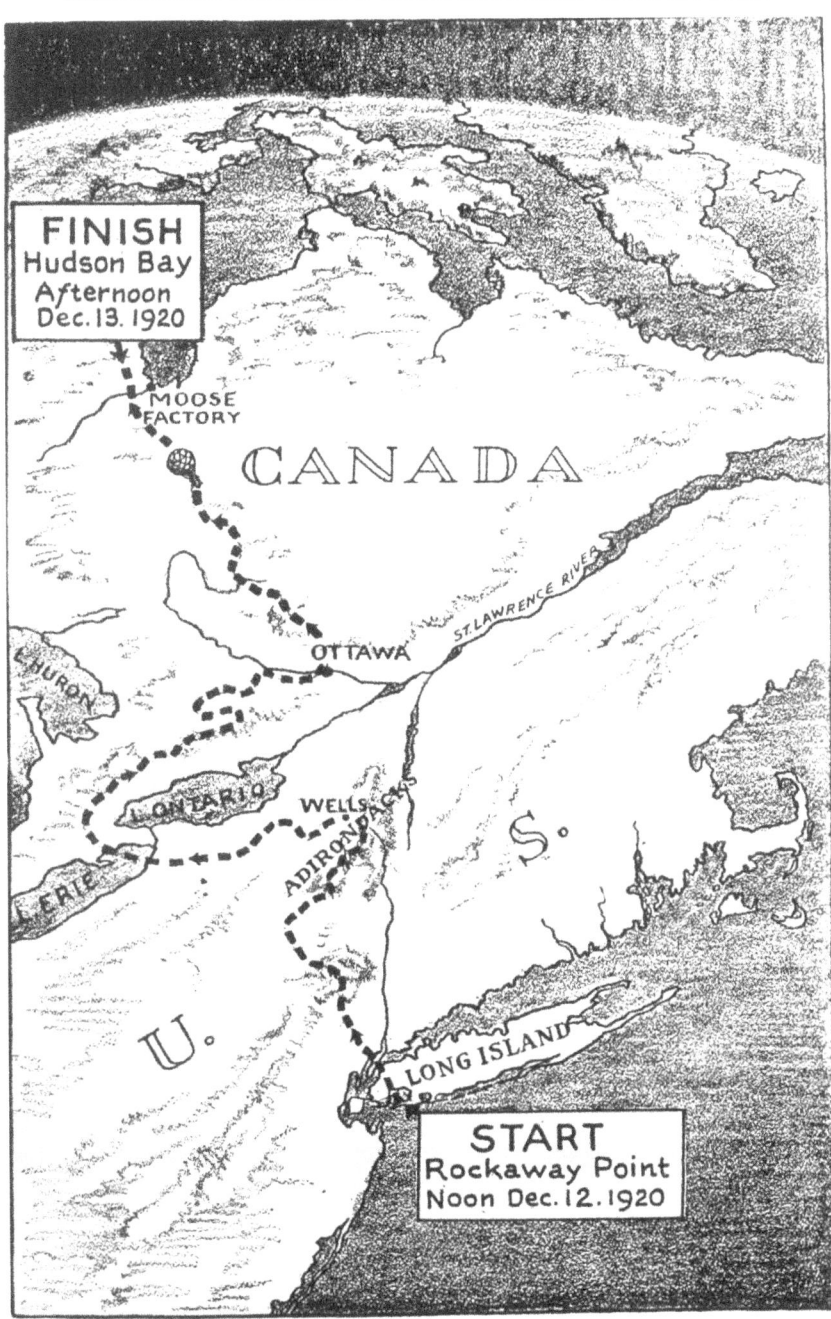

An artist's rendering of the route taken by the balloon as it got blown north. It crossed into Canada on the north shore of Lake Erie (Burns collection).

claimed again that the other officers had planned to refuse all reporter interviews and sell their story to the newspapers.

When Hinton arrived at the Hudson Bay clerk's home with Daniels' instructions he said: "Come on, Lieutenant, we want you to come up to the car. We have some orders we want you to see before you talk." Farrell cursed him. "Get out, you rat," Farrell shouted. "I can lick you. I can lick you both, and I will lick you if you don't get out of here."

"Now, Steve, don't get your Irish up, keep cool," Hinton pleaded, according to the *New York Times* account.

"That's got nothing to do with it," Farrell shouted. "Your letter was printed. It said I wanted you fellows to eat me. It said I wanted to commit suicide and was praying for my sins to be forgiven. Kloor's the only man who prayed or said he did. These were lies."

"You must not talk now," Hinton begged. "Come on and get together and we can make things all right."

"Farrell burst into a torrent of abuse and Hinton flatly denied he had written any such letter. Farrell insisted that a summary of the letter the correspondents showed him be read again. Hinton hung his head and fidgeted as the words sounded in the still room. At the conclusion of the reading Hinton made an effort to disclaim the letter," the *Times* reporter said.

"I may have exaggerated. I'll say, I exaggerated," he said. "But in a general way it was true, and it will come out. You're all right, Lieutenant. Come along with me to the car."

But the agitated Farrell went into another room in the hut, saying he was through with the argument and wanted to have tea. Hinton followed and said: "Now, Farrell, be quiet. These men," pointing to the newspaper men, "are taking down every word you say and it will all be printed."

The reporters protested they were just trying to get Farrell's side of the story since Hinton's had already been printed. Hinton repeated that he had three messages from Daniels that Farrell should read and Farrell shouted, "Get out of here, you damned rat, and let me alone." Hinton's response was lost in the hubbub and Farrell pushed through the reporters and attacked Hinton.

The *Times* correspondent's account said: "Putting his full weight behind the blow," Farrell "planted his right fist on Hinton's jaw. Hinton staggered, closed his eyes and fell on to a serving table by which he stood. Farrell followed his blow with a vicious left hook, which glanced off Hinton's head. Hinton stood bent over the table. For the second occupied by the attack those who looked on stood motionless, too startled to intervene. The American newspaper men thrust themselves into the breach. Some of them grabbed Farrell and held him, others lifted Hinton from his half prone position over the table.

Then in stern and uncompromising words, the newspaper men told both officers the scene was disgraceful and must not be prolonged."[6]

Hinton retreated back up the hill to the railway car to get Kloor and along the way told reporters the story was essentially true. Kloor returned and got Farrell away from the reporters, but the damage was done. The newspapers had a sensational story about suicide, cannibalism, and a fight between two Navy officers, one of them the famed Atlantic flyer.

The banner headline spread across the top of the front page of the Times on January 12 read in three lines of all caps: "AIRMEN, SAFE AT MATTICE, BRAWL OVER REPORTS SENT HOME; FARRELL, ENRAGED BY 'SUICIDE' TALE, KNOCKS HINTON DOWN; CONGRESS LIKELY TO ORDER INVESTIGATION OF FLIGHT."[7]

By that afternoon a Utah U.S. Senator was asking for an investigation as to why a balloon flight was made in mid-winter and Daniels had ordered a Naval Court of Inquiry into the trip, the loss of the balloon, and the fight at Mattice.

The *New York Times* correspondent speculated that any Congressional inquiry would "almost certainly be directed toward ascertaining the truth of reports that the aviators sought to make a long flight in order that they might furnish a sensational story which they could sell to the newspapers."[8]

The fliers rested in Mattice for two days and then left by rail on January 13 to return to New York via Toronto. They arrived at New York City's Penn Station shortly after 10 AM on January 14 and were escorted back to Rockaway where they arrived about 3:30 PM.

The Court of Inquiry into the loss of the Navy Free Balloon A-5598 and "all matters connected with its flight" opened January 17 at the Rockaway Naval Air Station. The Inquiry Board included Rear Admiral George W. Kline, Capt. Henry H. Hough and Lt. Commander Joseph P. Norfleet. Lt. Commander Archibald McGlasson was Judge Advocate.

The court started its inquiry by hearing testimony from the officer who had been sent to Canada to search for the missing airmen, the commander at Far Rockaway, and the men who helped make Balloon A-5598 ready for flight. On the third day they got to Lt. Kloor and Lt. Hinton. They had each man detail the experience and their understanding of the orders, the intent of the flight and the story of being lost in the woods.

When Hinton got to the part where Lt. Kloor sent him to advise Lt. Farrell not to talk to the press and he was attacked by the gunnery officer, he said:

> Upon entering I requested him to return with me to the car as we had received some very important telegrams which concerned him. He flew into a rage and made statements which I do not consider fair to repeat due to his over wrought nerves and condition. I do not consider that he was responsible for what he said

or did. I left the house and returned to the car. Lt. Farrell came over about fifteen minutes later and all differences were made right, and no further controversies on the matter mentioned from that time on.

The Court halted proceedings and declared Farrell "an interested party," meaning that some action might be taken in regard to him. They asked for Farrell to appear before the Court. But Lt. Farrell was too ill to attend that day. A note from the station's senior medical officer, Julius F. Neuberger, informed Admiral Kline that Farrell had a 102-degree temperature, a high pulse rate, tonsillitis, and a general malaise and was suffering from exhaustion psychosis. The court resumed listening to Hinton's narrative of the trip. He told them that the landing site estimated by the Hudson Bay Company officials at 20 miles north of Moose Factory was probably in error. "There is no way that the Hudson Bay people could estimate this as the parties they have sent out for the balloon were unable to get into the woods far enough to see it," Hinton testified.

Dr. Neuberger then testified on the physical conditions of the three:

> The one to have least suffered was Lt. L.A. Kloor. Mr. Kloor did not lose any weight, still weighing 137 lbs., as before the flight. His nostrils were slightly hardened due to freezing. His left ankle was slightly swollen due to mal de racquet. His both feet showed slight scars from blisters. He complained of pains in both hips. He showed a marked rash on the anterior surface of both thighs which he claims was the result of exposure to the cold....
>
> Lt. Hinton suffered more than Mr. Kloor. He had lost twenty-one pounds. The tip of his nose was markedly frozen and the region around the alae of his nose was still hardened, making it difficult to breathe at times. The extensor muscles in both legs are still very stiff due to mal de racquet and are slowly responding to treatment. He particularly complains of pain in his right knee and left ankle.... He complains of slight soreness in the gastric region, and claims that this pain was due to eating a moss, and the food to which he was not accustomed....
>
> The officer who suffered most severely was Lt. Stephen A. Farrell. His loss in weight was eleven pounds. The tip of his nose was frozen.... He complained of pain in his toes. His feet showed scars and blisters. He complains of pain in the gastric region which he attributes to the drinking of water out of moose holes, stating to this medical officer that immediately after drinking this water he became short of wind and fainted. His vision is slightly impaired.... His heart is fast and there is a slight roughening on the first heart sound. He presents a sluggish circulation giving him a bluish appearance.... In addition to the above physical signs this officer showed mental symptoms. The condition is known in medicine as "exhaustion psychosis." I believe this condition to be due to the severe exhaustion, anxiety and worry and extreme exposure during this trip. He shows extreme restlessness and irritability.... This condition is similar to shell shock.

On the afternoon fourth day of the Inquiry, Dr. Neuberger said Farrell was able to tell his story. Farrell brought an attorney with him as counsel,

David Senft. In his testimony before the Court, Farrell confirmed much of what Hinton had said in his letter that the *New York World* published. He admitted praying, but said:

> I think I said a little prayer out loud that began asking God to assist us in our efforts as we all had a hunch that we would hit something on this, the third day. This was the only prayer that was said by any of the party that I heard at any time. It was said, not in a very devout way, bu simply as an ordinary fellow would try to say a prayer.
>
> That morning we started out. The going seemed to be particularly rough, especially for myself. I had been walking in my underclothes since the previous afternoon. I kept following behind and Hinton suggested I take off the heavy flying suit. This I did and he generously volunteered to make a blanket roll of it and swung it over his shoulder.
>
> After going for perhaps two and a half or three hours I had two very bad falls. The ground seemed to be covered with logs and holes and when I'd step on one I would either slip and fall or go through a hole. Kloor was well in advance of the party, and Hinton second. I guess it was about a quarter to twelve when I had a very bad fall. My stomach had been bothering me all morning, especially after the first fall. I appeared to want to vomit but could not. I was quite thirsty and made a couple of trips to the river for water which put me further behind the party. When I got up after the last fall I was very weak. I called to Hinton to come back.
>
> He came back and I told him I could go no further and asked him to make a fire. He sort of "razzed" me to keep on."

On their arrival in Matice, Farrell testified he thought he had arrived at the settlement about two or three o'clock.

> I was absolutely dog tired though the moving picture men kept continually bothering me and I smiled for them. I smoked cigarettes for them. I did everything they asked me to do, everything to please them. I was absolutely all in.
>
> When they got through with me which must have been an hour later, some fellow got me aside and said, "Come over here you are supposed to report to the Hudson Bay Company." He was a decent sort of a fellow and I went with him.
>
> Kloor and Hinton had come in perhaps about half an hour before myself as they got a ride from a movie man we met perhaps six or seven miles out, while I walked the last part with our Indians and our dogs and in that way we became separated.
>
> I went with this fellow to his house expecting to see Kloor and Hinton there as I knew the Hudson Bay people had us in charge. He offered me a cup of tea that his mother was making. I went to the kitchen and his mother asked me if I wanted some fish. I said, "I don't mind. Yes," and she said, "All right, wait a few minutes until I can cook it."
>
> This man took me out in this room and began talking to me and asked me about the men at Moose Factory as he knew most of them. While we were sitting there one man came in, then another man came in, and they began asking who I was and that sort of thing, then another and another until the room was full of men.

I began to answer questions. I was absolutely tired, dead-tired and was growing impatient but it seemed I could not resist the questioning. Each would ask something and start something new.

I said, "If you want to get the story see Kloor," and they said, "You will tell us something of the story," and so on. The result of the whole questioning seemed to drive me silly. They'd ask questions about balloons, they say, "How big is the balloon? What was the number of the balloon." I was absolutely worried sick of the questions and decided to tell them a general story of our trip.

I seemed to be fast losing my senses of reasoning power. I would answer questions and tell them general what we come through in the woods.

I remember one fellow telling about the things that had been published about me in the papers. I seemed to get all excited. I really did not know what I did or said, but I heard somebody say, "you must stop this swearing." I apologized for swearing to this man who had first brought me in there and after general movements around the place I seemed to lose all sense of reason. I was shaking all over with nervousness when this man took me out of he place and down to the Hudson Bay store. From there I was taken up to the car where the Canadian National Railroad people were looking out for us.

I seemed to be dopey, dog-tired, all in and Mr. Way suggested that I lay down. I did but I was so nervous I could not sleep. Kloor told me after I got up that I had had a muss with Hinton and the newspapermen. I scarcely remember seeing Hinton. I told him that I was going nutty if he didn't look out. They put me to bed and kept me there for a couple of hours. When I got up and they said supper or dinner was ready. I could not eat but sat around with them, smoked a few cigarettes, and finally got to bed and got to sleep.

The next morning Kloor said that I had better apologize to Hinton as I had treated him rough, and I did so and him and I have been friends and always were friends before and even since. After leaving Mattice we traveled on the railroad down to New York and were treated very kindly on the way.

I seemed to get very nervous at times and got very little sleep. After getting to our own station the Captain gave us permission to go ashore until Monday, which we did.

I went home with my people and everybody seemed to want to shake hands and all this sort of thing, and I really got sick, I think, trying to please everybody. The result was that Doctor (Julius) Neuberger, (Senior Medical Officer, Rockaway Beach Naval Air Station) made me go to bed and kept me there for a couple of days. I felt better and was able to come on and tell you the story as I have told it to you.

After taking Farrell's testimony the court adjourned for the day at 3:30 PM.

On the fifth day Farrell's attorney David Senft asked the court to call Hinton back to attempt to establish that Hinton didn't really know who struck him at Mattice. It was obvious that Hinton was sympathetic to Farrell's plight. For example, Senft asked, "Will you explain to the court what you meant by 'flew into a rage?'"

"I might state that he was in an excited condition," Hinton replied.

"Would you say that this condition was caused by the strain of the trip?" Senft asked.

"I consider that it was," Hinton answered.

"Well, have you anything to base your opinion on outside your own experience?" Senft asked.

"Only from what I have heard, and I have here a telegram from F. F. Sainsbury who came through from Toronto to Mattice with dog teams and sled and met us about seven or eight miles from Mattice. Mr. Sainsbury said that he had been ten years in the Arctics as an explorer. Upon reading newspaper accounts he decided that he would come to New York, stop at the Continental Hotel, wired me to call him by phone which I did, and said that he would remain in New York another day as he would like to explain to people what it meant to be lost in the woods or hit the trail for any length of time, which he was certain no one could understand except those who had actually encountered these difficulties," Hinton said.

The Court concluded Farrell "was not fully responsible for his actions," that the trio should have carried a chart of the Canadian territory and had incorrectly estimated their flight speed, but that no further proceedings should take place.

But Naval Operations bounced the report back saying: "While it is recognized that the extent and details of a free balloon flight can not be definitely controlled beforehand," they felt the Far Rockaway station was being laxly run and recommended disciplinary action against Commander A. H. Douglas and that before such action he should be asked for a statement. Naval Operations also felt that "to a more limited extent" Lt. A.D. Brewer, USNRF, the senior Lighter-than-Air officer, bore responsibility "for the laxity evident at the U.S. Naval Air Station, Rockaway, in connection with this flight."

They also held that Lt. Kloor "evidenced a lack of realization of the necessity for or of knowledge of aerial navigation and aerology, but that his subsequent conduct under trying circumstances in Canada was commendable."

Secretary Daniels ordered them to reopen the inquiry because "there was ample and excellent opportunity to effect a landing of the balloon between 8 and 10 o'clock PM on 13 December, 1920 at Wells, New York when the altitude of the balloon was only 100 feet. Despite these facts it was none the less determined to fly all night. In this connection it is to be borne in mind that Wells, New York is approximately but 100 miles from the Canadian border."

The court re-interviewed most of the participants and the full proceedings were eventually sent to Lt. Commander A. H. Douglas, who by this time was ironically serving aboard the U.S.S. *Aroostook* with the Pacific fleet in San Pedro, California. (The *Aroostook* was the mother ship for the transatlantic flight.)[9]

Douglas said he did not believe the claim that a flight into Canada was intended was substantiated by the evidence and said he had no knowledge of such a contention. The Judge Advocate General Department on review in May 1921 recommended no further action be taken in the case.

By then the handwriting was on the wall for Hinton. He had been promoted to lieutenant temporarily for the Atlantic flight and held at that rank, but with an elementary school education, he had little future in the naval service. He was advised that when his appointment ended December 31, 1921, he would revert to enlisted status, so Hinton chose to take an honorable discharge effect January 1, 1922.

His wife, Sally Adline Hinton, who was called Addie, knew this and knew that Hinton's future in the Navy was limited by his education. When asked by the seemingly aggrieved *New York Times* reporters why she gave the letters to *The New York World*, Addie said:

> It was entirely on my responsibility that the letters were made public. My husband, at the time I permitted the publication of his story, was on his way from Moose Factory to Mattice, and naturally knew nothing about the letters being given out.
>
> As was pointed out in the *World*, which first printed Mr. Hinton's messages to me and to Lieutenant Talbot, they were not written with any idea that they were for the general public. They were for us alone. In fact, there was a paragraph at the end of Mr. Hinton's letter to me, advising me not to give any information to the press.
>
> I would not have done so, in the ordinary course of affairs, but I received a special permission from the Navy Department to release the news that my husband sent "because the whole country was eager to hear from the missing men" and on that account I allowed *The World* to print the letters.[10]

The Navy Department denied that anyone had given Sally Hinton permission to release the letters and she carefully avoided identifying the source of her authority.

"I would like to make particularly clear the fact that there was no thought in my mind that the letters would reflect upon the courage or ability of Lieutenant Farrell — quite the contrary. Indeed, when I read my husband's remarks about Mr. Farrell I at once declared, and so did such friends as read the letters, that Lieutenant Farrell was a true hero, and we all said we thought he was the bravest man of the party, since he offered to sacrifice himself so that the others might proceed faster.... Again I would like to say that I gave them out only because there was such a great public demand for information about the men who had been rescued after their great adventure."[11]

Hinton was in great demand immediately to speak to various clubs and civic groups. Jake Muller carefully guided him in his new speaking career and may actually have guided Addie on the release of the letters to his friends at *The New York World* and what to say to the press. That early *New York World* connection took Hinton on his next adventure.

14

Hopping Down to Rio

> *"The only life worth living is the adventurous life. Of such a life the dominat characteristic is that it is unafraid."*
> — Raymond B. Fosdick[1]

It was after 8 PM and the sun had disappeared in a foggy bank of clouds on the western horizon. The twin 400-horsepower Liberty engines of the Curtiss H-16 flying boat roared rhythmically as Walter Hinton kept the craft on a compass heading for Guantanamo Bay, Cuba.

Hinton strained to find the lights of the naval base that would spell safe harbor as the stormy tropical night fell, black and muggy, around them. Hinton and Brazilian co-pilot Euclides Pinto Martins watched the dimly lit gauges as they descended through the blackness toward the surface of the Caribbean. The weather had been fair and the seas were reportedly calm, but atmospheric pressure was affecting the altimeter gauges. Hinton was landing so flight engineer and radio operator John Edward Wilshusen, a Curtiss employee, could get a radio fix on the Guantanamo base and they could taxi the craft into the harbor rather than risk missing the base entirely.

The altimeter gauge spiraled down 2,000 feet, 1,500 feet, 1,000 feet, 500 feet, 300 feet, 100 feet. When the gauge said they were at 100 feet, according to Hinton's reckoning, the 16,000 pounds flying boat struck the surface of the sea like a rock.

Hinton had made a horrible mistake. As the bottom ripped out of the *Sampaio Correia II*, the gas tank in the main cockpit area shot upward. Hinton flew forward and struck his face on the dashboard, cutting his lip. George T. Bye, the *New York World* reporter who was chronicling the adventure for his newspaper, which had sponsored the first air mission from New York City to Rio de Janeiro, flew into the air and would have gone overboard except he caught hold of the wing guy wires and dangled over the water. Water flushing past him through the fuselage almost tore Bye loose. The three other men on board were soaked and shaken, but unhurt. Supplies and journals sloshed in

14. Hopping Down to Rio

The crew of the *Sampaio Correia II* pose for photographers in the uniforms made for the trip from New York City to Rio. Left to right: Bye, Pinto Martins, Hinton, Wilshusen and Baltzel (Burns collection).

the hull. Pathe News movie cameraman John T. Baltzel had protected his equipment aft by turning his back to the water deluge.

The H-16, which had been provided by the U.S. Navy, was a smaller version of the giant NC-4 flying boat that Hinton had piloted across the Atlantic in May 1919. Since that day the Atlantic had been spanned numerous times and daring aviators had moved on to other record setting adventures — flying from England to Australia, flying across the Pacific, flying around the world. It seemed like each week and each month, someone announced a new flight or claiming a distance, altitude or endurance record.

All five men climbed on to the upper wing of the biplane as the cabin and hull submerged beneath them. They stood knee deep in warm seawater mixed with gasoline, oil and garbage. Hinton suffered from burns on his legs from the gasoline for the rest of his life. For 15 minutes the bow stayed above water and the men rescued some of the baggage. Pinto Martins and Bye found a signal lamp. Bye flashed the lamp. They had landed in a naval garbage dumping grounds off Cape Maisi at the eastern end of Cuba and about 10

The crew of the *Sampaio Correia II* pose for newspaper photographers. Left to right: John Baltzel, the *Pathe News* photographer; George Bye from *The New York World*; Hinton; Pinto Martins; and mechanic John Wilshusen (Burns collection).

miles from the Guantanamo Bay anchorage. As the bow sank the men clambered back up onto the upper wing, which was awash.

Shortly after 8 PM, a night lookout aboard the U.S.S. *Denver,* which had been steaming out of Guantanamo, had seen the red glare from the two Liberty engines in the sky and assumed it was a shooting star.

But an officer had read a story about Hinton's plan to make the first flight from New York to Rio de Janeiro and that they were on the seventh leg of their journey. When he mentioned that to Captain Y.S. Williams, the captain ordered the ship to head for the spot where the glow was noted. A half hour later the ship pulled up near the stranded fliers, sent a lifeboat to the airmen, and took them aboard.

While the ship crew made attempts to get grappling hooks on the crippled flying boat, Bye filed a dispatch via ship wireless to his newspaper: "In attempting to land off Cape Maisi in utter darkness at 8:11 o'clock to-night the bottom of our flying boat was smashed through and the fuselage totally wrecked," he reported.

The story was exclusive to the *New York World* because they paid for part of the cost of the 8,500-mile flight. The staid *New York Times* and other papers noted the progress of the flight and the crash landing in a few paragraphs. But the exploits of 1919, when planes and dirigibles crossed and recrossed the Atlantic, had set off a fever of long-distance attempts at firsts.

The World, owned by Joseph Pulitzer, pioneered the idea of using travel to promote the newspaper when it sent investigative reporter Nellie Bly on a trip around the world after she had read Jules Verne's *Around the World in 80 Days.*

The newspaper held a competition to guess how long it would take Bly to circle the earth and more than 1 million people reportedly entered. On the morning of November 14, 1889, Bly, with only one piece of hand luggage that was just 16 inches wide and seven inches high, set sail from Hoboken, New Jersey, aboard a liner named the *Augusta Victoria.* Back in New York, when she arrived 72 days, 6 hours, 11 minutes and 14 seconds after leaving, a huge crowd greeted her.[2]

Earlier, in April 1922, *The World,* a three-times-a-week newspaper, and *The St. Louis Post-Dispatch* paid for exclusive North American rights for Sir Ross Macpherson Smith's proposed around-the-world flight. Smith had flown a Vickers Vimy bomber from England to Australia in 1919. But Smith was killed during a test flight at Brooklands on the eve of the mission.

After Hinton left the Navy January 1, his mentor and promoter advertising man, Jake Muller, an avid fan of aviation, suggested he should take advantage of his fame and helped Hinton explore various proposals for a long, record-setting flight. Muller introduced Hinton to Pinto Martins, who explained his dream of showing that New York City and Rio could be linked by air.

Pinto Martins, 30, had come to the U.S. in 1909 to study engineering mechanics at the Drexel Institute in Philadelphia. He worked in the Baldwin Locomotive Works and earned his degree in 1911. He got his pilot's license in 1921 and had been fascinated by the accounts of Hinton's exploits. After meeting in January, they convinced banker Andrew Smith Jr., Pinto Martins' friends in Brazil, and the *New York World* to sponsor the flight. Curtiss built the H-16 which had a wing span of 92 feet for the Navy and the Navy Department, feeling a successful mission would promote their brand of aviation, sold it to the fliers and agreed to tune it up at the Navy Aircraft factory at Philadelphia.

"Everybody in his place," Hinton had shouted a few minutes before 3 PM on August 8 at the Essington, Pennsylvania, naval dock. Hinton gave the signal to cast off the newly assembled plane from the Marine railway for its first test flight. Crowds on shore cheered while Hinton maneuvered around yacht moorings on the Delaware to mid-steam, where he lifted the plane into the air a minute later and headed east toward Atlantic City, where they turned north and flew along the coast line to New York. The crew included Pinto Martins, Wilshusen, Bye and Smith Jr., one of the financial backers.

In spite of strong headwinds and some bumpy flying as they approached the Atlantic coast near Atlantic City and as they passed over Sandy Hook, the plane made good time and descended from a height of 1,200 feet at 6:13 PM over the Hudson and was moored to a buoy at Duffy's Landing, the New York air pier.

Hinton was reportedly delighted with the test. "The motors never missed once," he said. Bye, however, in writing about the flight, noted that while the plane flew as steady as a canal boat that it sounded like a canal boat with "a thousand machine guns firing salvos" on board.

On August 9, Hinton flew the *SC* as the crew called her to Rockaway Naval Air Station to load spare parts and radio equipment for the trip. She was beached there in order to keep her out of the water until it was time for the flight. The full name of the craft was in honor of a Brazilian senator who was also the president of the Rio de Janeiro flying club.

On Friday, August 11, *The World* announced that official start would be from the Columbia Yacht Club seaplane harbor off West 86th Street on Tuesday, August 15.

Pinto Martins' daughter, Adelaide, and Shirley Tribken, daughter of I. Bennett Tribken, one of the flight's trustees, would baptize the flying boat. The Brazilian American Chamber of Commerce hosted the fliers and presented the nations' flags on Monday and the crew appeared in special blue uniforms that had been made for the mission. The flight was planned to arrive in Rio about September 7, the opening day of the World Exposition there celebrating the centennial of Brazilian independence from Portugal. In addition to the *Sampaio Correia II*, the U.S. was sending a handpicked contingent of U.S. Marine veterans of World War I to the Exposition. All of them were six foot tall. Various folks doubted whether the *SC* could make the journey over uncharted territory, but at least one Brazilian official wagered $200 that the *SC* would make it to Rio.

Since the legs of the 8,500-mile journey would be mostly within sight of land there was no request for Navy patrols to watch for the airmen.

When Hinton brought the *SC* back from Rockaway at 1 PM on August 15, he hit an empty lemon crate floating on the incoming tide as he landed and smashed the starboard wing pontoon. The men on board said they barely noticed the jar when it struck. "It was trival but aggravating, Hinton said. "If the boat were an F-5-L we could replace it in five minutes. As it is, I am afraid it will be necessary to send to the Navy aircraft factory at Essington, Pennsylvania."

Navy officers called Essington, and T.E. Pell, hangar superintendent at the factory, got a duplicate pontoon and then learned he couldn't take it on a passenger train unless it was crated — a two-hour job that would make him miss the train.

So he commandeered an old truck at 5:15 PM and drove the pontoon to New York, covering 220 miles in a little over six hours. Before midnight the pontoon was in place and officials announced a 10 AM start. Various dignitaries were on hand, including Glenn Curtiss and Rear Admiral Carl T. Vogelsang, who had approved using Rockaway as a hopping-off point.

At 3 PM on August 16, Hinton taxied away from the 86th Street basin and made the short hop to Rockaway without incident. The *Revista Semana* newspaper of Rio de Janeiro reported the scene:

> The dock of the north River, ahead of 86th St., appeared to be a human anthill. More than a million people had crowded on the wharf, with all eyes fixed on the great mechanical bird. The hydroplane *Sampaio Correia*, newly painted, bore on its sides the starry flags of the two great sister republics. As the clocks of the city approached 3 PM the powerful motors began to roar grimly. By means of four or five skillful maneuvers, the device moved, maneuvering between the massed private boats, looking for the widest and most open areas of the river. Then a miracle occurred. Out of that million crazy spectators, perhaps a hundred million cheers roared into the air. For a long time, they had been hearing all the rumors in that tumultuous and seething metropolis. New York throbbed in that shout, which broke from the mouths of all ages of all shapes and of all conditions. One could say it was the mount of the city that cried out.[3]

After loading all the radio equipment and supplies, Hinton concluded the *SC* was overweight and would have difficulty getting off the water, so they taxied back in and unloaded 300 pounds of gear. Hinton ordered Bye and Wilshusen to move forward and stand directly behind him and Pinto Martins so the craft wouldn't be tail heavy. At 8:49 AM on Thursday, August 17, Hinton once again taxied across Jamaica Bay, lifted off, and turned the *SC* south into heavy headwinds of 20 miles an hour and more.

About 10 minutes after takeoff, Pinto Martins gestured to Bye and motioned to his goggles, which Bye removed and hung them over a cockpit support wire. Pinto Martins gave him a disapproving stare, so Bye put the goggles in a suitcase only to again get Pinto Martins' look of reproach. Bye got the message and polished the salt spray off the goggles with a pair of Wilshusen's BVDs that were hanging on a wire.

All of the men were wearing rubber earplugs to protect their hearing, although they could hear the roar of the unmuffled engines anyway. It was smooth sailing down the Jersey shore and when they got over Atlantic City, Hinton dropped down to 500 feet so Baltzell could shoot a panoramic of the boardwalk, where they saw only one woman promenading in "a dahlia yellow dress" and she ignored their passing. "After Atlantic City we ran into snorty weather, into which the *Sampaio Correia II* tore along disdainfully," Bye reported.

With the fuel load lighter, Hinton motioned Wilshusen to take the suitcases to the aft compartment. The men decided they needed coffee and coffee cake to settle their stomachs so Baltzall got the food and drink out and Pinto Martins served it. Since Hinton had to keep both hands on the wheel they fed him his cake. They drank the coffee out of paper cups and Bye reported himself as "the finicky historian lay on his back in the bottom of the amidship's cockpit sipping leisurely from a sanitary cup which was placed between sips in one of Hinton's old shoes."

Waves breaking around Cape May created a soapy froth and Hinton took the SC up to 3,500 feet over Delaware Bay and pointed out ships down below in a deep blue sea. "What looked like gentle combed riffles must have been fairly hefty waves judging by the bounce they gave yachts in the Bay," Bye wrote.

The crew had been up until midnight walking around Rockaway and only got four hours' sleep, so Wilshusen rigged a pillow from a tarp and invited Bye to take a nap in the drafty passageway. About three hours later, running low on fuel with all the Roanoke bayou islands looking alike as Hinton searched for the Navy refueling station for flying boats at Manteo, he landed on the marshes near the Roanoke Marshes Lighthouse to ask for directions.

"'Manteo is back eight miles on the other side of Roanoke Island,' shouted Charles Hugh, [the] lighthouse keeper from the veranda of his pagoda cottage, the cupola of which is the channel beacon at night," Bye reported.[4] Hugh then got out his boat and, with his daughter, Mary, rowed out to the flying boat. Tommy Baltzell, the Pathe News photographer, insisted on getting a picture of Hugh and his daughter so they tied to a piling in the lee of a stiff wind with squalls blackening the sky to the west, according to Bye. "Hinton meanwhile took a nap on the port wing and Dr. E. Pinto Martins, our debonair navigator, scion of an old Brazilian family — in athletic gear and barefooted — helped our infallible mechanician, John Wilshusen to oil up."

Hinton took off again at 1:35 PM and coasted down at Manteo 15 minutes later. But Baltzell, who had been assigned to bring in the bow anchor and the towing cable, got busy taking down his big camera and forgot to haul in the cable. When they landed at Manteo the shackle on the end of the cable smashed a hole in the hull of the *SC*, which Bye was now calling the "Longitude Express."

14. Hopping Down to Rio

A carpenter put a foot-square piece of copper plate over the hole and a veneer panel and the crew went ashore for lunch at 3 PM and decided because of "puffy weather and predicted squalls," they would not try to make Charleston, but would overnight at Manteo, fly to Charleston early the next morning and on to Nassau in the Bahamas before noon, the longest hop out of sight of land planned on the journey.

Lighthouses had flashed the word ahead that they were arriving at Manteo and dozens of motor boats were out, including one from the Tranquil House where Hinton stayed. The host there had four chickens killed for their lunch, anticipating their arrival, and also fed the crew hot biscuits, broiled potatoes, stewed cabbage, tomato salad and iced watermelon.

The crew was also greeted by A. W. Drinkwater, the weather officer representative and telegrapher who had sent out the first news of the Wright brothers' successful glider flights in 1903 and again tapped out the first news of their powered flight in 1908. He let Bye write his story in the parlor of his home where he kept the telegraph key.

The hop to Charleston the next day was uneventful, as was the flight south that got off the water at 7:34 AM. They rose early Sunday and loaded the *SC*. Hinton was unable to lift her off the Cooper River even at full throttle in two long runs, so they moved the emergency gas and oil forward, some of it into the bow and Wilshusen and Bye again stood close behind the pilots and on the third run (at 8:22 AM) "we shook loose" and "were soon out to sea."

Bye reported the weather as surly. "We made out five storm centers around us. Our complexions got the benefit of a rainwater soaking as we swung through the tail of a shower cloud. The sea was muddy color beneath us and of a leaden bluishness in the distance. The air was constantly bumpy as we made altitude, but we were cheered by a gush of sunshine that caused an enormous semi-circular rainbow landward." A quarter hour after getting airborne they picked up a 15-mile-an-hour tail wind that pushed them along at 93 miles an hour. Wilshusen made a forward gesture of triumph with his fist. Savannah was reached in 36 minutes. But the favorable wind only lasted an hour before shifting again. Hinton flew at altitudes ranging from 200 feet to 4,200 feet, trying to avoid strong winds that buffeted them as they continued south. They ate cheese sandwiches as they flew and at 10:22 AM the aft altimeter showed 3,000 feet and they were still climbing. When they got abreast of the northern Florida coast they struck a series of squalls. With more storms brewing around him, at 11:50 AM, Hinton pushed the nose of the *SC* down and they spiraled earthward over "a painted green sea" and landed on the Indian River at Titusville for their first views of palm trees and alligators. When the squall line passed Hinton took off, quickly hit more fierce storms, and landed again near the hamlet of Rockledge along the Intracoastal Waterway. It became apparent to Hinton as they progressed south again along the coast that they would not make Nassau before dark so he decided to land the *SC* in Lake Worth at West Palm Beach.[5]

Bye typed his story in mid-air at an altitude of 3,500 feet with his typewriter on his suitcase, standing endwise and held between his legs, while seated on an upside-down oil can face aft in the amidships cockpit.

"In a few minutes we're going to spiral down to West Palm Beach for tonight. The exact time of landing I shall insert when I go ashore to file this telegram," he wrote on August 20 for the next day's front page. It was 6:26 PM.

At 11 AM the next morning, the *SC* took off from the Palm Beach Inlet and crossed the Gulf stream to Nassau in the southern Bahamas without incident. The following day, they headed south, planning to make Port-au-Prince, Haiti, when they ran into continuing strong squalls that slowed their progress. Hinton tried flying higher and it didn't help, so they flew lower in conditions Martins described as "grim." As night fell and they still had the Windward Passage to cross between Cuba and Santo Domingo, Hinton made the decision to stop at Guantanamo at the southern end of Cuba where there was a safe harbor and ample support from the U.S. Navy.

He alerted all hands to watch for the Windward Passage Lighthouse so they would know they were at the entrance to the Bay. When they saw lights he took the craft down.

But what he had mistaken for the lighthouse was the U.S.S. *Denver*, a battleship. Luckily the captain had heard of Hinton's flight and ordered the ship to the scene where the red glow of its exhausts had disappeared. After rescuing Hinton and the others from the downed plane, sailors attached ballast tanks to it to keep it afloat so a tug could tow it into Guantanamo where the Liberty engines were salvaged and sent to Philadelphia for repair since Wilshusen's Liberty tool kit had gone to the bottom of the Carribbean in the crash.

The five men then caught transport on a Navy ship to Jacksonville, Florida, where they arrived at 1 PM on August 28. They transferred to a train and arrived after a 16-hour train ride at the Pensacola Naval Air Station where Hinton had learned to fly. Urged on by Rear Admiral W. A. Moffett and Acting Secretary of the Navy Theodore Roosevelt Jr., the Navy sold *The World* and Andrew A. Smith Jr., one of the original backers, another H-16 so they could complete the mission. They called it the *Sampaio Correia II*.

On September 4, they were ready to go again after waiting for a shipment of replacement film for Baltzall's movie camera. They got up at 6:30 AM. The Navy assembled a crew of 50 men to help them with final details and takeoff was delayed while the camera base mount in the bow was installed and adjusted.

Bye waxed hyperbolic in his description for *The World* readers: "Our wind tanned skipper, Hinton, took a squint at the impermanent ether waves, through the medium of a curl of smoke from a nearby stack, just before we plugged up our ears, and suggested with brilliant optimism that we might find smooth air at 500 feet. As sure as I am sitting here in this flirting tail with a typewriter machine on my lap we have been climbing the sky ladder from zero to 2,000 feet without finding anything but ruts and gullies and what we Westerners from the open spaces of bare chests call buttes and arroyos. Don't trust smoke. Never have I been so deceived."[6]

Bye and Wilshusen, who described themselves as "moving ballast," had been moved forward again for the takeoff along with seven cans of gas as the overloaded flying boat was tail heavy. After they got airborne the two lugged the gas cans back through the two-by-two crawl passage to the aft cabin.

Hinton paralleled the shore line as squally weather was forecast all the way to Key West as the hurricane season was in flower. About 10:50 AM Wlishusen handed Bye a note saying Panama City, Florida, was off the port wing.

At 3 PM Hinton decided not to push his luck with another squall looming to his west in the Gulf and told the crew he would land at St. Petersburg. Shortly after they touched down and had the *SC II* refueled, the storm burst over the city.

Local officials had hastily arranged for the Kiwanis Club to entertain the men. Bye noted in his dispatch that it was the 17th day after their official start from Rockaway Beach and only the seventh day of flying and they had been in the air 31 hours and 50 minutes.[7]

The hop to Key West the next day was uneventful, but Hinton and Wilshusen were concerned about the engines and Key West Navy personnel bathed parts in kerosene to remove sticky buildup while a carpenter made a new, lighter base for the Pathe camera.

They had trouble getting off the water the next morning at Key West and Hinton failed twice to get the *SC II* airborne. They returned to the naval base and took off 300 pounds of equipment and substituted a lighter anchor and a smaller coil of rope before getting into the air at 11:50 AM after a run of one minute and 35 seconds.

Hinton predicted they would have to lighten the load on board daily as they approached the Equator because of the light air. A half hour out of Key West two cylinders of the 12 on the port engine started missing and Hinton decided not to try to make Nuevites Bay, 150 miles further along the north shore of Cuba, and instead landed at Caibarien, Santa Clara Province, after flying 186 miles.

The *SC II* immediately drew a crowd of pleasure craft and small boats and when Bye, Martins and Hinton went ashore, they were mobbed by curious

Cubans. Baltsell climbed onto a nearby building to film the scene. The group paid a visit to the American consul. Local shipping-line officials put them up at the Hotel Commercial, "one of the best in Cuba," for the night.

They refueled in the city of Caibarien and hopped the next day to Nipe Bay, a sheltered inlet about 50 miles north of Santiago de Cuba at the eastern end of the island. The next morning, September 7, they left the water shortly after 7 AM for the 4-hour-and-21-minute flight to Port-au-Prince, Haiti, where they were greeted by thousands of people crowding the docks. A Marine quartermaster in a motor barge took them to meet the American High Commissioner Brig. Gen John H. Russell and they were then taken to the palace, where they were received by the President Louis Borno. Gen. Russell entertained the Hinton party at dinner and Pinto Martins sent a cable to the president of the Brazilian Exposition expressing their regrets that they had failed to reach Rio de Janeiro in time for the opening of the World Fair.[8]

The plan, according to Bye, was to fly on September 8 another 234 miles to San Domingo City, escorted by two Marine Corps seaplanes. They would fly overland at 6,000 feet, hoping to use lakes if an emergency arose. Hinton had predicted the air along the mountainous shore would be bumpy. But that would be a huge understatement about the rest of the mission. It would be a disaster.

What Bye didn't write was that the engine radiators in the tropical temperatures were overheating and Hinton, Pinto Martins, and Wilshusen were concerned about their ability to continue. The equatorial humidity and temperatures played havoc with the machinery. Bye filed no further dispatches until this short item appeared at the bottom of the front page of *The World* on September 24:

"Another test of the flight ability of the S-C II, was made to-day by Pilot Hinton. He was up for half an hour, making a height of 3,000 feet. He found, however, the radiators would not hold water and that the motors overheated. He hopes to correct this and we may get off to-morrow."

On September 28 the *New York Times* noted on page five Hinton's predicament with this small item:

> Walter Hinton, commanding the seaplane *Sampaio Correia II*, which started some time ago on a flight from Florida to Rio Janeiro, has cabled the Philadelphia naval aircraft station for new radiators and new propellers for the machine, which has been unable to resume its flight owing to the overheating of the engines because of insufficient radiation. It is estimated that the wait for the new equipment will cause an additional three weeks delay in the departure of the plane.

Opposite page: **Brazilians were so excited to have their native son Eugenides Pinto Martins involved in the first flight from New York to Rio de Janeiro they had already erected a monument to Hinton and Pinto Martins by the time the pair finally arrived (Burns collection).**

But it didn't take three weeks to get the parts and the *SC II* crew hopped to San Domingo, capital of Santo Domingo, to be greeted by a huge crowd most of whom had never seen an airplane, far less a flying boat.

From San Domingo they got off early on October 8 and landed after four hours and four minutes at San Juan, Puerto Rico, at 1 PM to another large, enthusiastic crowd and legal complications. The crew didn't have the proper documents to be entering Puerto Rico and officials took them into custody. U.S. diplomatic officials intervened and they got belated permission to land, refuel and continue.[9]

From San Juan they arced southward along the chain of volcanic islands leading to South America and landed at Pointe-a-Pitre, Guadaloupe. The flying boat was surrounded by swarms of small boats manned by curious folks trying to get a look at it, one of which ran into a wing and put a foot-square hole in it. Guadaloupe officials arrested the boaters and put them in jail while the damage was quickly repaired by Wilshusen, and they then flew on.

Flying at a speed of slightly under 60 miles per hour they approached Martinique at a height of about 6,000 feet in order to avoid hitting the 4,582-foot-high volcanic Mt. Pelee on the northwest corner of the 424-square-mile island.

Mt. Pelee was shrouded by white clouds and mist, but no smoke. Its "red sides looked like kiln-baked clay and the lava sluices looked like gravel walks," according to Bye.[10] Twenty years earlier Pelee had proved to be one of the most dangerous volcanoes in the world when it erupted on May 8, 1902, and destroyed the city of St. Pierre, and 20 ships and killed 30,000 people, leaving only two or three survivors.[11] The *SC II* hit fierce, buffeting winds near the volcano that slowed their progress and it was so cold that Hinton had to pound his hands together to get feeling back in his fingers.

The good news, according to Bye, was that the starboard engine, which had been threatening to boil over, cooled down to about 200 degrees. Hinton spiraled the craft down from the great height to Fort-de-France, Martinique, where they arrived shortly after noon on October 12 to an estimated 40,000 people crowding the docks.

"Gendarmes with fixed bayonets had to charge the crowd to clear a way for the landing of the airmen," reported Bye, in a page-one article in the *World*. As was in the case in earlier stops, the crew was treated like royalty. Hinton, Bye and Pinto Martins accepted a tour of Martinique from the island's governor while Baltzell and Wilshusen were taken on a climb up Mt. Pelee. On Saturday, October 15, they departed for Port-of-Spain, Trinidad, closer to the South American coast. Enroute to Trinidad, a propeller was damaged and when they landed at Port-of-Spain, they discovered it was beyond repair. Hinton cabled Philadelphia for a new one and the crew, after the arrival celebrations, sat and waited more than a month.

The new propeller finally arrived aboard the steamer *Mayaro* on Friday, November 17. Wilshusen installed it on Saturday and on Sunday, with a large crowd gathered, they tried to get off the water, but failed because the prop still didn't work properly. They returned to their anchorage and Wilshusen did some additional adjustments and finally, on November 20 at 10:30 AM, they left for Georgetown, British Guiana.[12]

They arrived at 4:30 PM on the South American coast that day and landed at the mouth of the Essequibo River about 25 miles from Georgetown and spent the night anchored there, planning to get additional oil in the morning. It was the first flight to link the two continents. It left only America to Asia and America to Africa on the list of intercontinental flights to be accomplished, Bye reported.[13]

They stayed several days at Georgetown, being feted and making repairs again on the engines before hopping to Cayenne in French Guiana and then on to the mangrove swamps of Maraca Island in the state of Amapa, where they could find additional fuel to continue the trip across the Amazon River delta to Para, Brazil. Hinton later characterized the 640-mile area between Cayenne and Para as "virtually uninhabited and not habitable, being marsh land overgrown with a brush called mangrove." He said it was far from the ship lanes and "the water was alive with man-eating sharks and its currents were extremely treacherous. He said the tides at Maraca created currents that would destroy a flying boat and if a flying boat landed in the Atlantic a steady southeasterly wind would prevent it from drifting into the seas lanes where the crew might be rescued.[14]

The *SC II* crossed the delta successfully and arrived at Para, Brazil, about 3 PM on December 2. The experience of crossing the delta and the ongoing problems with keeping the *SC II* in the air caused Hinton to scrub a proposed flight from Para up the Amazon. Instead he announced they would leave Thursday, December 7, at 10 AM for Maranhao with a stop at Braganca, Brazil, for gasoline.[15] Engine trouble again plagued the craft on the flight and Hinton sent a telegram to the Associated Press office at Maranhao that they would have to stop over in Braganca for several days and overhaul the engines again.[16] They flew the 200 miles on December 14 to Maranhao, where they were greeted by 50,000 people, according to Bye. The crowd clamored for speeches, "flags were fluttering, whistles blowing and cannon salutes being fired" as they anchored.

A marble monument depicting Hinton and Pinto Martins was unveiled and a three-day carnival ensued. The four Maranhao newspapers honored Bye at a dinner and toasted the *World* as "the most enterprising newspaper on earth." A estimated crowd of 80,000 gathered to send them off on the morning of December 19 and, bucking strong headwinds, they left the muddy waters of the Amazon delta behind for the "green seas" of the Atlantic as they flew on to Pinto Martins' birthplace in Camocim, Brazil. The flight took four hours and seventeen minutes to cover 231 miles. Bye reported that Pinto Martins' village of 7,000 seemed like 100,000 as they spiraled down to earth from 4,000 feet.

Local officials honored Pinto Martins with speeches. One got so excited that he got his feet wet as the *SC II* crew was rowed ashore. The aviators were taken on a parade through town with a band leading the way and residents waved palm leaves decorated with the flag colors of the U.S. and Brazil.[17]

On December 21, they again had trouble getting off the water. They dumped 25 gallons of gas overboard and still ran aground four times before getting airborne in 30 seconds on the fifth run. Fifteen minutes later the port Liberty engine started losing oil and Wilshusen crawled out on the wing and discovered the tank cap had not been properly tightened. A quarter hour later water started spewing out of the starboard motor. Hinton throttled it down and Wilshusen, clinging to the support wires, worked with tape and tools for 20 minutes to patch an intake manifold so they could get to Natal. The *SC II* rounded the "right shoulder" of South America as they continued to parallel the coastline. They flew over ugly rock reefs and heavy seas during the four-hour-and-fifteen-minute trip.[18] The flight was so rough, Bye reported, that the *SC II* had to come down almost vertically. Once again they were paraded

At every stop in Brazil the flying crew was feted and mobbed. Note the lighted signs for Pinto Martins and Hinton (Burns collection).

through the streets led by bands and the streets were roped off to prevent citizens from rushing to the airmen.

From Natal the crew hopped to Parahyba, Brazil, and once again had serious engine problems and had to wait three weeks for parts. When they arrived and Wilshusen had repaired the motor, Hinton came down with dysentery and was bedridden for a week. It was January 26 before he was well enough to fly and they flew to Pernambuco that day and arrived at noon.

Given all the delays the folks in Pernambuco had plenty of time to prepare to honor the fliers, and the festivities went on for three days. Five hundred couples and civil and military officials attended a ball at the British Country Club on the last day of their stay. Bye was entertained by the newspaper editors and reporters of the 10 newspapers in town and four gold and silver tablets and two large cups were presented to Hinton and Pinto Martins.[19]

The battered and bruised *SC II* finally arrived at its destination on February 8, 1923, about five and a half months behind schedule. Enroute they circled over Cape Frio to show off the flying boat and spent 15 minutes over Rio before heading for the Exposition site. Cars lined the roads on the shore of the harbor and thousands jammed the Exposition grounds.

"At an altitude of only 200 feet *The World*'s friendship airplane, the S-C II, reached the zenith of her glory this morning when, under the guidance of her skipper and pilot, Walter Hinton, she groped her way through the fog and thundered over cheering Rio de Janeiro, 5,641 nautical miles from New York."

The timed arrival at 11:30 AM had been arranged a week earlier by Senator Sampaio Correia, for whom the craft was named. Escorted by three squadrons of Brazilian seaplanes, with Pinto Martins at the controls, the plane flew over the Centenary of Independence Exhibition at 11:25 and coasted up to the reception pavilion on the waters of Gunabara Bay at 11:37 AM Bye wrote. Wilshusen and Bye waved U.S. and Brazilian flags as they landed and the *World*'s green and white house banner was draped over the center strut after Hinton shut off the engines. The harbor forts fired their guns and steamers sounded their sirens as church bells rang throughout the city.

Sen. Sampaio Correia boarded the *SC II* from his yacht and they were received by Dr. Alaior Praia, prefect of the Federal District of Rio, who praised the flight "as a symbol of eternal peace and harmony between the two Americas." They were also greeted by Alberto Santos-Dumont, a famous Brazilian balloonst, who was the first man to fly a powered balloon around the Eiffel Tower in Paris.

The car carrying the airmen was saluted from diplomatic expositions as it crept through the crowd. A police guard formed behind the procession as some fans fainted and were trampled in the crush.

The jitney that Hinton and Pinto Martins were riding in was mobbed when the crew finally reached Brazil. No one seemed to care that it had taken the flyers six months to make the trip from New York City (Burns collection).

"Flowers, confetti, streamers and paper airplanes showered upon us. The crowds were so dense it took us nearly three hours to reach the Gloria Hotel," Bye wrote. It was the beginning of two weeks of banquets and receptions arranged for the fliers and their crew.[20]

"Every newspaper gives us the front page tonight, some covering the entire page with nothing but a design working the flags and eagles of the United States and Brazil and sketches of Hinton and Pinto Martins, our Brazilian navigator," Bye observed. "The two general thoughts expressed are that the flight has added greatly to the relations of Brazil and the United States and that it is a 'final triumph of perseverance and bravery.'"

The flying time for the 5,581 miles from Pensacola to Rio was 100 hours and 21 minutes. While that could hardly be claimed as a huge aviation achievement given the fact that Jimmy Doolittle had already flown across the U.S. in September 1922 with one stop and a pair of pilots flew 2,500 miles in November 1922 from San Diego to Indianapolis, it had helped make both Hinton and Pinto Martins famous.

During speeches on February 9 at a breakfast sponsored by the Aero Club, it was suggested that the *SC II* continue its journey to Buenos Aires,

Argentina. Hinton told the crowd that the machine was in good condition and that the members of the crew were willing to make the trip.

The Rio celebrations marked an ending and a beginning because, as Hinton was traveling back to New York by steamer, a man asked him if he would like to do any more flying in Brazil. Hinton told the man that he had hoped to explore the unknown regions of northern Brazil on the Rio flight, but it had proved impractical. The man offered to arrange for Hinton to meet a friend who had led six expeditions to that region and was planning a seventh — Dr. Alexander Hamilton Rice, a wealthy geographer, who financed his own trips. On this trip Rice proposed a journey to explore the upper reaches of the Orinoco River valley, part of the Amazon system, and chart the area from the air, the first aerial exploration of lands unknown to the civilized world.

15

Exploring the Amazon Basin

"We who fly do so for the love of flying. We are alive in the air with this miracle that lies in our hands and beneath our feet."
— Cecil Day Lewis[1]

Walter Hinton flew over the landing site that he had scouted out by air several days before. Rocks and ledges stuck out of the river surface like teeth and bones. The water level had dropped. Landing was impossible. He would have to find another place to put the *Eleanor III* flying boat down for the night.

On December 23, 1926, Hinton and Army Capt. Albert W. Stevens had been exploring and charting the Amazon basin ahead of the main Rice expedition party for 10 months. The advance party, headed by Dr. Charles Bull, a one-time Harvard footballer and geologist, worked up to 100 miles ahead of the main party. Hinton and Stevens would fly ahead of that and Stevens shot aerial photos and charted the maze of twisting waterways, blind alleys, and islands so the expedition could progress without heading up hundreds of deadends. Each night the pair picked a place where the plane could land so Bull's party could deliver gasoline, oil and food before continuing upriver to a campsite suggested by the aerial reconnaissance. If the plane couldn't land, they would make a parachute with cloth and a canister and drop it to Bull with Stevens' sketches of the false channels and dangerous rapids.

On seeing the rocks, Hinton flew low looking for another place to set up an operating base. They identified a possible spot and Hinton coasted the noisy Curtiss Seagull down for a perfect landing.

But as the craft touched the surface, a terrific jolt shot through the plane. A boulder hidden just beneath the silvery surface had crushed the hull. River water gushed into the plane. Hinton gunned the engines. If they sank here, far ahead of Bull's party and nowhere near a place where they could get the craft out of the water and repair it, they were lost.

The *Eleanor*, engines roaring, crippled sluggishly back into the air, water spewing from the gash in the fuselage. The two men both knew they needed

15. Exploring the Amazon Basin　　　　175

This artist's rendering of Amazon natives seeing the Rice expedition *Eleanor II* airplane for the first time was used in advertisements during the era for files and other tools. Hinton and Stevens actually cut the file they used in half to reduce weight (Burns collection).

to locate a place where they could beach the craft to make hull repairs. Hinton headed downriver, searching for a sand bar. It was an hour before they found what looked like a suitable sand spit on an island at midstream. They had traveled 60 miles. Hinton put the plane smoothly on the water and rammed it hard onto the sand. Hinton and Stevens climbed out and waded ashore.

They had no radio and no way to contact Bull or the main party, but they had emergency supplies — a 12-by-14 foot piece of canvas with lines on all sides, two hammocks, fishing tackle, an axe, two aluminum kettles, matches, a flashlight, and several pounds of a bland-tasting grain product called farina, which is still sold by Nabisco in the U.S. as Cream of Wheat. They had no way of alerting anyone of where they were and the fact that they were safe. Stevens, on loan from the U.S. Army for the expedition, was armed with a .25 caliber pistol. It would be of little use against hostile natives or any creature large enough to attack the men.

The pair built a shelter with the canvas and hung their hammocks under it. They gathered a couple armloads of firewood to maintain a fire at the campsite so they would be prepared when darkness fell. Then the men looked at the damage to the aircraft. By now the sand spit was under water. Luckily they had moored it with a line to a nearby tree. A peculiarity of the Amazon tributaries is the uncertainty of the water levels. With all the rainfall, rivers could rise three to ten feet within 24 hours and then take several days to fall back to normal levels.

They were trapped on the unnamed island — one of thousands in the river system — until the water levels dropped again, exposing the bottom of the plane so they could repair it. They would then have to wait for the river to rise again after another rain to float the machine so Hinton could get it airborne. It would be the third Christmas that Hinton was either lost in the wilds or stranded somewhere thousands of miles from his home on Long Island, New York. In 1920 he had been lost in the frozen north near Hudson Bay in 40-degree-below-zero temperatures and presumed dead or at least stuck at some fur outpost until the spring thaw. In 1923 he was stuck in Parahiba, Brazil, located on the Atlantic shoulder of South America, waiting for parts to repair the *SC II* that he was piloting, the first flight from New York to Rio. Folks knew where he was, but the plane wasn't going anywhere until parts were shipped by slow boat from the U.S.

Hinton, who had piloted the first airplane across the Atlantic, met Amazon expedition leader Alexander Hamilton Rice in a club in New York City in March 1923 after a shipboard acquaintance introduced them. He told Rice of his dream of flying over the Amazon basin and Rice said: "If you are sincere in what you told, my friend, and I think you are, you can have anything you want to do it with."[2]

Rice laid a map of the 500-square-mile area on a table between the two adventurers and traced the routes of his previous six expeditions there.

"This was as far as we could go last time," he said, pointing out the location on the map. "Here we encountered the warlike Guaharibas, a tribe of cannibal Indians who attacked us, forcing us to return down the river."[3]

Rice, who was one of those larger than life figures of the 1920s, was a descendant of the governor of Massachusetts and mayor of Boston. A tall, gray-haired man who was noted for his poetry as well as his geographic studies, he had spent a quarter-century exploring and mapping in northern Brazil.

Rice was married to Eleanor Elkins Widener, the widow of George Widener who died with his son when the *Titanic* sank on April 15, 1912. Ham Rice, as he was called, and Eleanor lived in a palatial Long Island estate called Miramar, which was described in news accounts as similar to the French palace at Versailles, only better.

15. Exploring the Amazon Basin

Rice explained to Hinton that the source of the Orinoco had never been located or mapped and he believed that it was possible to reach its source by going up the Parima River via the Amazon and its tributaries. Rice believed that there was a mountain pass by which the warlike Guaharibas could cross into the Amazon basin and they had been blocking access to the region for hundreds of years, since the days of the Spanish conquistadores.

Rice agreed with Hinton's view that a flying boat would be able to make aerial photographs, map the route, reconnoiter ahead of the main party, make sketch maps, and carry food and medical supplies between the various bases and the advance party.

A day after meeting with Rice, Hinton looked up his friend John Wilshusen, who had been the mechanic with him on that frustrating odyssey from New York City to Rio de Janeiro, Brazil, that was supposed to take about 30 days and wound up taking six months with numerous breakdowns and repairs.

"John could sit down with a file and a piece of metal and turn out a part that many a mechanic might feel was an accomplishment with modern tools and a lathe to work with," Hinton later wrote. "His [Wilshusen's] reply was an immediate and enthusiastic, 'Yes.'"

The crew works on the *Sampaio Correia II* at one of the many stops they made (Burns collection).

Familiar with Curtiss equipment from his days as a Navy test pilot and instructor, Hinton turned to his friend Glenn Curtiss to purchase a flying boat. Curtiss had only one in stock—a Seagull, rated as "probably the best small flying boat of the period" (1919–1938) with a Curtiss C-6A 160-horsepower, six-cylinder, water-cooled, pusher engine. It had a range with two men and photographic equipment of about 300 miles, a cruising speed of 60 mph and a maximum speed of 76 mph. It could climb to 3,000 feet in about 10 minutes and had a service ceiling of about 6,000 feet. It had a mahogany plywood veneer hull over a wood frame and fabric-covered wings which spanned 49 feet, 9 inches. It was almost 29 feet long and 12 feet high, weighed almost 2,000 pounds empty, and in a pinch could seat three.[4]

From his previous learning experiences in the tropics on the disastrous Rio trip, Hinton had a larger radiator installed to keep the engine cool in the burning heat "where a forced landing meant death by starvation or at the hands of cannibal Indians," he said.

They also put inflated auto inner tubes in each of the four watertight compartments so the plane wouldn't immediately sink if they damaged the hull in a rocky river.

On March 29, 1924, Hinton, Wilshusen, Stevens (the photographer and cartographer), and John Swanson, on leave as radio inspector of the Federal Department of Commerce, sailed for Rio aboard the steamship *Southern Cross*. They were joined later by Hamilton and his wife.[5]

Rice and other party members were finally ready to set out on the mission July 6 from Manaos, Brazil, 1000 miles upriver from where the Amazon met the sea at the junction of the Rio Negro in the midst of a great forest. The group included Dr. Theodor Koch-Grunberg, a German ethnologist; Dr. George Shattuck, a physician, an interpreter, a film operator; and Indian porters and paddlers, bringing the total to 100.[6] Expedition members found Manaos to be a modern 40,000-person city laid out on a grid system with electric streetcars and an opera house with a gilded dome with a local theater showing American movies.[7]

With hundreds of miles from the ocean and surrounded by impenetrable forest, Manaos is a seaport handling tons of supplies from ocean steamers.

The plan was to map the Rio Branco and the Rio Uraricoera and find the source of the Uraricoera in the Serra Parima mountains and discover the passage if it existed that linked it to the headwaters of the Orinoco. Five years earlier, Dr. Rice and a small party in two canoes had attempted the same trek, but were attacked by Indians near a spot where the Guaharinos fought the Spanish in 1763.[8]

As Capt. Stevens, the noted Army photographer who was given leave through Ham Rice's influence, later put it in his National Geographic account:

15. Exploring the Amazon Basin

The *Eleanor II* comes in for a landing on the Amazon River (Burns collection).

"Our expedition started off with a bang — several bangs. On the night following our arrival at Manaos a revolution broke out."

While Rice Expedition party members dined by an open window in the lobby of the Grand Hotel, a troop of soldiers marched by carrying rifles and machine guns; light artillery and explosions and bangs that sounded like a Fourth of July celebration started in the city square.

When a hotel employee tried to close the window, Rice party members shooed him away and watched entranced as a man ran down the street and threw himself futilely at the light streaming from the window. Dr. Bull and Stevens jumped up, leaned out and caught his wrists and pulled him in. Stevens was convinced that his cabin mate on the trip up river from Rio had fomented the revolt that resulted in a dozen casualties.

At each port of call his cabin mate, a distinguished sort, would don a silk hat, dress up, and spend the day ashore, and subsequently revolts broke out. Stevens said the Rice expedition crew was lucky to be on the boat with the man because after the revolt, shipping on the lower Amazon was halted by the military for two months.[9]

The shop owners and store keepers of Manos viewed the arrival of the

The *Eleanor III* anchored to an Amazon River bank during the Rice expedition (Burns collection).

Rice expedition with its exotic flying machine as an excuse to have a holiday and closed for the day as Hinton and Wilshusen assembled the parts of the Seagull. It had been named *Eleanor III* in honor of Mrs. Rice. The docks were lined with curious people and the river was so jammed with small boats that Hinton had trouble finding a clear path to get off the water for a test flight.

A few weeks later on August 20 a chartered stern-wheel steamer and the airborne Curtiss Seagull headed up the glossy, black waters of the Rio Negro to spend nine months "in, beside and over the world's greatest forest."[10] A few miles north of Manaos, the Rio Negro, so named for its black waters, broadened to more than 10 miles across and was dotted by hundreds of irregularly shaped islands that created a labyrinth as the steamer threaded through the main channels.

Each morning Hinton would take off early and fly about 100 miles upriver with Stevens snapping pictures with a giant Fairchild aerial camera mounted on the plane and sketching the river. Then they would fly back and anchor at the same place as the steamer. On one occasion when Hinton gave another expedition member a sightseeing ride, the plane lost fuel pressure and the passenger had to get out a hand pump and work it for an hour and half while they flew back to camp.[11] The surface of the river was frequently so smooth and mirrored that it could cause Hinton problems in landing because it was difficult to tell exactly where the surface was. When possible he landed in the wake of a boat or where ripples marked the water.

The expedition followed the Rio Negro that was three and a half miles wide at Manaos and sometimes broadened to 15 miles wide for 200 miles to Carvoeiro where they saw the "milky waters of the Rio Branco pouring into the Negro like cream into black coffee."[12]

Hinton wrote: "We hurdled miles of solid woods and dense undergrowth through which no human could have made his way. There were vast areas of swamps, mountains with towering cliffs and chasms — all the extremes afforded by nature through more than a thousand miles of tropical waterways. We took them in at a speed rivaling that of the birds which sped away before '*o bicho grande*' or the 'big animal,' as the natives, speaking Portuguese, termed our airplane."

Stevens — ever careful — had glued together two large pieces of rubber so they made a life preserver which he could drape around his neck. Hinton said it looked like a huge hot water bottle on Stevens' stomach when it was inflated.

The pair put aboard canoe paddles so if they landed and the engine was damaged they could detach the wings, tail and motor and use the hull as a canoe. The steamer carried tons of food in watertight cases, a spare engine, wings, tail structure, wires, struts, instruments and propellers so everything except the hull could be rebuilt. It also had 3,500 gallons of gasoline and oil on deck in five-gallon tins, five canoes, outboard motors and special flat-bottomed boats. Dr. Rice's launch was towed alongside.

While Hinton tried to hold the Seagull at 6,000 feet in order to make the pictures a uniform scale, Stevens shot photographs and made his sketches on a drawing board with graphed paper held to it by cords and rubber bands. Pencils and erasers were secured with string so the wind couldn't snatch them out of the cockpit. Each inch section of his graph paper represented a four-mile area of river and jungle.

The pair would return to the mother ship at noon for a meal and to rest in the heat from the midday sun. Hinton described flying in the heat of the day as "torture" and Hinton's and Stevens' faces were as red as raw beef. The winds blew from the east in the afternoon and evening and they learned to respect them.

"One day we had swung farther off to the west than good judgment would have warranted," Hinton wrote. "Turning around to come back we felt a steady insistent opposing force that cut down the speed to a few miles an hour. We were over the Rio Negro which is fifteen miles wide at that point and treacherous. Narrow islands appeared below, dotting the surface and clinging tenaciously to the shoreline, forming channels miles long. We found ourselves repeatedly over blind leads so extensive that they appeared like smaller rivers with their ends blocked by the jungle. The steamer always hugged the banks to avoid the current. It would be out of sight for hours, hidden by the overhanging foliage. Now as we tried to find the vessel it was nowhere in sight. Without warning the engine commenced missing. We were out of gasoline. At that instant the steamer appeared, a tiny moving speck on the edge of a limitless waste. We glided to the surface within fifty feet of it. Had we been forced down in one of the blind channels we should never have been found."[13]

When they returned to the steamer at dusk, riding lights would be attached to the wings and the engine and propeller covered with canvas to protect them from the continuous rain. A canoe would then ferry them to the steamer.

Days would pass between each aerial reconnaissance, as the plane covered so much territory on each flight. On off days Hinton and Wilshusen would work on the plane checking for problems, but they couldn't inspect the hull, which was constantly in the water. Meanwhile Stevens developed his film so he could show the expedition what it would be facing upriver.

As they left on the last flight they took, while working with the steamer, the plane dragged and had trouble getting into the air. Hinton turned and flew low over the boat and Wilshusen climbed to the top deck and confirmed that the veneered bottom on the tail had pulled off in a six-foot-long section that was four feet wide at one point and tapered to two feet wide. The fabric wing surfaces had been coated with aluminum dope to protect against the equatorial sun, but the mahogany tail section had softened from constantly being in the warm water.

Hinton flew on and Stevens carried out the mapping program for the day. When they saw a clearing on shore with a gentle bank and a village, they landed. The pair recruited help by handing out cigarettes to the villagers, who were a mixture of Indian and Portuguese. The men helped lift the tail out of the water, which revealed the extent of the damage.

The residents then escorted Hinton and Stevens to the best thatched house in the village and the pair was surprised to see pictures that featured Hinton's year-earlier flight from New York to Rio pinned to the walls. When Hinton explained he was the pilot of that flight the villagers "became wildly enthusiastic." The steamer arrived at that moment, ending the plans for a celebration in Hinton's honor, and Wilshusen patched the bottom well enough that they could fly on to a larger village Sororoca, one degree from the Equator.

At Sororoca Stevens satisfied a childhood dream to stand exactly on his own shadow with the sun directly overhead at noon. Hinton and Wilshusen

15. Exploring the Amazon Basin

Walter Hinton in cowboy hat trades with Amazon Indians as the Rice expedition moved upriver in search of the source of the Orinoco (Burns collection).

spent two days amid clouds of mosquitoes and gnats, re-planking six feet of the bottom with solid wood where the tropical weather had separated the mahogany veneer. They then stretched canvas over the bottom and with the help of 20 Indians pushed the flying boat back into the water. Hinton, suffering the effects of the second of nine malaria attacks, was able to fly the Seagull on to Vista Alegre, the end of the steamer line.

There the steamer unloaded the flat-bottomed boats, gasoline, oil and food supplies for the expedition to carry on upriver in canoes, while Hinton, who had recovered from his malarial fever, flew back down to Sororoca with Dr. Richard Strong, who had finished his research, to pick up a collection of biological specimens and then meet the steamer returning downriver.

It wasn't until they saw the lights of the steamer in the dusk that they remembered the vessel had lost its only canoe and all the other boats were at Vista Alegre. Hinton couldn't shut off the engine and coast up to the ship because, alone, he would have no way to spin the pusher prop and get off the water. "But the others on deck had seen our difficult position before we came within shouting range," Hinton wrote. "We saw a deck chair hurled overboard at the end of a rope." Hinton taxied past slowly and Dr. Strong jumped overboard and swam to the chair and was hauled aboard through a nasty swirl of piranha, "a small fish rarely more than fifteen inches long. Yet it is voracious with a jaw like a circular saw, and it has been known to snap a piano wire in two."[14]

With the steamer sending a farewell blast on its horn, Hinton turned back up river in the waning light, fearful that he wouldn't cover the 40 miles to Vista Alegre before the pitch darkness of an equatorial night descended. He flew low over shallow water, reefs, floating logs, rapids and sandbars to make sure he didn't leave the main course of the Branco, straining for 25 minutes to see the lights of the town.

At last Hinton saw a lantern in a canoe. It was Wilshusen waving it at midstream to signal the *Eleanor* in and ready to rescue him if the landing went bad. Others on shore waved lanterns to signal the camp's location; Hinton set the Seagull down safely and taxied to shore.

The men spent the next month in Vista Alegre waiting for Rice to return from business affairs in Manaos. Six of the men, including Hinton, cane down with malaria even though they were all taking quinine each day and sleeping under mosquito netting.

Dr. Theodor Koch-Grunberg, the internationally known German ethnographer, died. He had refused to take his quinine dosage and didn't use mosquito netting because he thought after so many years in the tropics he was immune. Koch-Grunberg had secretly feared his heart would not withstand the negative effect of the drug, Hinton wrote. The German scientist was buried next to an Englishman, marked by a white stone cross, and some Brazilians and Portuguese, marked by wooden crosses, who had also succumbed to the disease.

After moving upriver from Vista Alegre, Hinton said, they experienced "the real hardships of the tropics, the plagues and the poisonous insects which carry deadly diseases. On shore we virtually lived under mosquito netting."

The men at times wore mosquito netting headgear that made them look like fugitives from early science fiction movies. There were ants — red, big, little, black, biting. Hinton one night left a shirt hanging on a branch and all that was left the next morning were tatters. The ants had eaten it.

As soon as the flying boat touched land ants were likely to stream on board.

The men painted ropes, guy wires and other surfaces with kerosene to block the pest invasion. Injuries, accidents and sickness took their toll. Wilshusen got a leg infection and had to be taken back downriver to a hospital in Manaos where he spent almost three months. Hinton, while trying to cut a tough root stuck on the bottom of the flying boat's tail, slashed his left hand to the bone, cutting the nerves. A tourniquet with a handkerchief and a spanner wrench stopped the bleeding and Drs. George Shattuck and Strong sewed him up after Bull anesthetized him with nine drinks of a sugar cane rum

Hinton models a shirt that, left out overnight, was eaten by Amazon jungle ants. They had to put sticky substances on the tent and hammock ropes to keep them out at night (Albert Stevens, National Geographic stock).

drink. Hinton's hand was in a splint for three weeks and was almost useless. He dropped the expedition's best wrench and a good screwdriver overboard because he had no feeling in his fingers. While working on a hot engine Hinton smelled something burning and realized it was the little finger on his left hand. He couldn't feel it.

In the air Hinton sometimes had to throttle back and dive to avoid hitting large buzzards or colorful macaws that were spooked by the engine noise. And almost every morning they would find a spider living within the airspeed indicator, according to Rice.[15] But the expedition moved forward with Stevens and Hinton flying upriver to Boa Vista, a town of about 1,000 people, which was their main camp for the final push to discover the source of the Orinoco.

Immense herds of cattle ranged on the open lands around Boa Vista and as far as 100 miles to the west where dense forests began and continued all the way to the Andes in Colombia. Two rivers — the Uraricuera and Takutu — join to form the Branca about 30 miles upriver from Boa Vista and it was 375 miles up the Uraricuera that Rice proposed to penetrate.

The powerful river dropped 750 feet in a 90-mile stretch and one fall was 95 feet high, Hinton reported as they continued reconnaissance flights while the main Rice party worked its way up to Boa Esperanza, the last settlement on the plains, 150 miles above Boa Vista.

When the herds of cattle and horses heard the Seagull engine, they stampeded away, and the Indians who heard the plane abandoned their villages and hid in the jungle for several days before their curiosity overcame them and they visited the Rice camp. Some wanted to go up in the "big animal," Hinton reported and most were delighted when someone would give them anything made of cloth — "a torn cap, or a tattered handkerchief."[16]

Days in the Amazon Basin would usually start bright and clear and by 10 AM clouds would form and it would rain in the afternoons. Nights were clear with stars twinkling brightly in the blackness. The Uraricuera splits above Boa Esperanza and flows on either side of an island 45 miles long. Over the south channel Hinton discovered "boiling rapids, huge rocks with narrow leads and small islands — all surrounded by a great forest as varied in colors as a rag carpet and stretching endlessly as far as we could see."[17]

Mist lay over the dark, sodden jungle in blankets and smoke spirals and steam-like clouds puzzled the fliers. "The channel gradually narrowed. Below, the unbroken river bed offered no chance of a landing and, fearing that we were flying into a cul-de-sac from which we could not escape if forced down, I swerved abruptly to the right and we flew over the island jungle for perhaps ten miles, striking the north branch and following it to the end where the two forks joined. Near there we found the only available camping site."[18]

There Hinton had another malaria attack and took to his hammock while Stevens oiled and gassed the plane. Hinton swallowed up to 100 grains of quinine a day to fight the disease.

The flying was particularly dangerous in February and March because of the rains. They had taken off the windshield to save weight and the rain drops would pelt their faces like birdshot, leaving them purple and welted. While the small area of sky they could see from a jungle campsite might be clear, when they got airborne they would find themselves detouring around storms. If they passed through them, they would lose sight of the river for minutes at a time, threatening to put them off course. Their lives depended on the steady hum of the engine.

The pair discussed what they would do if it stalled and they had to crash land over jungle. "I'll wear my parachute, and jump," Stevens said. "That will lighten the load and reduce the landing speed." On second thought, he added. "No, that will not do. We would be separated." They got rid of the parachute even though both agreed it was the most dangerous flying that either had ever experienced.

In late afternoons the pair would look for a clearing and land in the river and taxi to shore where Hinton would ram the nose of the Eleanor into the vines and trees and plants and Stevens would cling to the branches as they brought her to shore. They would set up camp and Stevens would take water from the river to develop the day's negatives, sometimes using the sheltering roots of a tall tree that could be shrouded with canvas for a darkroom.

Hinton and Stevens were making a reconnaissance flight to locate a supply base at a place the explorers called Kuleikuleima Rocks on December 23 when the Seagull was badly damaged. After landing, Hinton was taxiing toward shore when they heard the quarter-inch thick wood hull splintering.

Taking the risk he would tear away part of the hull, Hinton revved his engines and got the Eleanor back into the air. They headed back toward Boa Esperanca 150 miles down river, but it was late afternoon and the sun had begun to set as they arrived at Maraca Island and headed down the north channel.

Rather than try to fly blind in the equatorial darkness, they looked for a place to land and selected the middle of three small islands in the channel. It was about a mile long and a quarter mile wide. They would be there — out of contact with the expedition — until the river fell and they could repair the hull and then rose again so they could float the craft.

They set up camp by stretching a line about nine feet up between two trees and hanging the canvas over it. The two hammocks were slung high underneath it, close together, with the men headed in opposite directions. They smeared creosote on the ropes to discourage insects from joining them in bed. Stevens and Hinton faced the prospect of a dismal Christmas. But they had their food supplies and could fish from the tail of the plane, careful to stay out of the water and attract piranha, which would strike at any living thing.

On Christmas night Stevens played old tunes and jazz on a harmonica and he set up his Fairchild aerial camera with its lens as big as a dish plate so he could take a picture of the two of them sitting by the fire. Stevens threw a handful of flash powder on the fire and got an image of both of them in profile,

Hinton and Army Capt. Albert W. Stevens spent Christmas Eve 1923 stranded on an unnamed island in the Amazon, lost miles from the main party with a gash in the bottom of their flying boat. Stevens threw flash powder on the camp fire to get this photograph (Albert Stevens, National Geographic stock).

peacefully tending a campfire that could have been shot at any campground in the civilized world rather than on an uncharted jungle island.[19]

"There we were hundreds of miles from the last outpost of civilization, in a wilderness never before penetrated by white men, even lost from the rest of our party, yet we had been able to fly in there and make a picture of ourselves inside of a few hours. Had our plane carried a radio we could have told the world about it in a few moments.[20]

On the third night Hinton heard something large in the brush and woke Stevens.

"Steve, wake up."

"What's the matter?" asked Stevens.

"Something's prowling around camp. It sounds like a great big animal," Hinton said.

Stevens heard a crunch, "a ponderous, a loud, a threatening crunch."

"Sounds like an elephant," whispered Hinton and Stevens agreed even though both men knew an elephant prowling around at night in the Amazon basin was not likely. Stevens wondered aloud if it could be an alligator and whether the reptile could reach the hammocks. He suggested they get up and cinch up the hammocks farther off the ground.

The pair got up. Stevens got out his pistol and they armed themselves with an ax and a machete. Stevens pointed his flashlight into the jungle. They saw nothing, but the sounds were coming closer. There was a final crash and trees shuddered as a large animal blundered off at full speed. For several minutes they heard it crashing away through the trees.

In the morning the men checked and found hoof prints which indicated it was a tapir, "a queer but harmless" prehistoric relative of the horse and rhinoceros that looks something like a large pig and can grow as large as 500 lbs and dines on aquatic plants, twigs, foliage and fruit. An ancient legend has it that "the tapir was made by God from odds and ends left over after all the other creatures were created."[21]

It was four days before the water level receded enough for the men to see the damage to the hull. Repairing the bottom with strips of mahogany and marine glue took a day.

On the fifth day, four Indians suddenly appeared in camp — three men and a boy. They had been paddling downriver and saw smoke from the campfire. At the camp Indians would appear suddenly and stare at the whites. For the most part they wore no clothing except an occasional small apron made of beads. They wanted to trade for metal goods, but had nothing to exchange except bows and arrows.

Stevens and Hinton thought about Dr. Rice having been attacked a few years earlier and reports that 68 members of an oil-prospecting party had been massacred two years earlier. They waved to the Indians to help themselves to the fish they were boiling for breakfast and they did.

Stevens noted that they looked almost Mongolian in appearance and had their hair trimmed in soup-bowl cuts. The men were short and came up to the aviators' shoulders. They had no iron goods and apparently had never seen white men. The Indians didn't seem to be bothered by the stinging, biting insects or the hordes of mosquitoes, or the ants that were everywhere and turned up in the food. Steven said when making coffee they would put a spoonful of sugar in the cup and then add hot water and skim off the ants, but this approach seldom removed all of them.[22]

The flying boat was on the other side of the island from the camp and when the Indians saw it, they were amazed and left muttering in their dugout.

It was four more days before the river rose enough to float the plane so two men could shove it off the sand bar. They flew away from their unnamed island home on January 2, 1925, and returned to Boa Esperanza, where they

Hinton in the cockpit, with Capt. Stevens behind him, shows off the *Eleanor III* to Amazon natives who had never seen a plane. They called him "The white-winged God on the big bird." Hinton discovered a poster of himself from the Rio flight in one chief's living quarters (Albert Stevens, National Geographic stock).

spotted a search party 20 miles upstream from the two hut village. They got an enthusiastic welcome from the men there, who had wondered what had happened to them and feared the worst. The main party, led by Dr. Rice, had already pushed upriver to another camp and no radio contact had been made with them, so they waited.

Finally after 10 days, Hinton and Stevens got impatient and flew upriver looking for Rice and found the party struggling to portage around roaring rapids and making slow progress in strong currents. Some of the tins of gasoline they had started out with were lost in accidents while pulling the canoes up rapids.

When the main party finally arrived at the Kuleikuleima Rocks there were more than 70 people in camp. They now prepared to push on to their objective, the sources of the Orinoco and the Parima, the land of the fierce Guaharibos.

Bull and the advance team left 10 days ahead of the Seagull to provide a refueling spot near the mouth of the Parima. As Hinton and Stevens flew up the waterway following Bull's course, the river banks rose gradually and became cliffs and then walls that twisted one way and another with the course of the river. When the radiator water started boiling, Hinton and Stevens realized they couldn't rise above the canyon walls to escape nor was the gorge wide enough to turn the flying boat around. They flew on making tricky lefts and rights and finally they turned a corner and there was Bull standing upright in a canoe a midstream waving them down. He had placed a large piece of cloth on a bush also as a signal to the aviators.

Hinton and Stevens made careful preparations for their last flight inland. They weighed everything that was put aboard the *Eleanor*. Cushions were pulled from seats, a file broken in half and one part left behind. They calculated they could get three hours and forty-five minutes of flying with the fuel the Seagull could carry. They knew that if they were forced down in the Parima mountains, nothing could rescue them. Hinton said that he and Stevens each carried a little package of opium "sufficient to end our lives if the machine came down" in hostile territory.

On March 12, 1925, they set out for their final aerial reconnaissance and Hinton climbed the *Eleanor* to about 5,000 feet. "The mysterious Sierra Parima lay ahead as far as we could see through the mist and the banks of cumulous clouds which at intervals surrounded us, soaking everything in the machine." Hinton write. "We passed through the rain, however. The mountains looked like a huge, rolling sea, vast and limitless, with the far horizon showing no sign of smooth country in any direction."[23]

As the river narrowed they saw two bridges that had been created by felling trees from opposite banks and tying the ends together. Deep ravines and canyons faced the gorge and they saw a waterfall dropping 600 feet and passed over two thatched huts and dropped two of their gift packages — large pieces of scarlet cloth fashioned into parachutes with various articles tucked into bundles underneath. They saw no more signs of life as they flew up a five-mile-long gorge lined with waterfalls and cascades. Gradually the river became a tiny stream and it was evident to Hinton and Stevens that there was no common source for the Parima and no secret pass that the Guaharibos used to attack their enemies. There was a 75-mile barrier of mountains between the source of the Orinoco and the Parima.

Hinton turned and headed back to base camp and they spent the night with the main party before heading back down river toward civilization, their mission accomplished. They had flown for more than 174 hours during the eight and a half months they were in the jungles, without a major incident. "We blazed the trail over which future generations will travel to develop this unknown wilderness," Hinton said later.

It took the men on the ground 10 weeks to travel 85 miles up the Parima to the waterfall Hinton and Stevens had noted on the charts, a trip that took the aviators and the Seagull three and a half hours.

Near the source of the Parima, the main Rice party met a tribe of what they called "white Indians" who were much lighter in color than the other natives in the Amazon basin and had been occasionally reported since the first European explorers got to South America.

As the main body pushed on upriver, Hinton and Stevens headed the *Eleanor III* back to Manaos. They had flown for 12,000 miles over the world's greatest river and forest in storm and heat and survived.

When Hinton and Stevens arrived back in Manaos, they received an enthusiastic welcome from a cheering group of British and Americans there, but a new city government's police force demanded to know who gave them permission for the flights. The police told them in the future they must be notified before any additional flights were made. The pair readily agreed since the mission was all but complete.

The pair made one last flight to shoot aerial pictures of the mixing of the Rio Negro's black waters with the yellow waters of the Amazon, which created a distinctive band in the water. There was a stiff cross wind on the four-mile-wide river and when they landed on the choppy surface to taxi back to shore, the banging of the hull on the waves proved too much for the many patches on the Eleanor, according to Stevens, and canvas strips pulled loose from the bottom. They quickly had the plane pulled ashore for the last time to be loaded on the steamer for the trip down the Amazon.

The Rice party finally returned to New York aboard the Cunard liner *Mauretania* on July 10, 1925.

16

Hinton the Celebrity

"Anyone can be taught to fly.... To an experienced pilot, a plane is a part of him and flying becomes second nature."
— Walter Hinton

Transatlantic flyer, Amazon explorer and celebrity pilot Walter Hinton walked out the door of Reuben's Restaurant at Madison Avenue and 58th Street in New York into the March night air. Hinton had cut short his remarks to patrons about his recent aerial exploration in Brazil looking for the source of the Orinoco, a tributary of the world's greatest river and the strange light-skinned Indians he had encountered there because he felt nauseated. His friend, socialite Richard E. Condon, had accompanied the 38-year-old divorcee that March 19, 1926, as Hinton made talks on aviation to the Junior Board of Trade and Transportation and later to American Legion members.

Suddenly the 38-year-old Hinton felt severe chest pains and told Condon he wanted to go home to his apartment at 76 Washington Square South. But Condon signaled a taxi and ordered the driver to take them to his nearby apartment at 480 Park Avenue. There, after Hinton collapsed fully clothed on a bed, Condon called his physician friends, Dr. Harold E.E. Pardee of 160 East 64th St. and Dr. Graham Biddle of 300 Park Avenue.

Hinton appeared to have had a heart attack. The doctors concluded he had been stricken with acute inflammation of the outer layer of his heart. He was also running a high fever. Feeling Hinton wouldn't survive the night, they summoned his ex-wife Sally, who lived in a Manhattan apartment nearby. But late in the night the fever broke and Hinton's condition improved enough that they could transfer him to a hospital.

The *New York Times* page-one headline the next day read:

> HINTON, OCEAN FLIER, STRICKEN ILL HERE;
> Heart Attack, After Speech, Puts His Life in Danger,
> but He Later Rallies.

16. Hinton the Celebrity

WIFE CALLED TO BEDSIDE; Taken to Home of Friend,
Air-Man's Recovery is Problematical, Specialists Declare.

The *Times* of March 21 reported that Hinton was much improved and had been moved Friday afternoon to the Naval Hospital in Brooklyn. It also stated that Mrs. Hinton had received messages of sympathy from "prominent fliers and officials in Europe" and Dick Byrd and the American Legion. Acting Mayor Joseph V. McKee visited the stricken flier's bedside. What it didn't report was that for four days Hinton's health was so precarious that hospital attendants didn't remove his clothes. It was three weeks before he was released.

No further story ever appeared on the incident. But once he was out of the hospital, Hinton recovered quickly and went back to the lecture circuit and continued to fly. There were no strict federal regulations about pilots passing health examinations.

After his return from his Amazon adventure, Hinton was the toast of New York and Washington, D.C. In New York he was accorded celebrity status with the *Times* deeming him recognizable in headlines by his surname alone.

The tall, one-time Ohio farm boy had many a tale to tell and a disarmingly modest way of telling them. He praised others, kept their failings to

Hinton poses next to the Fairchild plane that he and his co-pilot flew to small towns all over the country to promote aviation (Burns collection).

himself and downplayed his own role. Hinton, with help from influential aviation fans, became a regular feature on the New York and Washington, D.C., lecture circuits.

Hinton could talk about flying the Atlantic in an open cockpit flying boat; consorting with royalty in Portugal and Britain; attending the Versailles Peace conference at a president's invitation; being lost and given up for dead on a balloon ride in the wilds of Canada and threatening to eat a companion in order to convince him to keep walking toward safety; experiencing a nighttime crash landing in shark-infested waters off Cuba; living through a revolution in Brazil; seeing the strange fish, fauna and people of the Amazon; crash-landing and surviving on an island in the Amazon jungle, and the famous and near-famous he had met along the way.

With help from his old friend George Bye, who had been on the Rio trip with him as a correspondent for the New York World, Hinton penned dozens of articles in popular magazines of the day, such as *Liberty,* where titles such as "Outguessing Death," "Flying for Life," "The Wildest Balloon Ride" and "Flying Rum Runners" appeared under his byline. Additional stories appeared in *Current History, World's Work, Literary Digest,* and the *New York Herald Tribune.* Bye, by 1923, had opened a literary agency at 535 Fifth Avenue specializing in handling celebrity books. He was the agent used by newsmakers and amateur authors with something sensational to say. He specialized in "stunt" books, according to the *New York Times.* He was a friend of the Roosevelts, General John J. Pershing, Heywood Broun, Westbrook Pegler and Charles Lindbergh. Bye "liked to describe himself as 'guide, philosopher and wet nurse,'" the *Times* reported. "On one occasion warming to the subject of literary agents and their clients, Bye commented: 'We arrange marriages and divorces for them and rush obstetricians to their doorsteps when they're having babies. The only time I ever failed was when a client came to me with a valuable dog who refused to have pups. I couldn't do a thing about that,'" a *Times* reporter wrote in Bye's obituary years later.

Bye helped his friend Hinton meet and greet the right people and get the right invitations to speak. Hinton was wined and dined and did radio appearances. When aviation feats were proposed, Hinton's name was published as the possible pilot. When aviation records were set — which was an almost weekly occurrence in the 1920s — Hinton was interviewed. When Lindbergh accomplished the first solo crossing of the great pond in 1927, the media turned to Hinton for comment, and a piece bylined by Hinton, "How Lindbergh Did It," appeared in the *New York Herald Tribune.* Bye later reportedly sold the movie rights to Lucky Lindy's biography to Hollywood for a million dollars.

Hinton's praise of Lindbergh's courage in a magazine articles about the younger flyer may actually have been written by Bye. Hinton put Lindbergh's fame in perspective in his piece for *Outlook*[1]:

> Nothing in aviation, no single achievement, no combination of aerial events since the Wright brothers made the first mechanical flight twenty-four years ago, has had such influence on the public mind as Charles A. Lindbergh's lone dash from New York to Paris.... Despite all that has been done, written, and told about the miracle that is flight, people generally have refused to accept it, take it into their minds, and treat it as they do the radio, motor car, or any of the other scientific marvels to which they have become accustomed. But Lindbergh has changed all this: his flight lasted 33 hours and 30 minutes. It will live forever.[2]

Hinton had a laconic style in conversation much like Lindbergh and other early aviation stars, who were self-taught mechanics in love with flying rather than educated raconteurs. Hinton's audiences felt they had to draw the tales out of him.

Jacob Muller, an advertising executive, whom Hinton had met at the Friars Club after the transatlantic voyage, was another mentor and impresario for Hinton, guiding him through New York society. Muller was also active in the National Exchange Clubs, a service organization, and he convinced the group to launch a "Service to Aviation" program that would garner it national media attention and make Hinton known to thousands of folks across small-town America.

The club passed a resolution at its July 1928 convention in its headquarters city of Toledo, Ohio, that said it would support establishing permanent landing fields with easy access to the business districts of towns and cities; proper field marking and night lighting; establishment of emergency landing fields; marking building roofs with the name of the town or city for easy identification by aviators; patronage of air transport for passengers, freight and mail, and cooperation with government agencies developing air transport.[3]

Muller, Bye, Richard Byrd and others helped Hinton found the Aviation Institute of U.S.A., a home-study correspondence school for would-be aviators. Its first address was at 71 West 45th Street in New York City. Hinton's backers produced a 32-page booklet, *Aviation and You*, hyperbolically touting the more than 50 occupations that students could consider once they completed the Hinton system ground school and took actual flying lessons at local airfields.

> Twenty-five years ago *the Movies* flickered feebly on a half-dozen white sheets stretched in a darkened room. Today the income of that single industry is almost beyond belief. You know how the pioneers in *that* field reaped *their* golden harvest.
>
> Only 5 years ago *Radio* offered the same marvelous chance for profit. Those who seized their opportunity are among the richest men of the day. Did you see

the future of Radio? Did you get your share of the millions spent as the industry grew? ARE YOU GOING TO GET YOUR SHARE OF THE BIG MONEY IN AVIATION?

What the telephone, the automobile, the movies and radio were in *their* day, aviation is NOW!

Prepare yourself! Don't wait until Aviation is entirely developed. Get into this new big industry while the opportunity and chance for making money are best. *Learn aviation at home, now!*

Letters of endorsement for the school came from World War I flying ace Eddie Rickenbacker, by 1926 vice president of Rickenbacker Motor Company in Detroit that built aircraft engines; Hinton's old friend and pupil, Commander Byrd, who had been first to fly over the North Pole; Frank Tichenor, president and publisher of *Aero Digest*; and F. Trubee Davison, the Assistant Secretary of War.

Aviation and You included testimonials from some of the hundreds of students who signed up for the course. Wilbur C. Damuth Jr of Seaford, New York, finished the course in two months and four days and said he then completed his flying lessons and had been commissioned in the U.S. Naval Reserve. "It was your instruction that made it possible," Damuth wrote. The testimonial is accompanied by a picture of the 21-year-old in a soft leather flying helmet, goggles, a jacket and bow tie. It was chosen at random from among thousands in Hinton's files, according to the booklet.

Alexander Aircraft Corporation, manufacturers of the Eagelrock plane with fields across the country, promised to teach budding aviators as young as 16 to fly at a discounted rate in eight hours after they presented their certificate from the Hinton system of flying instruction.

The booklet, probably one of the earliest incarnations of the infomercials of the 20th and 21st centuries, promised that Hinton would personally supervise the grading of test answers, would personally respond to questions, and would personally negotiate for a

Walter Hinton in his dress uniform (Burns collection).

reduced rate for flying lessons for the would-be pilot if a Hinton-approved airfield was not near the student's home.

The booklet even had a section of "Questions and Answers," the 1920s version of Frequently Asked Questions (FAQs).

Typical were "How does it feel to fly?" and "Is it true that pilots are born and not made?"

"Not as you would think," Hinton replied on the feel of flying. "The ground appears to leave or return to you when taking off or landing. The dizziness experienced when looking down from a tall building does not exist, due to the absence of a reference point, which is the cause of the unpleasant sensation. Height and speed are not realized."

"Anyone can be taught to fly," he said in answer to the second question. "To an experienced pilot, a plane is a part of him and flying becomes second nature. You glance occasionally at instruments to assure yourself that your motor is functioning properly, checking on your map the distance covered as you pass over the towns beneath you, thus determining the speed of your plane, which varies as the wind is with or against you. Inasmuch as the plane is a part of the air, a wind blowing across the path of flight will alter the course, this being termed 'drift.' In case the plane passes through clouds or rain, sight of the ground being cut off, the knowledge of air navigation will be your rule and guide."

The 16 lessons in the course outline covered everything from the history of aviation to air craft terminology, nomenclature, popular engines and the weather. The history lesson quizzed the student on aviation firsts, from the Wright brothers' successful launch at Kitty Hawk to "What was the date of the first 'TRANS-ATLANTIC' flight" and "Who first 'looped the loop' in an airplane?" If followed carefully, the course of instruction would obviously provide the student with considerable knowledge of all aspects of flying and airplanes, short of actually going up in one.[4]

By 1928 Hinton had moved his home-study aviation institute to Washington, D.C., with offices near the Mayflower Hotel, a few blocks from the White House, and he had become active in local civic organizations, including the Chamber of Commerce and, with help from Jake Muller, the National Exchange Club where Muller was slated to be president of the D.C. club the next year.

Hinton suffered what was identified as a second heart attack early in 1928. He spent five weeks in a Washington hospital with little or no public notice. In any event, he was well enough by December 1928 to trek south along with 3,000 other celebrities, governors, U.S. Senators, delegates from 40 countries, and lots of average citizens to commemorate the 25th anniversary of the Wright brothers' first flight at Kitty Hawk, North Carolina. Despite the advances in aviation during that first quarter-century, you couldn't get to Kill Devil Hill by air. Planes couldn't land in sand and there was no nearby airport. New Yorkers headed for the December 17 unveiling of a granite monument to the accomplishment of flight took steamships to Norfolk, Virginia, and made their way by bus and car from there.

Wilbur Wright and about 200 of the delegates to the International Civil Aeronautical Conference in Washington, D.C., including Hinton, took busses from Norfolk to Currituck County Court House, North Carolina, according to the *New York Times* correspondent.

At the Virginia–North Carolina line, Wright was met by the governor of North Carolina, Angus McLean, and war-years Secretary of the Navy Josephus Daniels as part of a welcoming committee. The party switched to 65 private cars for a push over rough roads to Point Harbor where they took a boat across Currituck Sound to Kitty Hawk. One man fell overboard, but was saved by a seaman with a boat hook who caught his heavy coat before he completely sank.

State highway workers who had been pressed into overtime service to complete a corduroy road across the swamps and mud holes helped them get through. A hundred cars awaited them at Kitty Hawk and took them through more swamps, sand and woods to Virginia Dare Shores, where they had a barbecue hosted by local citizens before pressing on to Kill Devil Hill, where an 80-foot stand had been built. An incessant wind threatened to blow anyone brave enough to go there off the top of the stand.[5]

Amelia Earhart, Hinton and other aviation celebrities gathered around the surviving Wright brother as the politicians and government officials extolled their feat of learning how to warp wings to sustain flight in a wind. Wilbur, who reputedly had never made a public address in his life, kept that record intact and was reported to look alternately nervous and agitated and focused on something on the far horizon.

Hinton asked Wilbur if he had thought, back in 1903, that aviation would ever reach its present state of development. "Yes," Wilbur answered, "but it has reached, in twenty-five years, the place that Orville and I dreamed it might reach in a hundred years."

In late 1929, again, probably with research and writing help from the hyperbolic Bye or someone he hired, Hinton wrote a 255-page book published by W. W. Norton, *Opportunities in Aviation*.[6]

It chronicled the advances and opportunities in aviation and also included predictions on the future of air transport, air freight and air communication. It even included Hinton's prediction that giant floating airports would be built to accommodate the trans-ocean traffic.

Hinton downplayed the danger of flying that had become an issue in the six months after Lindbergh completed his solo aerial journey from New York to Paris. The dozens of tragic accidents and disappearances of would-be aerial record setters caused various governmental bodies to enact regulations against foolhardy attempts.

But Hinton wrote:

> To insist that flying is not yet safe is to say that traveling by steamship, rail or automobile is not safe, for all of these involve the ordinary risk that attaches to any form of travel. A wreck is a wreck, whether it be of a steamship or an airplane. There is not nearly so much hazard in taking a trip in a licensed plane flown by a licensed pilot as there is in crossing Fifth Avenue when the traffic light is against you. Yet thousands of jay-walkers thread their way among the mazes of speeding traffic every hour of the day and night, careless of a danger held in contempt through its familiarity....
>
> It is not so spectacular to be crushed under the wheels of a motor truck as it is to be involved in an airplane accident. For that reason alone the airplane accident is "circussed" on the front page of your newspaper, while the motor accident is hidden away among the three columns of casualties on the inside of the last sheet.
>
> When the Wright Brothers made that first flight, lasting only twelve seconds, it was shouted to the world in headlines half a foot high. Today, when a plane remains in the air, in continuous flight, for longer than three weeks, the name of the man who made that flight is forgotten within the month!
>
> When the Wright Brothers flew a few hundred feet, the world applauded. Today, non-stop flights of thousands of miles attract scant interest.
>
> Those who are familiar with the trend in aviation today cannot help but realize that the first twenty-five years of aviation history, remarkable as they have been, are but a foreshadowing of the tremendous development that will arrive within the next twenty-five years or even within the next decade.[7]

Hinton predicted:

> Travel will become an essential part of education. Languages will be taught by actual visits to the lands in which they are spoken; geography is already being taught by flying over the territory being studied; history will be impressed on the scholars' minds by showing them the scenes where history was made.
>
> Aviation is changing the mode of living of each of us. The rising generation will be a generation of flyers — of men and women who take easily and naturally to the air, who put the airplane to a myriad uses in business, and who derive from it a vast amount of pleasure.
>
> Planes are already being developed that will carry 50 or 100 passengers, and that will fly all night. "Diners" are already operated on some air lines. Some day we may have barber and beauty shops on the largest airliners!
>
> In a few short years floating airports of vast proportions, anchored permanently in the oceans, will link all continents. I firmly believe that when these floating landing fields are in daily service, and air transportation is in scheduled operation over the Atlantic and Pacific, it will be found that the trans-oceanic air service, in competition with steamships, will save more money for business than is saved by air transportation over land in competition with railroads....

The steamer that maintains an average speed of 20 miles an hour is a fast ship. Thus it is very easy to see that airplanes, utilizing floating landing fields (or seadromes), will speed up trans-oceanic travel by at least five hundred percent.

Fifty years ago it was 3,000 miles from Atlantic to Pacific—*weeks* of toilsome travel over trackless plains, craggy mountains, virgin forests and forbidding deserts. Twenty years ago it took a week of travel by railroad. Today, it is less than *48 hours* away! Forty-eight hours of swift, smooth, luxurious flight in comfortable, well ventilated and heated cabin planes, over miles of changing scenes unfolding beneath you as you fly.

The airplane has annihilated distance and time, and every American business man knows that time is the essence of progress. Time is money, true; but is more than that—it is opportunity.

Before many years go by, planes will fly on frequent schedules between the United States and Europe, utilizing a chain of seadromes anchored at intervals across the Atlantic. At the terminals of this trans–Atlantic route, airlines from the business centers of the interior will connect all the great cities of this country with the business centers of Europe. Documents and money that took, formerly, five to eight days to pass from London to New York or ten days from Berlin to St. Louis will be delivered in less than forty-eight hours. Again, savings in time and money—in interest on money—will be tremendous.[8]

Hinton also wrote about an auto manufacturer who discovered flying parts in from a supplier would save thousands of dollars in down time, a practice that continues to this day. And he reported on a typewriter company that dropped its products by parachute to customers wanting immediate delivery where there were no landing strips.[9]

In February 1929 the Exchangite sponsored a national dinner to tout the progress of aviation. Muller, the National First vice president, handled the planning and underwrote the financing for the January 29 affair at the Hotel Commodore in New York City. Hinton, Earhart and dozens of other aviation record holders were on hand as 1,000 persons turned out for the black tie-affair.

In August 1929 the Department of Commerce reported there were already 1,485 private, commercial, military airports and marked auxiliary fields in use and that it had received notices of 1,174 proposed additional fields to be completed in the following year.[10] But the Exchange Club goal was to promote 800 more and Muller had the idea of sending Hinton as the national Exchange Club spokesperson, on an aviation tour to big and small towns across America to promote signage and airports for aviation.

At the same time Hinton actively promoted a national airport for Washington, D.C. As late as 1929 the nation's capital was using a U.S. government mail landing airport—Bolling Field—for landings and takeoffs and in wet weather the field was soft and soggy.

Hinton appealed through the *Exchangite* to members across the nation to contact their Congressmen to support an airport for Washington. "Then someday when you fly to Washington you can say: 'This is our airport. We did our bit to make it suitable for the Capital City.'"[11]

On November 25, 1930, Hinton—with assorted notables on hand, including National President Muller, who financed the whole trip—took off in a single-engine, blue and gold Fairchild monoplane christened *Exchangite* with "Walter Hinton" written on the rear fuselage to tour cities in Ohio, Michigan, and Indiana promoting the marking of national highways with their numbers and of roofs with identifier signs and establishment of airfields. He held the titles of National Marshal and Aviation Chairman and third vice president of the group. His co-pilot and mechanic for most of the tour was Bob Chew, who did much of the flying since Hinton had suffered another heart attack. An escort plane carried the mayor of Put-in-Bay and a few others.

The first destination was a short hop to Put-in-Bay, Ohio, an island on Lake Erie where Hinton would dedicate the new airfield and speak before 300 fans of aviation the next day.

Toledo Blade aviation editor Dick Roberts reported the scene at the airport:

> Lieutenant Hinton whose brilliant aerial career reads like a page from a modern book of fiction, took off from the Toledo Transcontinental airport late Tuesday afternoon carrying with him the well wishes of the nation's renowned airmen, who gathered at a noon luncheon to bid him Godspeed and happy landings.... A typical American flier, Lieutenant Hinton thrilled hundreds attending the luncheon with a word picture of his flight across the Atlantic, the first ever made. As seems to be the custom with the majority of America's air notables, he gave all the credit for the success of the aerial venture to his companions, reserving none for himself.[12]

It was an inauspicious start in cold, snowy weather after University of Toledo student Molly Crowder christened the Fairchild as the *Exchangite* because an hour later Hinton returned to Toledo defeated by a storm over the lake that they couldn't penetrate. When they did arrive on November 30 the weather was still snowy and cold so the air strip was dedicated from inside a building.

Hinton's next stop was Saginaw, Michigan, where on December 2 he addressed both high schools, the Exchangites at their noon lunch meeting and the Wholesale Bureau of the Board of Commerce. Saginaw Exchange officials accompanied him to tiny Caro, Michigan, where he talked to the high school and general public in the afternoon and to Exchange and Rotary Club members from a number of nearby cities at an evening banquet. The Caro Club secretary said it was the best meeting they ever had in town.[13]

The goal, according to Hinton, was to paint the highway numbers in large figures at intersections, near bridges and all villages, towns and cities and every 10 to 20 miles so pilots could refer to highway maps to tell where they were in the air.[14]

From Caro, Hinton flew to small towns across Michigan, Ohio and Indiana, like Three Rivers, Michigan; Fostoria, Napoleon and Bryan, Ohio; Richmond and Marion, Indiana, speaking to hundreds of eager listeners at each location. In Three Rivers he held "everyone spellbound." Local radio stations broadcast his talks and in Bryan, Ohio the Exchange Club president said, "Lieutenant Hinton could almost have the handle off the old town pump out here."

By December 14 Hinton had headed east toward home and spoke in Elizabeth, New Jersey, the next day and then to more than 1,500 in Wilmington, Delaware. After that he flew off to Washington for the holidays with plans to head south during the winter weather.[15]

February 9, 1931, found Hinton landing the Fairchild in Stamford, Texas, where he was greeted by the mayor, civic club officials and celebrities and spoke to high school students and later the general public in the city auditorium. Fifteen hundred students heard him in Abilene and in Fort Worth he talked to 500 students at Texas Christian.

Bad weather prevented them making a scheduled February 12 appearance in San Antonio. "I regret that we were unable to meet with your San Antonio Exchange Club last Thursday," Hinton wired from Austin:

> That would have been our 38th stop uninterrupted although we have had some bad weather conditions. We left at daybreak and got about three-fourths of the way when fog closed in so tight that we couldn't much more than see the end of our wings. We landed in a field a mile and half from the nearest telephone and about five miles northwest of Briggs.
> It rained and thundered and lightninged the rest of the day and night. We spent a miserable night sitting in the plane with the wind blowing so hard we were afraid it would blow the plane away.
> The next morning at daybreak we took off and flew for twenty minutes. In this dense fog we realized that it might have been folly to try to get through and headed over for Austin. We picked up a highway and flying about five or ten feet over the tops of trees, follow(ed) it into Austin. We realized that we didn't dare follow it all the way as we might hit a building if it were to carry us over the city. We passed over a field that looked as though we might be able to get in and turned around but couldn't find it again so we landed in another and it happened to be just four miles east of the airport we were looking for. We landed in front of a Mexican's house, set our brakes and slid right up to the fence. I think both Bob Chew and myself aged about five years.[16]

They then flew to Houston in a bleak, gray sky and spent three days there. The Texans put two yachts at their disposal and the Hinton party steamed off to a well-known seafood restaurant.

Hinton did several radio talks and his lecture to a "mammoth" aviation lunch in his honor was broadcast. The pair then hopped to Dallas on February 17 and 18 where Hinton was presented a medal for distinguished service for aviation and was presented at a gathering of 10,000 people. As result of his visit, the Dallas Exchangites promised to mark all highways leading into the city for passing aircraft. After visiting Paris, Texas, on February 19 and Fort Smith, Alaska, on February 20 and repeating his visits to high schools and civic organizations they were escorted by 14 planes as they approached Kansas City, Missouri, on February 23. The tour continued on to Montgomery and Selma, Alabama; Miami, Lake Worth, Tampa, Vero Beach, Tallahassee (March 13), Winter Haven, Orlando, St. Augustine and Jacksonville, Florida. In Miami residents took Chew and Hinton to the horse races, the jai alai fronton and the dog track where a race was named in Hinton's honor.[17]

They headed west after leaving Jacksonville March 12. It was Pulaski, Tennessee (March 16), Nashville, (March 17) and then back to Indiana, landing at Evansville on March 18. The itinerary included Louisville, Kentucky (March 19), Indianapolis (March 20), and an unscheduled visit to Terre Haute (March 22) where he renewed a friendship with an old friend — Clyde Bennett — with whom he entered Navy training 23 years earlier.[18] The drill was the same in most communities with governors, mayors and civic leaders turning out. They would pick up local dignitaries and national officers of the Exchange Clubs in one town and fly them with them to the next stop. Frequently a delegation of military and private planes would fly out to greet them and then escort them to the target city where they would be greeted by more dignitaries and paraded in open cars through the streets. Stamp collectors would mob Hinton at every stop, asking him to sign a special air tour cachet.

Other clubs, seeing the turnouts at aviation dinners and high schools, clamored for Hinton and Chew to add them to the itinerary. After a scheduled stop in Decatur, Illinois, on March 23, they added a stop in Peoria the next day after the National Club signed off on it. Chew and Hinton reached Des Moines, Iowa, on March 25 and then hit Davenport before flying over the Rockies to San Bernardino and hopscotching around eight California cities in April, ending with Los Banos on April 15.[19]

Almost every month during the tour, *The Exchangite* featured an article by Hinton detailing one of his adventures or his take on the future of aviation to build local interest in hearing him speak. And the reports that came in from the clubs were excited, including phrases like "a prominent role was given Lieut. Hinton in the impressive ceremonies dedicating Fargo's new airport, bringing 12,000 air-minded citizens thronging to the port;" "a rousing welcome wafted up to Lieut. Hinton as he glided gracefully down at the Freeport Airport"; "Lieut. Fay O. Dice zoomed into Kewanee Airport leading an attack flight of three U.S. army ships from Chanute Field ... in honor of

Lieut. Walter Hinton.... Thousands of aviation fans were on hand"; "three big electric signs blazed Milwaukee's welcome to Lieut. Hinton.... An escort of 14 planes ushered him to the airport"; and "winging his way through rainy skies, Lieut. Hinton dropped down at the Paris [Illinois] airport."

High schoolers, middle schoolers, boys clubs, civic leaders, the parents of pilots who had died in accidents all heard Hinton speak or met with him. By the end of six months, the June issue inside the front cover trumpeted that Hinton and Chew had covered 16,000 air miles, been heard by 200,000 persons at 325 speech appearances, had visited 100 cities and were still going strong.

In May Hinton and Chew worked their way back across country, stopping at Sioux Falls and Fargo, South Dakota, then on to Freeport, Kewanee, Rockford and Elgin, Illinois, up to Milwaukee and Racine, Wisconsin. And then back through half a dozen Illinois and Indiana cities like Danville, Paris, Galesburg and an officially scheduled stop in Terre Haute. Chew was then replaced as co-pilot by William S. Green of Kansas City, Missouri, for a two-day trip in June to Wilkes Barre, Pennsylvania, where Walter Hinton Days were celebrated with an air show and the usual round of talks.

By the time the Fairchild flew into Memphis, Tennessee, Municipal Airport, Hinton had visited more than 120 cities and a few others twice. One delegate from each city Hinton visited was on hand on September 20 when Hinton's plane arrived in Memphis, for the National Exchange Club Convention to end his tour and his duties as third vice president. Hinton was a household word in cities big and small and hamlets across America and more than 300 aviation projects had been promised by local Exchange Clubs.

He was probably better known than some national politicians, but in the fall while back at his home in Washington, D.C., he was struck again with what the doctors called a heart attack. It was a mild one this time compared to the previous two and he recovered in a matter of days. But the doctors advised that he give up flying. His days of piloting an aircraft were finished. He was not at the controls when the Fairchild was flown to Keene, New Hampshire, in December. "Despite poor visibility, low ceilings and an ice-coated plane, Lieut. Hinton dropped into Keene on December 7 just six minutes off schedule on his flight from Washington, D.C.," the *Exchangite* reported.

The next day it was 8 degrees below zero and oil was frozen in the lines, but Hinton quietly took off for Rutland, Vermont, escorted by that city's airport plane. Heavy snows prevented him from continuing to Montpelier on December 9, so he borrowed a car and was driven 75 miles over ice-covered mountain roads to meet the governor, mayor and members of the City Council.[20]

In working so closely with Jacob Muller, Hinton had gotten to know

Carrie Susan Knapp, Muller's daughter, who was married to George Knapp. The 1930 census showed the Knapps and Muller, a widower, living together at the same address in New York, but Susan, as she was known, apparently was starstruck by Hinton and his accomplishments. The Knapps were divorced and on New Year's Eve 1931 at a church near Times Square in New York, Susan and Hinton were wed. It was a marriage that lasted more than 40 years. An acquaintance who had known both Walter and Susan for decades said, years later, "She set her sights on a trophy husband and she got one."

17

Touring the Country for the Exchange Clubs and Beyond

"The boast of heraldry, the pomp of power, And all that beauty, all that wealth e'er gave, Awaits alike th' inevitable hour: The paths of glory lead but to the grave."

—Thomas Gray[1]

Eventually Walter Hinton had flown into 135 cities on his "Service to Aviation" tour. Nicknamed in the media as "The Air Crusader," he had been credited for saving an airport in Keene, New Hampshire, that was in danger of closing down. He also won praise for getting local leaders and citizens excited to build airports near Newark, New Jersey, and Washington, D.C. In the late '20s he spoke out in the press about the need for a Newark airport to serve the New York market. In the '30s he served on a D.C. commission to pick a site and promote the building of what became National Airport in Virginia, the facility that is now called Reagan International.

The U.S. Congress, moving with its customary speed, finally established an NC-4 medal in February 1929 to be awarded to Commander Towers and the crew of the Four. It was awarded to Hinton and the others in ceremonies at the White House by President Herbert Hoover. The ribbon has the U.S. colors—red, white and blue—and the Portuguese colors—green and red. One side shows a gull flying over waves with the inscription "First TransAtlantic Flight United States Navy 1919." On the reverse side "NC-4" is inscribed with the words "Newfoundland" and "Portugal" and "Presented by the President of the United States in the Name of Congress." On the top half of the medal are the surnames and initials of the recipients. The name of Eugene Saylor Rhoads, the Four's laconic mechanic, is spelled wrong: "E. Rhodes."

By the mid–1930s airports and airfields had sprung up all across the nation and it was obvious that most of the predictions except for floating airports in the Atlantic that Hinton had made in *Opportunities in Aviation* were coming true. Air freight and passenger businesses were thriving.

17. Touring the Country for the Exchange Clubs and Beyond

Hinton founded an aviation school for ground training with the support of his flying friends (Burns collection).

Hinton's health remained suspect and he suffered from a variety of complicating illnesses. He sometimes reduced his speech schedule to an occasional appearance. In 1934, for example, Jake Muller organized a luncheon honoring Hinton at the McAlpin Hotel in New York City for the Exchange Club.

A. Hamilton Rice, who hired Hinton for the Amazon expedition, introduced the guest of honor and half a dozen others spoke in praise of Hinton. These included veteran race pilot C.S. (Casey) Jones, Danish explorer Peter Freuchen, Augustus Post (an American balloon racer), and a past president of the Adventurers Club.[2]

That same year *Washington Post* reporter Harris B. Hull penned a piece suggesting the era of scheduled ocean service across the Atlantic was about to begin. He referred to the NC-4 transatlantic crossing as opening an era in the development of aviation. "The completion of that great pioneering flight, undertaken without the splendid navigational instruments of today, still stands as one of the two or three most outstanding achievements in all aviation history," Hull wrote. He pointed out that 28 of the 57 later attempts to fly across had no loss of life, but that more than 20 aviators died trying.[3]

Later in 1934, Jacob Muller, Hinton's mentor, fan and now father-in-law, had a stroke. It was the first of several that eventually caused his death in July 1937. Muller had dropped out of school at age 12 to work as an office boy in the office of a morning New York newspaper. That office focused on theatrical advertising and Muller worked his way up until he knew all the folks in the theatre business that made commercial decisions.

He left the newspaper and started his own advertising agency, the J. P. Muller Advertising Agency at 512 Fifth Avenue and arranged to coordinate the ads from the theaters, saving the managers the task of dealing with each newspaper individually and the newspapers the task of hiring sales people to make the rounds of the theaters each week. He was an early member and official of the Friars Club that had been founded in 1904. When Prohibition went into effect at midnight on January 16, 1920, making it illegal to sell liquor, Hinton fondly remembered helping his future in-law load Friars Club cases of booze that night in a car and taking them to a safe haven on the off chance the Manhattan club might be raided.[4]

In its first year of existence, Muller's advertising agency recorded $250,000 worth of business and Muller invested his profits in a Queens County garage and auto supply operation and bought Long Island real estate.

When he died from a final stroke at age 63 on July 11, 1937, Muller left all of his property to his daughter Susan, who took up Muller's interest in buying and selling real estate for the rest of her life. At one time Hinton identified himself as a real estate investor when asked for his occupation.[5] And he did help out friends and acquaintances in various management roles. At one time he contemplated buying a real estate brokerage from a friend who was ill.

Hinton continued to be in demand as a speaker and radio guest throughout the thirties. For example, in March 1935 he appeared on the popular Thornton Wilder Show on NBC and recounted his wild Canadian balloon ride again.

Wilder gave him a hyperbolic intro on the show:

> And now, ladies and gentlemen, on behalf of Briggs and Muriel (cigars), I am proud to present to you a distinguished American flyer, my old friend, Lieut. Walter Hinton, formerly of the United States Navy.... His record sounds like wild fiction.... He had a plane burst in mid-air; the breaking of a propeller on a pusher type plane which almost severed the tail of the ship.... As a pilot he headed out over the broad expanse of the North Atlantic bound for Europe on the first transatlantic flight in the NC-4 over 15 years ago and made it.... He landed in the middle of the night in the rough Caribbean waters 17 miles off the coast of Cuba, sinking in his plane in a shark-infested sea, being rescued by a naval vessel.... He was the first to fly over the unexplored jungle territory in Northern Brazil, where a forced landing would have meant death or falling into the hands of cannibalistic Indian tribes who had never laid eyes on a white man.... The men of the service salute you, Walter ... a gallant officer, indeed ... Mr Hinton, jump into the cockpit with me....

"All right, Thornton ... give me the controls," Hinton replied and they were off.⁶

Two years later, in 1937 the Canadian Press Association moved a story from Cochrane, Ontario, that the A5598 — the balloon that carried Lt. L. A. Kloor, Lt. Stephen A. Farrell and Hinton on their 1,200-mile adventure to the Canadian wilds — had been found a few yards from an Indian trail not far from James Bay and about 20 miles north of Moosonee. The article noted that the tattered bag was caught in the branches of a tree and the basket was on the ground, but no one seemed to know what would become of the battered relic that was worth $5,000 when it was lost.⁷

The Hintons continued to be a part of the social circuit and show up in society columns in both Washington and New York and at various times in the '30s and '40s claimed home addresses in both areas. The Aviation Correspondence school operating primarily under others' leadership, ran until 1944 when it closed down.

Susan and Walter spent a lot of time traveling both by oceanliner and air. When the luxury liner *Normandie* sailed from New York in 1937 the Hintons were listed as two of the celebrities on board by the *New York Times*. When they flew the Atlantic or elsewhere on airlines, Susan would quietly make sure a flight attendant knew of her husband's achievements and flight captains would invariably announce they had a hero on board and sometimes sent back champagne or invited Hinton up to the cockpit.

In 1940 Hinton's father, Millard, and stepmother, Louvinia, were injured in an October 31 car accident when a car driven by a Convoy friend was hit broadside on Main Street in Van Wert. Mrs. Hinton, 81, died of a head injury and shock. Newspaper accounts noted that the victims were the "famous flyer's" parents, but there is no record that Walter attended the funeral a few days later.⁸

The world moved on and Walter Hinton gradually dropped from public view in the 1940s. After Pearl Harbor on December 7, 1941, Hinton, 53, stepped forward to volunteer, but was turned down because of his record of heart attacks and the lingering effects of malaria from the Rice expedition, spots on his lungs from the Canadian balloon ride and leg burns that he still suffered from as a result of standing in gasoline on the wrecked hulk of the *Sampaio Correia I* off Guantanamo Bay.

During World War II Hinton said he toured the South Kensington Science Museum in London to take a look at the *Eleanor III*, which had been on display on previous visits. The plane, which had been damaged slightly in the German bombing blitz of London in 1941, was missing. When he inquired after it the museum officials told him that the craft had some "very advanced mechanical features" that the British military didn't want to fall into enemy hands. After the war the plane was traded to the Canada Aviation Museum for some other airplane parts and it was restored in Canada.

Hinton remained close to his sister, Florence Hinton Slade, who with her husband, Clarence, had moved to the Lansing, Michigan, area, but he had not been particularly close to his father, Millard, and stepmother Louvinia, who had moved back to Van Wert after unsuccessfully trying their hand at farming in North Carolina.

At Susan's insistence they maintained many close ties to the various Muller relatives — the Tousleys and Makaras — and saw a great deal more of them. However, when Florence, who had been his surrogate mother, was rushed to a Lansing area hospital with a burst appendix, Hinton visited, paid the medical bills, and hired a nurse to care for her. He also bought a new dress for his niece, Marjorie Slade (Tubbs).

The Hintons were in the Far East on one of their trips in 1949 when Rear Admiral (Ret.) A. C. Read and NC-4 mechanic Eugene Saylor Rhoads took part in a modern-day re-enactment of the first Atlantic crossing.

Read and Rhoads were guests aboard the twin engine *Truculent Turtle* that had set a world's record for range in 1946 flying 11,235.6 miles from Perth, Australia, to Columbus, Ohio, without refueling. It was a record that reportedly stood for 16 years.

The re-enactment flight took off From Floyd Bennett Naval Air Station not far from where the NC-4 had taken off from Rockaway Bay 38 years and eight minutes earlier. (The reason the takeoff of the 61,000 pounds aircraft was eight minutes late was that the official speeches ran long.) The *Turtle*, a Lockheed Neptune P2V-2, re-traced the Four's route and dipped low and circled over Chatham, Massachusetts, where the Four taxied to get a new engine; Halifax, Nova Scotia, Trepassey Bay, Newfoundland and the Azores. It landed a little over 15 hours later in Lisbon. The plane flew at 160 miles an hour and its two 3200-horsepower Wright engines delivered almost four times the power of the NC-4's Liberties.[9]

From 1946 to 1952 Hinton worked for the Civil Aeronautics Board as an aviation accident investigator, then he formally retired. Hinton told friends in a letter in 1949 that he had had a couple of temporary jobs — one selling building maintenance for a former Manhasset neighbor and the other running a real estate agency while its owner had an operation and went through alcohol rehab.[10]

In 1950 Hinton was honored along with retired Admiral John Towers and other early aviation record setters at the Wings Club in New York. The Hintons were living in Manhasset on Long Island at the time.[11]

In May 1969 Smithsonian Aviation Museum Director Paul Garber finally managed to assemble in a Maryland aviation repair shop all the pieces of the

NC-4 he had recovered from sites in New York, Pennsylvania and Virginia. Workmen cabled her to the ground on the Washington Mall on the 12th Street overpass near the Freer Gallery.

Hinton and Rhoads, the last two survivors, were on hand for the 50th anniversary celebration on May 8. But even then the Four got little respect. Here is what *New York Times* writer Christopher Lydon wrote about the upcoming ceremonies:

> If all the official guests show up on time for the ceremony on the mall, it could mark the first event in the life of the NC-4 to go off as planned.
>
> Despite its undisputed place in the record books, the NC-4 remains a stepchild of aviation mythology.... The NC-4 was too "corporate" an adventure to entrance the nation as Charles A. Lindbergh's solo dash in the *Spirit of St. Louis* did eight years later.
>
> Slighted from the start by an awkward name, the NC-4 is now too old to be popularly remembered and not old enough to seem ancient and original, like the Wright Brothers' craft at Kitty Hawk, N.C.
>
> The story of the NC-4 is a chronicle of sad miscalculation.[12]

And to add insult to injury, a *Washington Post* letter writer added this remark on the display: "It uglifies the Mall."

When the Hintons visited Michigan, Walter would visit the Slades in Charlotte, south of Lansing, while Susan visited her cousins, the Tousleys in Grosse Pointe, and the Makaras, in Gibralter, a downriver Detroit suburb. The Hintons eventually built a home on Bishop in Grosse Pointe Park to be closer to Susan's relatives.

During the winter months the Hintons migrated to Florida and eventually they bought a large home on the Intracoastal Waterway in the Landings, an upscale Fort Lauderdale suburb. An iron silhouette of the NC-4 graced the wall next to the garage. One of Hinton's nephews, Florence's son Theron, tried to visit him there and said he knocked on the door and it was apparent someone was home, but no one answered.[13]

As their friends put it, Susan ran the show. She continued to invest in stocks and bonds and real estate. She would buy a condominium unit or two in one of the new high rises going up along the Florida Atlantic beaches every couple of years, sell the one they were living, and move into one of the new ones.

They continued to travel extensively around the world. Susan made the plans for four trips a year and Walter happily went along for the ride. He loved to travel and enjoyed sending postcards to friends and acquaintances back home with no message, but his distinctively plain signature — "Walter Hinton."[14] Vienna was a favorite destination and Susan had various knickknack collections that she added to on the trips.[15]

During spring in 1961, worried about her real estate purchases and the fact some of the properties were not selling, Susan had a serious heart attack and wound up in the hospital for two weeks. She recovered, but it somewhat curtailed the couple's travel abroad. They still traveled, but not as frequently. Ten years later she was still buying and selling condo properties, though, and had apparently lost interest in hearing Walter's tales of adventure re-told. Although she was civil to reporters who learned about Hinton's accomplishments, she would no longer sit in on them and when he was urged to talk of his exploits in her presence would chide him about the oft-told tales.

In 1972 at a Christmas visit to Michigan by the Hintons, Barbara and Frank Tousley's daughter, Gwyn and her husband, John Makara, recognizing the historical value of Hinton's stories, started audiotaping and later videotaping them. While Mrs. Makara always referred to Hinton as "Uncle Walter" in reality she was not related to him, but was a second cousin to Susan.

Susan remarked in the background on one tape: "They used to write him up every couple of years in the Sunday supplements just to see if he was still alive."[16]

In a 1971 letter to her cousin, Barbara Tousley, Susan wrote: "New Year's Eve will be our 40th anniversary (How have we *ever* been able to stand each other *that long?*).... I have 'unloaded' 7G apt. in Plaza East but still have 19H empty. The mortgage and maintenance and the taxes are eating my income up fast; wish it could have been the expensive one sold. Bottom just dropped out of condominiums, just as I put them on market. It's been dragging for everybody, houses as well, and yet actually thousands come to live permanently in Florida every month. God knows where they set up housekeeping, must be out in the sticks where the ocean breezes never get but the mosquitoes do."

In August 1974 Hinton alerted Frank and Barbara Tousley that Susan was back in the hospital suffering from pernicious anemia and not likely to survive. He offered to pay the expenses for them to come south to Fort Lauderdale to visit if they could. "I don't want to be an alarmist, but she is convinced that her days are numbered," Hinton wrote. "I'm reasonably sure that if she gets home again that she will never be able to leave the house."[17]

In 1976 at a ceremony celebrating the dedication of the National Museum of Naval Aviation in Pensacola, Florida, and the dominant place of the reconstructed NC-4 in the center of the main floor, Hinton saw the flying boat for the last time. "It looks like it will still fly," he later told a reporter. "But I wouldn't want to try it."[18]

He told another reporter: "That's my baby. I was on her every flight she ever flew."[19]

The *Pensacola News Journal* reported there was "so much brass, in fact, that four of America's most famous astronauts were not granted seats on the

The reconstructed NC-4 is a centerpiece of the National Naval Air Museum in Pensacola. It dwarfs visitors and a film of the successful flight is shown periodically (Ben Burns Photograph).

speaker's platform." The 4,000 persons who jammed their way into the museum gave their most rousing applause to the men they were there to honor for their contributions to naval aviation.... That combination was perhaps best represented by Walter K. Hinton, the man, and the NC-4, the machine."[20]

The keynote speaker, U.S. Sen. John Stennis (D-Mississippi), chair of the Armed Services Committee, was quoted as saying: "Back in 1919 the NC-4 represented brilliant foresight in concept and design. It truly pushed the then state-of-the-art in terms of weather, instruments, aircraft construction, the art of aerial navigation and engines. I don't have to tell you that a trans-Atlantic flight in 1919 was hazardous and dangerous indeed."[21]

Hinton's 1974 prediction proved incorrect. Susan, in ill health for the next three years, died in August 1977. Most of Susan's estate went to the Muller/Tousley family relatives, but one generous donation went to the Smithsonian Air & Space Museum to set up a special fund to support research and public education.[22] A trust had been set up to protect Walter's financial needs.

That same year the crew of the Four was inducted into the "First Flight Shrine" at Kitty Hawk. Charles Lindbergh had been honored the year after the tribute opened with the induction of Wilbur and Orville Wright in

1966. Others named to the Shrine before the NC-4 crew included Admiral Richard E. Byrd in 1968, the first to fly over both North and South poles; Glenn Curtiss in '69, who built and flew the first Navy seaplane; Lt. Thomas Selfridge, the first Army officer to fly and the first airplane crash fatality in '71; and Col. John Glenn, the first American to orbit the earth in '78.

The Canadian Broadcasting Corporation sent a crew to interview Hinton for a 60th anniversary show on *Front Page Challenge*. The show was aired in Newfoundland on March 9 and Hinton spent 12 minutes on the air talking about the transatlantic crossing and the other aviators in the air race. His appearance drew at least one enthusiastic two-page letter from a 70-year-old man who had lived in St. John's, Newfoundland, when Hawker, Grieve, Raynham, and Morgan were getting ready to fly. "It's a magnificent story of astounding and astonishing accomplishment and one which posterity should be made [to] appreciate. To the best of my knowledge, the story of the NC-4 flight has never been made into a movie. I wonder if the Television people realize what a wonderful feature presentation that story would make. Thank God that there are some of us who appreciate your achievement and would like to see you honored…. You have helped me re-live a historic moment from our glorious past."[23]

Whether Susan and Walter got on well during their last years or not, Susan was the strength that managed their affairs and kept their finances in order. Walter was lost without her. "Susan ran the family and called the shots," a social friend Albert Bakker said. "I had the feeling she felt, 'my father gave me this war hero trophy.' Walter was very modest. He never bragged. It was one of the things I liked about him…. He was a very modest man. You had to really draw him out to find out information about his past life as a Navy flyer. Susan did the talking when they were together. He was very quiet."[24]

After Susan's death friends noted that Hinton "became very suspicious of everything, including people. He changed a lot."[25]

If you believe the reports of Hinton's blood relatives from the Midwest, the aging aviator had some reason to be wary. While he was befriended by the Bakkers and naval history author Richard Knott, who interviewed him for his books and others, some of his caregivers and folks around Hinton seemed primarily interested in who would get Hinton's money when he died.

Hinton's niece, Marjorie Slade Tubbs, his sister Florence's daughter who was a schoolteacher for 30 years, said that one of his caregivers was a former prostitute and escort service employee who would show up in the late morning at the posh oceanfront condominium, make Hinton a frozen Stauffer's TV dinner for lunch, sit in another room and smoke cigarettes, and then put another frozen entree out for his dinner before leaving in mid-afternoon.

Mrs. Tubbs said that letters, anniversary and Christmas cards, and phone calls from her and her brothers would go unanswered and that she was reasonably sure that someone was screening the mail and not letting Hinton see them, trying to cut off the involvement and connection with the Slade relatives.

Hinton remained close to Susan's relatives as they had become family over the decades and when he visited Gwyn Makara in Gibraltar, Michigan, for the holidays in 1979, they arranged for him to be interviewed by the *News-Herald*, a chain of weeklies serving that Detroit suburb. Gwyn presented Hinton with a stuffed Snoopy dog dressed as the Red Baron with an NC-4 patch embroidered on its sleeve. It drew a good laugh from Hinton.

Hinton recounted the Four's transatlantic crossing one more time and told reporter Pat Andrews that when the flight reached England, "everyone turned out to welcome us — the Prince of Wales, even Churchill.... I guess we took chances, but at that time, we didn't know they were chances," Hinton said.

"His eyes unclouded by age — his repertoire of adventure stories intact — Hinton admits to relishing his family visits at this point in his life and reminiscing with younger pilots, say those in their 70s and 80s," Andrews wrote. "And Hinton appears to have a fondness for reporters. Interviewed by journalists the world over for nearly 60 years, obviously it is still Hinton who 'could write the book.'"[26]

That same year on May 17, the 50th anniversary of the NC-4 flight was celebrated at the Smithsonian Institution's National Air and Space Museum and the Chief of Naval Operations at the Pentagon and Hinton journeyed there to be honored during the ceremonies.

In 1980 Hinton returned to his birthplace in Van Wert for the last time to serve as grand marshal for the Isaac Van Wart Days parade. It was the first time he was in Van Wert in a quarter century. The Makaras and Marjorie Slade Tubbs also attended the ceremonies and dinner honoring the now thin, stooped, white-haired 91-year-old former aviator, but the two families avoided talking to each other.

At a dinner at the Holiday Inn Express — a far cry from the dinner venues in Manhattan and Washington, D.C., that Hinton frequented in his salad days — he was presented a hand-carved key to the city mounted on a plaque by Mayor Stanley Agler, eight wooden nickels and two booklets on the history of Van Wert. He presented the Historical Society with two photographs, a booklet on the NC-4 flight and a framed collection of replicas of the 36 medals and decorations he had received from the U.S., Great Britain, France, Portugal and Brazil.[27]

The Brazilian government also tracked him down in 1980. They invited him to Washington, D.C., in late December where diplomats awarded him

A collection of Hinton's medals. Most of these are now at the National Naval Air Museum at Pensacola (Burns collection).

the Santos Dumont Medal of Merit for his flight from New York to Rio and his first aerial exploration of the Amazon basin. Santos Dumont was the first to demonstrate controlled flight was possible in October 1901 when he flew around the Eiffel Tower in a dirigible balloon. He also made the first public flight of an airplane in Europe in 1906 and is revered in Brazil as "the father of aviation." On receiving the medal in a ceremony, Hinton simply remarked, "I knew him." And he had as he had known most of the pioneering fliers and aviation inventors of the early days.

The Makaras planned to take Hinton for his first blimp ride ever on December 16 that year as a present for his 92nd birthday and alerted the *Miami Herald*, which sent reporter Peter Slevin to witness the event. But when Marjorie Tubbs, who was staying with Hinton, couldn't be dissuaded from accompanying the aged flier on the trip, it got cancelled. They told Slevin it was because of high winds, but Hinton later noted that the Goodyear blimp made a couple passes by his high-rise condo that day.

Slevin called Hinton "a flier growing old against his will."

"The oft-repeated accounts of Hinton's charm and gumption have blurred a bit with age, for the teller, the telling grows stale," Slevin observed.

"It gets kind of boring. It's been so long, and ... my age."[28]

"'I could talk in those days, just the opposite of now,' Hinton said, clenching his bony fingers into a fist. Interrupting one story when the words wouldn't come, Hinton explained, 'I get that way and I can hardly think of my name sometimes.'"

The failing Hinton said he spent most of his time in his apartment, only going out for haircuts or to share lunch with his maid.

Referring to the NC-4 flight, he said: "It was just another experience. We didn't think much of it at the time."[29]

During his last few years, getting more paranoid and more suspicious of people being after his money, Hinton became enmeshed in a battle among various parties over his estate. At one time his trust agreement allowed the real estate agent that Susan had used on her purchases and sales exclusive right to sell the condominium after Hinton's death at any price she deemed reasonable and it said she would be held harmless from any action from other heirs.

After his niece Marjorie Tubbs learned of the document, the will got rewritten, but Hinton was adamant that while he wanted her in the will he did not want to include her surviving brothers.[30] He did include Capt. Richard Knott, a retired naval officer and aviation author, who had befriended the aging flyer and interviewed him extensively for books. Hinton visited Knott in the Washington area and Knott visited him in Lighthouse Point near Fort Lauderdale. Because of Knott's expertise, Hinton asked Knott to help him select materials to be sent to the Naval Aviation Museum in Pensacola.

Hinton's health declined rapidly in his final year. He couldn't sleep. He had trouble with cogent thoughts and expressing himself. One night, while up pacing the apartment, he fell and broke his hip. There were five phones in various rooms, but Hinton was in such pain he couldn't crawl to any of them so he lay there for more than five hours until his caregiver showed up the next day. Knott checked on his friend by phone and Hinton's doctor said he would be fine. Knott planned to visit, but before he got to Florida, Hinton had been moved to Colonial Palms Nursing Home in nearby Pompano Beach.

On October 14 the National Naval Aviation Museum enshrined 12 early fliers as the first men in its Hall of Honor. They included six men associated in one way or another with the NC transatlantic flight. They were Adm. John Towers, commander of the mission; Rear Adm. Richard Byrd, whom Hinton taught to fly and later was the first to fly over both North and South poles; NC-4 builder Glenn H. Curtiss; Vice Adm. P.N.L. Bellinger, Commander of the NC-1; Rear Adm. Albert Cushing Read, Commander of the 4; and Capt. Holden C. Richardson, co-pilot on the NC-3.

Others were Eugene B. Ely, naval pilot No. 1, Lt. Col Alfred A. Cunningham, the first Marine aviator; Rear Adm. William A. Moffatt, the first chief of the Naval Bureau of Aeronautics, who died in the crash of the airship *Akron;* Lt. Com Godfrey de Courcelles. Chevalier, who made the first carrier landing while a ship was underway; and Warrant Officer Floyd Bennett, who flew with Byrd over the North Pole.

Hinton, who had been promoted to Lieutenant Junior Grade (temporary) for the flight and been bucked back to the enlisted ranks on his last day of service, December 31, 1922, was not on the list. Nor has he been among the more than 55 subsequent names in recent years added to the honor roll displayed at the museum in Pensacola. Three others with

In his 80s Hinton would still reminisce about the flight and downplay his role. It was just a job to do, he said to more than one feature writer (*Miami Herald* photograph by Bob Eighmie).

Walter Hinton during a 1980s interview with the *Miami Herald* (*Miami Herald* photograph by Bob Eighmie).

connections to the NC mission have been added to the Roll of Honor in the upper reaches of the Museum — Adm. Marc Mitscher, co-pilot of the NC-1 and a hero in the South Pacific in World War II; Capt. Kenneth Whiting, who got Hinton into aviation; and Hinton's co-pilot, Commander Elmer Stone, the first Coast Guard aviator. The official web site for the Museum in its bio on the NC-4 lists Stone as the pilot and doesn't mention Hinton at all.

While Colonial Palms Nursing home went out of its way to accommodate its celebrity guest, Hinton languished, confined to a bed, an old and broken man. When friends and relatives tried to comfort him Hinton would roll over and face the wall.

"He was the only fearless person I ever knew, but he had a fear of nursing homes," Knott said. "He told the nurses, 'Call Capt. Knott and have him come down and get me out of here.'" The nurses called Knott. "I said, 'I will call his niece and see if we can arrange something.' But within hours he had just died. It was a strange thing."[31]

Two weeks after the first dozen men were enshrined in the Naval Aviation Museum's Hall of Honor — on October 28, 1981 — two weeks before his 93rd birthday and 55 years after that first heart attack on a street in Manhattan, the last of the NC-4 transatlantic fliers died. A broken shell of the intrepid aviator of the '20s and '30s, Walter Hinton had simply outlived his time and his colleagues.

Epilogue

"Trouble in the air is very rare. It is hitting the ground that causes it."
— Amelia Earhart[1]

About a dozen persons from the condo, the bank, relatives, friends and hangers-on attended a short memorial service at the funeral home for Walter Hinton. Then his cremated remains along with his wife Susan's, were flown to Washington, D.C., and interred at Arlington National Cemetery.

The various heirs immediately started squabbling over the multiple wills and trusts that Hinton left behind and what each meant. While Susan and Walter had had considerable money and a comfortable upscale lifestyle with lots of world travel while she was alive, by the time Hinton died it was mostly gone, in bits and pieces to the folks who specialize in helping ease old age for the elderly, ailing wealthy. Eventually each person named in the final will got $10,000 to $25,000. "The lawyers got most of it," his niece, Marjorie Tubbs, said.[2]

Gwyn and Francis Makara, Susan's relatives who were close to the Hintons, had hoped to obtain the hand-carved key to Van Wert that Hinton had promised to their adopted son, John Francis Makara, but it had disappeared. They blamed Marjorie Tubbs for its being missing, but Mrs. Tubbs, in an interview at a modest Lansing area nursing home, denied she had even seen the item. It was never recovered.

NC-4 and Hinton memorabilia and recognitions can be found at the Naval Air Museum in Pensacola, where the flying boat, looking like a mechanical version of some prehistoric, bi-winged, beached whale, dominates the center of the museum. The NC's 126-foot wingspan is slightly greater than that of a 757 jetliner, naval historian and later Hinton friend Richard Knott noted. "It was a biplane, an ungainly looking machine with a maze of booms, struts and guy wires, but to Walter Hinton, one of the NC pilots, 'it was beautiful.'"[3]

The preservation and resurrection of the NC-4 can be attributed primarily to the efforts of one man — Paul Garber — a Smithsonian official, who over the decades campaigned to have the hull and the wings, which were stored in different locations, reunited and re-constructed and put on display. How much of the actual original parts are in the NC-4 on display at the Naval Air Museum in Pensacola is anybody's guess. On a visit several years ago the pilots' cockpit was empty except for a circa 1990s metal card table chair.

Garber was a friend of Hinton's and the first pitch he made to preserve the NC-4 and built a suitable display facility, which would have cost $100,000, was in the 1930s and it was ironically turned down by then Assistant Secretary of the Navy Theodore Roosevelt, son of Teddy and nephew of Franklin.

Other mementoes of the Four and Hinton are in the Van Wert Historical Museum and the Brumback Library in Van Wert, Ohio, and at Kitty Hawk where the Wright brothers first flew. There are plaques at various stopping points along the NC route, including Chatham, Massachusetts, Trepassey Bay, Newfoundland, and Plymouth, England, but there is none in evidence in Lisbon, Portugal, where the plane made its first landfall on the European continent.

For years the Smithsonian sold framed pictures of the NC-4 in flight with a small square of fabric similar to that used to cover the wings of the flying boat. One of these popped up as recently as 2007 on a national PBS television show called *History Detectives*. The show features scenes from the Naval Air Museum in Pensacola, Florida, and the Glenn Curtiss Museum in Hammondsport, New York.

Narrator Elyse Luray interviewed Shelly Monfort from Saratoga, California, about a piece of supposed NC-4 wing fabric that has been passed down, according to Ms. Monfort, "from my grandparents."

"Yeah, it's been in the envelope for years and years. And there's an inscription on the other side that's written by my grandmother." Ms. Luray read it: "This is a piece of the original fabric that covered the wings of the NC-4, the first plane to cross the Atlantic by our Navy, May 31st, 1919."

Of course, the *History Detectives* investigation concludes that the piece of coarse, linen fabric couldn't have been actually part of the NC-4 since all the surfaces of the Four were coated with yellow dope, but the hunt led them to the Naval Air Museum and historian Hill Goodspeed, who showed them a piece of fabric that they had received from Sally Hinton sometime in the 1960s or 1970s. It was inscribed, my husband, Lieutenant Walter Hinton August 1919." She also included a picture of the NC-4 anchored near a seawall, which was shot on the NC-4 publicity tour, probably in St. Louis, Missouri.

The irony there is that Sally Hinton had divorced Walter Hinton in the 1920s, accusing him in later years of having had an affair on the long, troubled

Rio flight. She then married the executive officer at Rockaway, Lt. Commander J.C. Monfort, who served there during the final preparations for the NC mission. Walter Hinton only said in response that his first wife wanted the security of a naval officer with a future in the service. Shelly Monfort wasn't Hinton's step-grandchild because Sally had divorced Walter before Ms. Monfort's mother was born. Hinton does have some distant relatives still alive in the U.S., but Ms. Monfort is not one of them.

In Chatham, Massachusetts, at the end of a deadend road, looking out over the bay, there are these words affixed to a granite boulder. "Here the Navy seaplane NC-4 put in for repairs after leaving Rockaway, Long Island, with two other NC's. After departing from Chatham with a crew of five [actually, there were six] on 14 May 1919, it came down at Halifax, Nova Scotia, caught up with the other planes at Trepassey, Newfoundland, reached the Azores on 17 May, Lisbon on 27 May and Plymouth, England on 31 May. The NC-4 was the only plane to complete this first historic crossing of the Atlantic by air."[4]

The restored *Eleanor III* is reportedly still on display at the Canada Aviation Museum at Rockcliffe Airport in Ottawa, Canada. The *Sampaio Correia II*, the first airplane to fly over the skies of Brazil, is still reportedly in a military museum in Brazil.

There is also a small, local airfield on the western outskirts of Hinton's home town, Van Wert, Ohio. On a sunbaked summer day early in the 21st century, heat rose off the asphalt and a Quonset hut hangar sat shuttered next to the offices. On its side a sign, peeling its white paint, read: " Honorary Walter Hinton Field." The airport itself is variously known as Van Wert Airport, Van Wert County Airport or Van Wert County Regional Airport and it serves this 10,000-person, mid–American center of corn and soybean fields. But a visitor stopping by the office and asking about Walter Hinton drew a blank look from the young man at the desk. He turned to a slightly older man, perhaps with more authority, "Did you ever hear of Walter Hinton?" Another blank look and then dawning recognition. "Just a minute," the older young man said. He went into an interior office, rummaged, and came out with a newspaper clipping housed in a simple black frame. "Here he is," the older of the two men said proudly. It was a copy of a *Van Wert Times* article about one of the city's most famous citizens, the man who piloted the first plane across the Atlantic, the man who flew the first plane from New York to Rio de Janeiro, the man who first explored the Amazon basin by air — Walter Hinton.

The folks at the Brumback Library — a fantastical edifice built like a small castle in the center of town — know all about Walter Hinton. So do the folks in the nearby Van Wert Historical Society Museum. But most of the public doesn't. Contrary to popular belief and even the uttering of one famous network television anchor, it was not Charles Lindbergh who first showed the Atlantic could be bridged and was precursor of our current space program. It was Walter Hinton and his Navy cohorts on the 1919 NC mission from Far Rockaway, New York, to Lisbon, Portugal, and Plymouth, England, organized with weather and station ships spaced out across the Atlantic, that was the first step toward putting a man on the moon.

Secretary of the Navy Josephus Daniels, a Carolina newspaper publisher, hoped that the 1919 mission and the follow-up tour of the country by the NC-4 would reap great publicity and financial support from Congress for naval aviation. While the mission was designed as carefully and scientifically as the technology of the time would allow, the equipment was primitive, the engineering flawed. Behind those chaotic final days of preparation the Navy wanted to be first across.

Lindbergh's 1927 flight was a heroic stunt. He flew the Atlantic alone, without support, and stayed awake for more than 30 hours, a feat in itself. Even he admitted that the aviation technology developed in the eight years between the NC mission and his flight made his a better proposition. Planes just weren't very safe in 1919. The men on board the NC flying boats were hailed as heroes, but most of them never thought of themselves that way. They were military. They had jobs to do and they did them to the best of their abilities.

Walter Hinton, who died at age 92 in Pompano Beach, Florida, was the last survivor of those men who set forth in wooden, canvas covered, open-cockpit flying boats to make history.

And they did. After all, despite our modern proclivity to award heroism and trophies to everyone in a contest, there can only be one first. Everyone who comes afterward comes with an asterisk. That includes John "Jack" Alcock and Arthur Whitten Brown who flew the first non-stop flight across the Atlantic to crash in an Irish bog in June 1919 as the NC-4 fliers were wending their way home on a slow ship dubbed the *Zeppelin*. Like Hinton, Read, Stone and the rest of the NC-4 crew, the Brits have been largely forgotten.

What Lindbergh did was capture the public and media attention and, as Hinton put it, that gave more impetus to the development of aviation than the men who crossed the Atlantic by air before the "Lone Eagle." There were actually 91 persons on 13 separate flights who made the crossing before Lucky Lindy. Those missions are chronicled in a book *The 91 Before Lindbergh* by Peter Allen.

People are still getting media play for aviation firsts across the Atlantic. They dream of conquering the Atlantic in another fashion.

On the 75th anniversary of naval aviation in 1986, 67 years after the NC-4 mission two PBY flying boats recreated the feat by taking off from

Rockaway on May 8. One was called the *Spirit of U.S. Naval Aviation* and the other, the *NC-4*. On hand to christen the *NC-4* before it flew to Rockaway was the widow of her commander, Bess Burdine Read. More than 150 guests watched as she banged a champagne bottle futilely against the nose of the old *Four*. Twice it failed to break. Finally one of the PBY pilots stepped in and helped and bubbly sprayed over both of them.

As early as 2002 a retired aeronautical engineer, Maynard Hill, attempted to bridge the Atlantic along the Alcock and Brown route from St. John's, Newfoundland, to Ireland with a remotely controlled model plane. He launched *The Sprit of Butts Farm* from a spit of land named Cape Spear, according to the *Washington Post*.[5]

A year later Hill, who was legally blind, and his team tried again. One of them said: "To be perfectly honest most of us thought he was crazy," said Dave Brown, president of the Academy of Model Aeronautics and a friend of Hill. "We didn't think it could be done."[6]

At about 6 PM on August 9, 2003, Hill tossed the red TAM-5 in the air. A ground pilot with a remote control sent it to about 1,000 feet and a computer took over and the balsa wood plane that was roughly six-foot long with a six foot wingspan headed for an Irish bog. They figured at 55 mph hour it had enough fuel to last 36 to 37 hours. But the model flew at only 42 miles an hour and the GPS unit conked out for three hours before turning itself back on. At the 38-hour mark the plane came into view of the ground crew in Ireland that was sure it was flying on fumes. With a remote control Brown landed the craft safely on August 11 about 90 feet from its target on Mannin Bay, Galway.[7] A crowd of about 50 cheered. Back in Newfoundland when Hill was informed of his success, he hugged his wife and cried.[8]

In 2005 a 60-year old investment executive, Steve Fossett, using the latest technology of the day, circled the world in a 110-foot-wingspan GlobalFlyer without refueling. It was a similar route to one early aviator Wiley Post took in 1932, making seven stops.[9]

On October 4, 2004, the SpaceShipOne, designed by Bert Rutan, rocketed 69.7 miles into space to claim the $10 million Ansari X Prize modeled after the early aviation contests such as the Ortieg Prize claimed by Lindbergh.[10]

Notes at the Naval Air Museum in Pensacola point out that the Discovery Space mission circled the earth at 17,000 miles per hour, each circuit taking 90 minutes, each astronaut weighing 400 pounds in his or her gear.

Planes don't fly from Rockaway Naval Air Station anymore. It no longer exists. A small park and parking lot mark the spot. Fittingly, the site is in the flight pattern of the great trans-oceanic jets that shuttle daily back and forth from the U.S. to Europe from New York's Kennedy Airport, almost all the passengers blissfully unaware of and not caring who flew first.

Epilogue 225

Here is what we know about what happened to those fearless fliers of 1919 and some of the other adventurers Walter Hinton associated with on his exploits.

Capt. John Alcock and Lt. Arthur Whitten Brown, who made the first non-stop aerial crossing of the Atlantic only to crash land in an Irish bog as the NC-4 crew were returning home, won the *Daily Mail* $10,000 prize. The flight from Lester's Field near St. Johns, Newfoundland, on June 14, 1919, took 16 hours and 27 minutes before landing near Clifden, Ireland. The pair was knighted and Brown got married and went to the U.S. on his honeymoon in October 1919. Alcock went back to work testing planes at Brooklands and in December 1919 he was killed delivering a Vickers Viking plane to Paris for an aeronautical exhibition. In rain and fog over Normandy the plane crashed. A farmer found the badly injured Alcock and identified him from an engraving on his diamond studded wrist watch. Alcock died December 18 before doctors got to him the next day.[11] Brown settled in Wales where he became General Manager of the Vickers factory. His only son was killed serving with the Royal Air Force in World War II. Brown died in 1948. He was 62.[12]

Lt. Louis T. Barin, U.S. Naval Reserve Force, was the co-pilot of the NC-1. Born in Portland, Oregon, in 1890, Barin was known as a daredevil test pilot and in 1917 survived a plane falling from 6,000 feet until he got control 200 feet above the water and crash landed. His helmet and goggles were ripped off and his clothes torn. After the NC mission he was awarded the Navy Cross and the "Knight of the Military Order of Tower and Sword," by the government of Portugal. His Navy Cross citation said in part: "for extraordinary heroism as pilot of a sea plane which was being utilized for the test of a new method of aerodynamic control. Realizing, from the performance of this device when on the water, that as pilot he was practically helpless to control the machine, he nevertheless took it into the air, and continued the experiment in order that the test might be complete." He was killed a year after the transatlantic mission while testing a plane on June 12, 1920 at San Diego, California. A Naval Medical Learning Facility in Foley, Alabama, near Pensacola was named in his honor. It was closed permanently in 1958.[13]

Rear Admiral Patrick N. L. Bellinger, who loved to play practical jokes, wore a long, white silk scarf over his flying uniform and was the first Navy aviator to take enemy fire in Vera Cruz, Mexico, had the bad luck to be in charge of naval aviation in Hawaii on December 7, 1941 when the Japanese attacked Pearl Harbor in their "Day of Infamy." That effectively ended his upward career. He later wrote his memoirs, but they were never published. There is a copy at the Naval History Museum in Washington, D.C. He retired and died May 29, 1962.

Lt. James L. Breese, engineer, the classmate of FDR's at Groton, who was willing to use that connection to get his aviation club into the Naval Reserve as officers, was a primary source for a 1961 book on the NC mission by HY Steirman and Glenn D. Kittler, *Triumph, The Incredible Saga of the First Transatlantic Flight*. While the pair interviewed Read and Lavender as well as Breese, the book is written in the style of some of the men's magazines — *True* and *Argosy*— that Steirman had written for. The authors put words in all of the participants' mouths as though they were there to take them down. It is apparent that Breese embellished his role and words, but there are admissions of considerable drinking and partying by Breese and Rhoads that were confirmed reluctantly by Hinton and other reported accounts. Smith did not mention the book or its authors when he crafted his meticulous 1973 prize-winning account, although he did list it as a secondary source. Richardson probably had it right when he told Towers before the flight that he wasn't enthusiastic about Breese, that he knew his engineering, but wasn't particularly involved in the mission.

Breese apparently harnessed that brilliance when he moved to Santa Fe, New Mexico, in the 1920s and founded a company that designed and built oil burners known as Breese Burners. The Santa Fe newspaper wrote that he was known as "a mechanical genius." His grandson said Breese "was the first high-tech entrepreneur in Santa Fe. He did a lot of work with the Army" during World War II and the Korean War. Breese reportedly had a huge home on Canyon Road that housed a laboratory. The house later served as a stand-in for the local high school in the movie *Red Sky at Morning* and as an interim site for a prep school. Breese died in 1959.

George Bye, the *New York World* reporter, who rode along on the long, accident-filled New York-to-Rio adventure to record Walter Hinton's exploits, parlayed the trip into a career as a literary agent, frequently for celebrities authoring "stunt" books. Among his clients were Charles A. Lindbergh, Alexander Woolcott, Westbrook Pegler, Heywood Broun and Army General John J. Pershing. In his obituary the *New York Times* reported he was close to President Franklin Delano Roosevelt and convinced Eleanor Roosevelt to begin her syndicated column "My Day." In 1954 Bye reportedly arranged for the sale of Lindbergh's book, The Spirit of St. Louis, to Hollywood for more than $1 million. A resident of New Caanan, Connecticut, he died at age 70 in November 1957.

Lt. Commander Richard E Byrd Jr, remained a lifelong friend of Hinton's. He continued to seek exploration first adventures and in 1926 claimed to be first to fly over the North Pole. He was awarded the Medal of Honor, but that claim was later disputed by explorers familiar with the capability of his aircraft. He was preparing with a crew to compete for the Ortieg Prize in 1927, but a crash while testing his craft allowed Lindbergh to get away first and win the $25,000. Byrd later became famous for Arctic and Antarctic exploration and was first to fly over the South Pole. "By the time he died, he had amassed 22 citations and special commendations, nine of which were for bravery and two for extraordinary heroism in saving the lives of others. In addition, he was awarded the Medal of Honor, the Congressional Life Saving Medal, the Navy Distinguished Service Medal, The Distinguished Flying Cross, the Navy Cross, and had three ticker tape parades," according to Wikipedia. He died at age 68 on March 11, 1957, in Boston and is buried at Arlington National Cemetery. His polar expedition papers are at the Ohio State University library in Columbus, Ohio.

Rasmus Christensen, engineer, and Chief Machinist Mate on the NC-1, was the only foreign-born member of the mission. He was born March 18, 1883, in Tombol, Germany. He was Danish and came to the U.S. as a teenager. He joined the U.S. Navy August 12, 1904, and joined the first aviation mechanics class at Pensacola. By December 1918 he had been designated Naval Aviator No. 1885. He served in various capacities until he retired as a Chief Machinist Mate in September 1934. He joined the Navy Reserve and was a Chief Warrant Officer at his death on July 24, 1960, in El Paso, Colorado. He is buried in Arlington National Cemetery. He was awarded the "Military Order of the Tower & Sword" by the government of Portugal for his role in the NC expedition. He watched his son, Ernest, graduate from the Naval Academy in 1934, receive his wings as a naval aviator, and eventually took command of the U.S.S. *Hornet*. His grandson, Ernest E. Christensen, Jr., also attended the Naval Academy and became a naval aviator. Ernest Christensen, Jr., rose to the rank of Rear Admiral before retiring in 1997. His son Lt. Commander Cory Christensen is also a naval aviator — the fourth generation.[14]

Harry Hawker and several friends formed the Hawker Aircraft Company after Sopwith went out of business. He lent his name to successful British military aircraft that fly to this day. He was killed when a Nieuport Goshawk he was piloting blew up on takeoff from Hendon Aerodrome on July 12, 1921. He was 32. An airport in Mentone, Australia, is named for him and a stamp honoring him was issued in 1987. He is buried at St. Paul's Church, Chessington, Surrey, England.

C.I. Kesler, engineer was the Chief Machinist Mate of the NC-1. There is little known about his subsequent life. Born in Dayton, Ohio, March 3, 1882, he joined the Navy in 1905. He was awarded the Navy Cross for the part he played in the Transatlantic flight and he retired July 1, 1935. Navy records did not show a date of death.

Lt. Commander Robert A. Lavender, the radio officer aboard the NC-3, went on to a distinguished career in the Navy. A Naval Academy graduate in 1912, he later earned a M.S. degree from Harvard in electrical engineering in 1921 and a law degree from George Washington University in 1927. He retired in 1939, but was recalled to active duty before World War II. He was attached to the Manhattan Project that developed the atomic bomb and his responsibilities included applying for patents to protect the various processes without revealing the fact that the group was developing a super bomb. He received the Legion of Merit for that work. The citation read in part: "As Patent Officer of the Manhattan Engineer District, Captain Lavender displayed high professional skill, splendid judgment and devotion to duty in supervising the compilation, investigation and processing to completing of the myriad patentable inventions produced by the Atomic Bomb Project. Through his skill and tireless energy, the great volume of complex inventions were processed to the best interest of the government in record breaking time under most stringent security requirements. Captain Lavender's accomplishments contributed significantly to the success of the Atomic Bomb Project. He has rendered service of outstanding value to the Government and assisted materially in the furtherance of the war effort."[15]

In addition to the Navy Cross for the NC mission and the Legion of Merit, Capt. Lavender held the Mexican Service Medal, the Haitian Campaign Medal, the World War I Victory Medal, the Yangtze Service Medal, the American Defense Service Medal, the American Campaign Medal and the World War II Victory Medal. When I interviewed Lavender in the 1970s at his apartment in northwest Washington, he showed a film of the NC mission and was in good health. But the Navy did not provide a record of his death or burial site in their biographical report. Copies of that film are shown at the National Naval Aviation Museum in Pensacola.

Euclides Pinto Martins, Hinton's Brazilian co-pilot on the unfortunate flight from New York to Rio from September 4, 1922 to February 8, 1923, was born in Camocim, Brazil, on April 15, 1892. He graduated from the Drexel Institute in Philadelphia with an engineering mechanics degree in 1911. He graduated from a flying school and obtained a pilot's license in 1921 and met Walter Hinton. A banker, Andrew Smith Jr., and *The New York World* agreed to underwrite Pinto Martins' dream of being first to fly from New York to Rio de Janeiro. Hinton was the primary pilot, but allowed Pinto Martins to fly the aircraft, the *Sampaio Correia II*, in Brazilian air space. Pinto Martins was treated as a hero, but fell into debt and his American wife refused to live in Brazil. He was found dead of a gunshot wound to the head in his room on April 12, 1924, a little more than a year after his triumphal flight.[16]

Lieutenant David H. McCulloch, listed as the co-pilot of the NC-3, was an outstanding aviator. He got interested in aviation in 1911 and had temporary duty at the Naval Air Station at Hampton Roads, Virginia, where he apparently met and befriended Commander Towers. He was released from active duty in December 1916. Towers had him recalled to active duty on March 24,

1919, to help with the NC preparation and testing. McCulloch was released from active duty again on August 2, 1919, and honorably discharged on September 30, 1921. He joined the Naval Reserves in April 1942 as a Lieutenant Commander and served throughout World War II. He retired on February 1, 1946. During his career he was awarded the Navy Cross "for distinguished service in the line of his profession as a member of the crew of the seaplane NC-3 which made a long overseas flight from Newfoundland to the vicinity of the Azores, in May 1919." He also received the "Order of the Tower and Sword" from the government of Portugal and a decoration from the government of Italy. He died September 20, 1955.

Marc Andrew Mitscher became famous in World War II as the Commander of Pacific Carrier forces for his "vigorous and fearless air attacks against the Japanese-held objectives." He was eventually award a second gold star in lieu of a Third Distinguished Service Medal and more than a dozen other medals and citations during his career. He is credited with refusing to turn off the landing lights on his carriers contrary to orders so that his pilots could find their way back at night. At the time of his death on February 3, 1947, he was serving as Commander in Chief, U.S. Atlantic fleet. Hinton described him as "short, lean, squared jawed and neither smart nor talkative, but he emerged as one of the top admirals in the Pacific."[17] He is buried at Arlington.

Boatswain Lloyd R. Moore, the lone mechanic left aboard the NC-3 after Commander John Towers dumped Lieutenant Braxton Rhodes to lighten the load, was nicknamed "Dinty" after a popular beef stew of the era. Born in Grand Island, Nebraska, a long way from salt water, Moore joined the Navy on August 19, 1909, at Denver, Colorado. He was named a warrant officer in 1917 and a Boatswain (Aviation) in 1918. He was promoted to Chief Boatswain in September 1919 after the NC expedition and was honorably discharged on April 28, 1920. He was awarded the Navy Cross and the "Knight of Military Order of the Tower and Sword" by the government of Portugal.

Frederick Raynham continued air racing and by 1924 became the chief test pilot for the Hawker Aircraft Co. After another test crash he turned to jobs in commercial aviation and traveled the globe. He was awarded the Order of the British Empire in 1935 and the George V medal. After World War II he and his wife moved to the U.S. and traveled the country "from top to toe" with a house trailer and car. At one point they lived in the Briny Breezes campground in Delray Beach, Florida. He died of a stroke in Colorado Springs, Colorado, in 1954 and is buried in Evergreen Cemetery there.[18]

Rear Admiral Albert Cushing Read was a lifelong Navy man. Secretary of the Navy Josephus Daniels' decision to overrule his Assistant Secretary Franklin Roosevelt and allow Read to continue to command the NC-4 on its final leg across the Atlantic created a lifelong distance between his superior

Commander John Towers and Read. Newspaperman Daniels' conclusion that the diminutive, fox-faced Read would make a popular hero was never borne out. Read continued to advance through the ranks, but despite both men's denials, it was felt that Towers, always the superior officer, chilled Read's chances. Read died in relative obscurity in Miami in October 1967 — where his wife Bess Burdine's family was a familiar name in a big department store chain. He is buried at Arlington.

Eugene Saylor "Smokey" Rhoads, the only enlisted man in the crew of the NC-4, replaced E.H. Howard just days before the mission launched when Howard stood up on the fuselage of the NC-4 and had a hand cut off by a propeller. Hinton said that Rhoads was the biggest man on the NC-4 crew at 195 pounds and more than six feet tall. Rhoads was talkative and complained a lot about things he didn't like in "a Pennsylvania Dutch" drawl.[19] The airport in Somerset, Pennsylvania, his birthplace, was dedicated in Rhoads, honor in 1929,[20] although today it appears to be called simply Somerset County Airport. After leaving the Navy, Rhoads worked for Douglas Aircraft in Santa Monica, California, and later as a Navy inspector for Lockheed Aircraft in Burbank, California. He was awarded the Navy Cross for the NC mission and received the NC-4 Congressional commemorative medal from President Herbert Hoover in 1929. He also held the Air Force cross, awarded by the British government and the "Military Order of the Tower and Sword" from Portugal as well as the Mexican Service Medal, the World War I Victory Medal and the Good Conduct Medal with two bars.

On May 8, 1949, on the anniversary of the NC-4 flight, he and Read boarded the Lockheed Neptune P2V-2 *Truculent Turtle* bomber, which flew them to Lisbon from Newfoundland and on to Plymouth, England in 16 hours and 50 minutes, compared to the 19 days it took the NC-4[21] Rhoads died in a California nursing home.

Braxton Rhodes, the engineering officer who never got to make the trip, was the engineer aboard the NC-3. When McCulloch and Richardson were unable to get the heavily loaded craft off the water in Trepassey Bay, Commander Towers ordered Rhodes, the sixth man, a five-gallon tin of water, the emergency radio transmitter, and about 50 pounds of the floor decking over the side. They mistakenly unloaded drinking water rather than radiator water.[22] It proved to be a fateful decision when they had mechanical problems and couldn't send a distress signal once they crash-landed near the Azores. Hinton described Rhodes as "medium-sized, red haired, freckle-faced, a pleasant, efficient officer, who knew his job." Rhodes had served for a year as officer in charge of the Mechanics' School at the Packard Motor Car Co. in Detroit, one of the manufacturers of the Liberty engines. Rhodes took flight training in June 1921 and in 1922 he served aboard the first Navy aircraft carrier the

U.S.S. *Langley*, taking part in the experimental phase of carrier landings. He rose to the rank of Captain and retired in December 1946. He held the Mexican Campaign Medal, the World War I Victory Medal, the American Defense Service Medal, the American Campaign Medal, the Asiatic-Pacific Campaign Medal, the World War II Victory Medal and the Good Conduct Medal. Portugal awarded him the Distinguished Military Aviator medal for the part he played in the NC flight. He died January 26, 1966, at the Naval Hospital in Pensacola.

Herbert C. Rodd, a Cleveland, Ohio, native, worked as a radio operator on Great Lakes freighters before joining the Navy. He was a tinkerer with his radio equipment and seemed to get more out of it than other operators. He didn't talk much and was quiet and unassuming. "He had his pet tubes," Hinton said.[23] Rodd was working at the Radio Experimental Station, Hampton Roads, Virginia when he was detached to accompany the NC mission in April 1919. Rodd flew on the publicity tour of the NC-4 after the flight's completion from Portland, Maine, along the east and Gulf coasts and up the Mississippi to St. Louis, Missouri. He eventually achieved the rank of Lieutenant Commander and received flight training at Pensacola in 1920. He served aboard the nation's first aircraft carrier, the U.S.S. *Langley*, and later aboard the U.S.S. *Virginia*. He received the NC-4 medal from President Hoover on February 9, 1929. He joined the U.S.S. *Saratoga* in September 1931 as aide and communications officer. He was killed in an airplane crash at Hampton Roads, Virginia, on June 15, 1932, while flying a O2U-4 airplane.

In addition to the Navy Cross and the Congressional NC-4 medal, Rodd held the Decoration of "Knight of Tower & Sword" from Portugal, the Air Force Cross, from Great Britain and the World War I victory medal. A satellite field of the Naval Air Station in Corpus Christi, Texas, was named in his honor and used as a training facility in World War II. There is now a storage facility at the site, but Rodd's name is still memorialized in Rodd Field Road, the access road.

Harry Sadenwater, in 1919, before the NC flight, demonstrated the feasibility of using voice radio and telephone relay for air to ground communications in an airborne flying boat, as the lieutenant (j.g) carried on a conversation with Secretary of the Navy Josephus Daniels, who was seated at his desk in the Navy Department some 65 miles away.[24] Sadenwater, the radio operator on the NC-3, was demobilized in October 1919 and discharged in April 1921. His honors included the Navy Cross and the "Knight of the Military Order of the Tower and Sword" from Portugal.

Elmer Fowler Stone, the Coast Guard's first aviator who surrendered the left-hand pilot's seat to Hinton because he recognized Hinton was the better flyer, successfully piloted a Loening amphibian plane from the deck of a barge anchored in the Potomac on February 27, 1926, catapulted aloft by a blank shell. It was believed to be the first time powder was used rather than air pressure. He set an air speed record for amphibian planes in 1934 by piloting a Coast Guard Grumman craft over a three-kilometer measured course at Hampton, Virginia, at 191.76 miles per hour.[25] He was chosen for the transatlantic mission because of the "skill, judgment and daring" he exhibited as a test pilot with the Naval Bureau of Construction and Repair. He was born in Livonia, New York, and grew up in Norfolk, Virginia, where he worked in the pressroom of the *Ledger Dispatch* until he entered the Coast Guard in 1910. As a seaman he helped rescue 12 men from a shipwrecked vessel by taking a lifeboat through stormy seas. He died of a heart attack at age 49 while inspecting an aircraft at the San Diego Coast Guard Base where he had been named commander a month earlier. He is buried at Arlington.

John Henry Towers, a consummate, careful and courageous officer, became Commander Air Force, U.S. Pacific Fleet as a Vice Admiral in World War II. He was responsible for designing the tactics to neutralize air and sea defenses and was key to developing the Pacific campaign. He received assorted awards including the Legion of Merit and the Distinguished Service Medal. Eventually he was made Commander in Chief, Pacific Fleet with headquarters at Pearl Harbor. He had more than a dozen other medals and citations and his biography." He died April 30, 1955, and is buried at Arlington.

Holden C. Richardson, the largest man on the mission at more than 240 pounds, designed the flying boats with their strangely truncated fuselages. While a British observer concluded the plane would never get off the water, Richardson had the courage of his convictions and gave the NC-1 its crucial test flight from Jamaica Bay, Long Island, on October 4, 1918. He was listed as the pilot of the NC-3, continued in naval aviation design, and was given the order of Maurice and Lazarus for his participation in the NC flight during a conference of trans-oceanic pilots in Italy before Word War II. He worked with the Smithsonian Institute after the war and various Navy departments as a consultant. Richardson died September 2, 1960.

Kenneth Whiting, the officer who once had himself ejected out of a torpedo tube to see if that was a safe way to escape a downed submarine and who got Walter Hinton into flying, helped convert the collier *Jupiter* into the first Navy aircraft carrier, the *Langley*. He commanded the *Langley* and the *Saratoga* and various air squadrons, prior to retirement as a captain in 1940. He was retained as General Inspector of Naval Aircraft, Eastern Division until 1943 and then commanded the Naval Air Station in New York until his death April 24, 1943. He was 61. His ashes were scattered off Execution Rock Light in the deepest part of Long Island Sound. An airfield in Milton, Florida, was named for him in 1943 and a seaplane tender memorialized him in 1944.

Chapter Notes

Chapter 1

1. Lamplugh, of the British Aviation Insurance Group in London, reportedly said this in the early 1930s. "Safety," *Great Aviation Quotes*, 2011, www.skygod.com/quotes/safety.
2. The definitive account of the transatlantic flight of 1919 was written by Richard K. Smith, *First Across: The U.S. Navy's Transatlantic Flight of 1919* (Annapolis, MD: Naval Institute Press, 1986). Smith, a historian on the staff of the Smithsonian Institution's National Air and Space Museum, relied on detailed records in Record groups 45 and 72 in the National Archives, plus hours of interviews.
3. Walter Hinton, interview, May 29, 1967.
4. Ibid.

Chapter 2

1. Walter Hinton, interview, May 29, 1967
2. Rudyard Kipling, "The Song of the Dead," *The Collected Works of Rudyard Kipling* (New York: AMS Press, 1970).
3. Walter Hinton, interview, May 1967; Marjorie Tubbs, interview, May 2005.
4. Hinton, interview.
5. Ibid.

Chapter 3

1. Wright speaking to the Western Society of Engineers in Chicago, Sept. 18, 1901. "Great Aviation Quotes," *Great Aviation Quotes*, 2011, www.skygod.com.
2. C. Douglas Sterner, "A Splendid Little War: The Spanish American War," *Home of the Heroes*, Military Times, http://www.homeofheroes.com/wallofhonor/spanish_am/03_manila.html (accessed 31 Oct. 2010). It gives an excellent account of Dewey's slipping his ships into Manila Bay under cover of darkness and defeating the Spanish fleet in the opening shots of the Spanish-American War.
3. Walter Hinton, interview, May 29, 1967.
4. The *Olympia*, the last surviving vessel from the Spanish American War, was scheduled to be permanently closed by the Independence Seaport Museum in November 2010 as the facilities directors faced a $20 million price tag to drydock and refurbish the historic cruiser. When the options of scrapping the *Olympia* or turning it into part of an artificial reef off Cape May, NJ, were published, it created a stir and a Friends of the *Olympia* group was formed and various proposals put forward to save the ship. An article from *The News Tribune* of Tacoma, WA, dated May 27, 2010, details the museum's plan and is reprinted at http://www.freerepublic.com/focus/f-news/2522532/posts (accessed Oct. 31, 2010). Fundraising efforts are detailed at Alan Jaffe, "Fundraising Plan Intended to Save the Olympia from Sinking," *PlanPhilly*, 11 Oct. 2010, www.planphilly.com/fundraisingplan-intended-saveolympia-sinking (accessed 31 Oct. 2010).

5. Mike McKinley, "The Cruise of the Great White Fleet," Department of the Navy, Naval Historical Center, www.history.navy.mil/library/online/gwf_cruise.html.
6. Compiled from Peter L. Jakab, P. L. Jaka, and Rick Young (eds.), *The Published Writings of Wilbur and Orville Wright*, Washington, D.C.: Smithsonian Museum, 2004); James Tobin, *To Conquer the Air: The Wright Brothers and the Great Race for Flight* (New York: Free Press, 2003).
7. "Flight of the June Bug," *Glenn H. Curtiss Museum*, 2007, http://www.glennhcurtissmuseum.org/museum/flight_of_the_june_bug.html (accessed 31 Oct. 2010); George Van Deurs, *Anchors in the Sky: Spuds Ellyson, the First Naval Aviator* (San Rafael, CA: Presidio Press, 1978).
8. Clark G. Reynolds, *Admiral John H. Towers: The Struggle for Naval Air Supremacy* (Annapolis, MD: Naval Institute Press, 1991), 13–15. This is the definitive book on the life of Towers. It was written with the cooperative of Towers' widow, Pierrette Anne Towers, who organized some of the materials and turned them over to Clark. It is a somewhat uncritical assessment of the great admiral.
9. Hinton interview, May 19, 1967. Hinton did not dislike Towers, but found him a coldly calculating leader. He respected Towers' ability and intelligence.
10. Van Deurs, *Anchors in the Sky*, 91.
11. Ibid., 99.
12. Clark, *Admiral John H. Towers*, 46–47.
13. Ibid., 65–68; *Baltimore Sun*, July 13, 1913.
14. Van Deurs, *Anchors in the Sky*, 124.
15. Navy Office of Information, Internal Relations Division, (01-430), 1964.
16. Papers of Vice Admiral Patrick N.L. Bellinger, Operational Archives Branch, Naval Historical Center, Washington D.C.
17. Clark, *Admiral John H. Towers*, 58.
18. Papers of Vice Admiral Patrick N.L. Bellinger, Operational Archives Branch, Naval Historical Center, Washington D.C.
19. Theodore Roscoe, *On the Seas and in the Air: A History of the U.S. Navy's Air Power* (New York: Hawthorne Books, 1970), 47.
20. Bellinger, unpublished memoirs.
21. Roscoe *On the Seas and in the Air*, 47–48.
22. Papers of Vice Admiral Patrick N.L. Bellinger, Operational Archives Branch, Naval Historical Center, Washington D.C.
23. Mary A. Renda, *Military Occupation and the Culture of U.S. Imperialism, 1915–1940* (Chapel Hill: University of North Carolina Press, 2001), chapter 1.
24. Undated *Baltimore Sun* newspaper clip, Walter Hinton clipping collection, Walter Hinton papers (Pensacola, FL: U.S. Naval Air Museum).
25. *True Magazine*, p. 108.
26. Van Deurs, *Anchors in the Sky*, 14.
27. Timothy J. Christmann, "A Fighter for Naval Aviation," *Naval Aviation News* (May/Jun 1984), in Van Deurs, *Anchors in the Sky*, 460–467.

Chapter 4

1. David L. Baker, "Safety," *Great Aviation Quotes*, 2011, www.skygod.com/quotes/safety.
2. Judy Rumerman, "The Curtiss JN-4 'Jenny,'" U.S. Centennial of Flight Commission, http://www.centennialofflight.gov/essay/Aerospace/Jenny/Aero3.htm (accessed 20 Nov. 2010).
3. Walter Hinton, interview, May 29, 1967.
4. B. Kimball Baker, "Lieutenant Walter Hinton: A Naval Aviation Pioneer," interview with Walter Hinton, University of Pittsburgh, Bradford, PA, 28 Oct 1981, Walter Hinton papers (Pensacola, FL: U.S. Naval Air Museum), 57–63. Baker interviewed Hinton shortly before his death and a copy of his article in an unidentified publication was given to the author.
5. Richard K. Smith, *First Across: The U.S. Navy's Transatlantic Flight of 1919* (Annapolis, MD: Naval Institute Press, 1986), 45.

Chapter Notes

6. "Pensacola, The Old and the New," Pensacola Historical Society, 35 pgs., 1986, p. 26.
7. Virginia Parks, "Pensacola: Spaniards to Space Age," Pensacola Historical Society, revised edition, 1996, p. 91.
8. Walter Hinton, interview, May 29, 1967. Hinton was reluctant to talk about his first marriage. Sally was a sales clerk in a big New York Department store. She had apparently been married once before.
9. There is a copy of the letter and a picture of Hinton in the Van Wert Historical Museum files.
10. Richard E. Byrd, *Skyward* (New York: Blue Ribbon Books, 1928), 27–42. Walter Hinton's copy has the pages marked where Byrd mentions him, but interestingly, some pages were never separated so he apparently didn't read the entire volume.
11. Hinton, interview. Hinton had affection for Byrd and later, when he started his aviation ground school in Washington, D.C., Byrd did an endorsement for him.
12. Ibid.
13. Ibid.
14. Baker, "Lieutenant Walter Hinton."
15. Smith, *First Across*, 43.
16. Record Group 45, Box 117, National Archives.
17. Hinton, interview.
18. Ibid.
19. Ibid.
20. Smith, *First Across*, 16–20.
21. Ibid., 11.
22. Department Office of Naval Operations, Washington, D.C., Op-Aire 068-A-494, 23 April 23.
23. Navy Office of Information, Internal Relations Division, (0I-430), 1964.
24. Hy Steirman and Gleen D. Kittler, *Triumph: The Incredible Saga of the First Transatlantic Flight* (New York: Harper & Brothers Publishers, 1961), 30.
25. John H. Towers, "The Great Hop: The Story of the American Navy's Transatlantic Flight," *Everybody's Magazine* (Nov. 1919).
26. Smith, *First Across*, 20.
27. G. C. Westervelt, H. C. Richardson, and A. C. Read, *The Triumph of the NCs* (New York: Doubleday, 1920).
28. Smith, *First Across*, 28–29.
29. Commander John Towers memo to CNO, OpAir S-63-1, 31 Oct. 1918, file 068-A, Record Group 72, Box 72, National Archives, Washington, D.C.
30. Ibid.
31. Smith, *First Across*, 31.
32. Percy Rowe, *The Great Atlantic Air Race* (London: Angus Robertson Publishers, 1977), 65; Graham Wallace, *The Flight of Alcock and Brown* (London: Putnam, 1955), 106–109.
33. Steirman and Kittler, *Triumph*, 33.
34. Ralph Cooper, *The Early Birds of Aviation*, www.earlyaviators.com; *New York World*, Feb. 19, 1919.
35. Smith, *First Across*, 58.
36. Westervelt, Richardson, and Read, *Triumph of the NCs*, 246; Smith, *First Across*, 58–59.
37. Smith, *First Across*, 63.
38. Walter Hinton, interview, 19 June 1967, and various published accounts. Hinton never bragged about being the primary pilot of the Four. It was an assignment and a job and he was good at it and did as he was told.
39. Record Group 72, National Archives, Washington, D.C.; Smith, *First Across*, 67.
40. Smith, *First Across*, 69–70.
41. Steirman and Kittler, *Triumph*, 51; Hinton, interview, 19 June 1967.
42. Steirman and Kittler, *Triumph*, 53–54.
43. Smith, *First Across*, 70–74.
44. Walter Hinton, interview, 22 Oct 1967.
45. "Louis Blériot: Centennial of the First Flight across the English Channel in a Heavier-

than-Air Craft," *First Fly English Channel*, 2009, www.firstflyenglishchannel.com (accessed 20 Nov. 2010).
46. Hinton interview, May 29, 1967.
47. Hinton interview, Oct. 22, 1967.
48. Steirman and Kittler, *Triumph*, 63–70; Hinton interview Oct. 22, 1967.

Chapter 5

1. Walter Hinton, *Liberty Magazine*, July 24, 1926, "Safety," *Great Aviation Quotes*, 2011, www.skygod.com/quotes/safety.
2. Walter Hinton, interview, May 29, 1967.
3. Walter Hinton interview with Cdr. Richard C. Knott, *Naval Aviation News* (Nov. 1976): 25. Knott, author of a number of books on naval aviation, became a good friend of Hinton's in his final years and looked after the aging aviator's interests. He was remembered in Hinton's final will and arranged for Hinton and his wife Susan's ashes to be taken to Arlington National Cemetery.
4. With the war over, it was a base without a purpose. But a year earlier, its aviators had bombed a German submarine, the U-156, off the coast at Orleans, MA. The sub had sunk four barges and set the tug pulling them afire. A large number of local residents and summer visitors watched as several German shots struck the beach — the only shots to hit American shores during the war. One of those aviators ironically was Chief Special Mechanic E. H. Howard, who had been scheduled to be aboard the Four until he lost his left hand to its pusher propeller. Howard manned the bombsight in the bow cockpit of HS-1L 1695 during the bombing runs on the sub. When the bomb release failed to function in runs at 800 feet and 400 feet altitude, Howard climbed out of the bow, crawled to the lower wing and, while holding a strut with one hand, released the bomb. It fell without a few feet of the U-156, but was a dud. Another U.S. plane also dropped a dud at 500 feet as the sub, on the surface, fired back at them and then proceeded north unscathed. Joseph D. Buckley, *Wings Over Cape Cod: The Chatham Naval Air Station, 1917–1922* (Orleans, MA: Lower Cape Publishing, 2000), 18–32
5. Ibid., 5–32.
6. Ibid., 95.
7. A copy of a transcript of the telephone conversation between Read and Whiting on May 9, 1919, is in file 068-A RG-72, BuAer Correspondence 1917–25, Box 73, National Archives, Washington, D.C. A second copy is in the Richard Smith collection at the Archives Suitland, MD, Facility.
8. Bess Burdine Read, "The Private Letters of Putty Read," *Pensacola Naval Avaiation Museum Foundation magazine* (May 1986).
9. Smith, *First Across*; Hinton interviews, 1967, Steirman and Kittler, *Triumph*.
10. Unlike Teddy Roosevelt, FDR was no athlete and not particularly fit. At Groton Academy, where he was an upperclassman when James Breese was a first former, since all students were required to participate in sports, FDR played with the scrubs. There was speculation that Breese, who got into the Naval Reserves on a lark with a bunch of his New York Racquet Club friends and established a training base at a Long Island mansion with a borrowed flying boat, used his Groton connection to win appointment to the transatlantic mission. So Roosevelt might have had a particular interest in the success of the Four and his classmate. Years later, Breese felt comfortable enough with the connection to ask FDR, who was then president, to arrange for him and his family to tour the new Boulder Dam in Nevada while they were on vacation.

Chapter 6

1. Roger Bacon, "Great Aviation Quotes," *Great Aviation Quotes*, 2011, www.skygod.com.
2. The information in this chapter is assembled from a variety of sources, including *The New York Times* during the period; Richard K. Smith, *First Across: The U.S. Navy's Transatlantic Flight of 1919* (Annapolis, MD: Naval Institute Press, 1986); Papers of Vice Admiral Patrick N.L. Bellinger, Operational Archives Branch, Naval Historical Center, Washington D.C.; Walton

Hinton, interviews, 1967; *The Flight across the Atlantic* (New York: Curtiss Aeroplane and Motor Corp., 1919); and Richard C. Knott, "Journey to Plymouth," *Naval Aviation News* (November 1976): 26.

    3. While newspapers across the United States had been publishing a Trepassey Bay dateline, there really wasn't a lot to the community. There were fewer than 500 residents. There was no hotel and five newspaper correspondents had set up headquarters in an old railway car on a siding at the station. (They dubbed the railway car "Nancy 5.") One news agency tried to buy both telegraph lines out of town.

    4. P. N. L. Bellinger to Commander Naval Operations (Aviation), 1 April 1919, Record Group 72, BuAer Correspondence 1917–25, Box 73, National Archives, Washington, D.C.

    5. "Article Title," *New York World*, 17 May 1919, p. 1.

Chapter 7

    1. Richard Bach, "A Gift of Wings (1974)," *Lone Star Flyers*, www.lonestarflyers.com/quotes.
    2. Walter Hinton, interview, May 29, 1967.
    3. Richard C. Knott, "Journey to Plymouth," *Naval Aviation News* (November 1976): 26.
    4. Walter Hinton papers, Brumback Library collection, Van Wert, Ohio.
    5. G. C. Westervelt, H. C. Richardson, and A. C. Read, *The Triumph of the NCs* (New York: Doubleday, 1920). Richardson provides a compelling account of the Three's misadventures and Read provides an account of the Four's flight. Read also wrote and was paid for an account of the flight in *The New York World*.

    6. Richard K. Smith, *First Across: The U.S. Navy's Transatlantic Flight of 1919* (Annapolis, MD: Naval Institute Press, 1986), 110–112; Hinton interviews.

    7. Report from Ensign H. C. Rodd to Towers, "Radio Report, Trans-Atlantic Flight, June 30, 1919," Record Group 45, National Archives, reprinted in Smith, *First Across*, 221–236.

    8. Various newspaper accounts and Hinton papers.
    9. Smith, *First Across*, 11.
    10. Ibid.
    11. Ibid., 115.
    12. Charlie and Jackie Cunningham, *Putty and Bess: Naval Aviation's Grand Couple* (Asheville, NC: Cunningham, 1997), 40–45. This account is based on Mrs. Cunningham's mother Bess Burdine Read's recollections and on Cdr. Ted Wilbur's monograph, "The First Flight Across the Atlantic, May 1919," *Naval Aviation News* (1969).

    13. Smith, *First Across*, 126–129. In Smith's account, a reader will note that he always refers to Elmer Stone as having the primary flying duties. The only explanation has to be that he assumed this because Stone outranked Hinton. Smith did exhaustive research in the National Archives and interviewed dozens of sources for his book, but for some reason never talked to Hinton, who was then living in the Fort Lauderdale area.

Chapter 8

    1. "Safety," *Great Aviation Quotes*, 2011, www.skygod.com/quotes/safety.
    2. Theodore Taylor, *The Magnificent Mitscher* (New York: Bluejacket Books, 2006), 170–180.
    3. Richard K. Smith, *First Across: The U.S. Navy's Transatlantic Flight of 1919* (Annapolis, MD: Naval Institute Press, 1986).
    4. *New York Times*, May 18, 1919; Hinton papers.
    5. Taylor, *The Magnificent Mitscher*.
    6. Ibid.
    7. Smith, *First Across*, 112–122.
    8. Taylor, *The Magnificent Mitscher*.
    9. Walter Hinton, interview, May 29, 1967.
    10. Taylor, *The Magnificent Mitscher*.
    11. Smith, *First Across*; G. C. Westervelt, H. C. Richardson, and A. C. Read, *The Triumph*

of the NCs (New York: Doubleday, 1920); Ted Wilbur, "The First Flight Across the Atlantic," *Naval Aviation News* (May 1969): 7–36; Hinton interviews, Record Group 45, Op-Air 068-A-635, Reports of Commanding Officer NC-1 and Lt. Com. M.A. Mitscher, National Archives, Washington, D.C., copy in Burns collection.

Chapter 9

1. Lane Wallace, "Eyes of a Child," *Flying* (Feb. 2000).
2. Walter Hinton, interview, Oct. 27, 1967.
3. Ibid.
4. Clark G. Reynolds, *Admiral John H. Towers: The Struggle for Naval Air Supremacy* (Annapolis, MD: Naval Institute Press, 1991), 144.
5. McCulloch report to the Navy Department, Record Group 45, Box 36, National Archives, Washington, D.C.
6. Reynolds, *Admiral John H. Towers*, 144.
7. Ibid., 147.
8. Ibid., 148
9. Ibid.
10. Ibid., 149.
11. Ibid.
12. Ibid., 151.
13. Towers, "The Great Hop," 9–15, 74–78; Richard K. Smith, *First Across: The U.S. Navy's Transatlantic Flight of 1919* (Annapolis, MD: Naval Institute Press, 1986), 133–143; Reynolds, *Admiral John H. Towers*, 150–158. Much of the Smith and Reynolds accounts is based on the article that Towers was paid to write for *Everybody's Magazine*.

Chapter 10

1. Muriel Hawker, *H. G. Hawker, Airman* (London: Hutchinson Publishers, 1922), 199.
2. Percy Rowe, *The Great Atlantic Air Race* (London: Angus Robertson Publishers, 1977), 68.
3. Hawker, *H. G. Hawker*, 213n.
4. Hawker, H. G., and K. Mackenzie Grieve, *Our Atlantic Attempt* (London: Methuem & Co. Ltd, 1919), 39.
5. Hawker and Grieve, *Our Atlantic Attempt*, 205
6. Graham Wallace, *The Flight of Alcock and Brown* (London: Putnam, 1955), 50–56.
7. Hawker and Grieve, *Our Atlantic Attempt*, 44.
8. Rowe, *The Great Atlantic Air Race*, 79.
9. Hawker and Grieve, *Our Atlantic Attempt*, 49.
10. For Hawker's account, *New York Times*, May 28, 1919, p. 1–2. Rowe, *The Great Atlantic Air Race*, 161–165; Richard K. Smith, *First Across: The U.S. Navy's Transatlantic Flight of 1919* (Annapolis, MD: Naval Institute Press, 1986), 192; Hawker and Grieve, *Our Atlantic Attempt*.

Chapter 11

1. "Safety," *Great Aviation Quotes*, 2011, www.skygod.com/quotes/safety.
2. "Two Daring Fliers Beat the Atlantic Before Lindbergh," in David Nevins, *The Pathfinders* (Alexandria, VA: Time-Life Books, 1980), 102.
3. Graham Wallace, *The Flight of Alcock and Brown* (London: Putnam, 1955), 136–172.
4. Bess Burdine Read, "The Private Letters of Putty Read," *Pensacola Naval Avaiation Museum Foundation magazine* (May 1986).
5. Hy Steirman and Gleen D. Kittler, *Triumph: The Incredible Saga of the First Transatlantic Flight* (New York: Harper & Brothers Publishers, 1961), 149–151.

6. Richard K. Smith, *First Across: The U.S. Navy's Transatlantic Flight of 1919* (Annapolis, MD: Naval Institute Press, 1986), 153.
7. Steirman and Kittler, *Triumph*, 302.
8. Smith, *First Across*, 153, 251–252; Clark G. Reynolds, *Admiral John H. Towers: The Struggle for Naval Air Supremacy* (Annapolis, MD: Naval Institute Press, 1991), 159.
9. Reynolds, *Admiral John H. Towers*, 160.
10. OpAir 068-A-545, Record Group 72, BuAer Correspondence 1917–1925, Box 73, National Archives, Washington, D.C.; also quoted in Smith, *First Across*, 155.
11. Ibid.
12. Smith, *First Across*, 157; Reynolds, *Admiral John H. Towers*.
13. *New York Times*, May 22, 1919, p. 3.
14. Smith, *First Across*, 158; Walter Duranty account, *The New York Times*, June 1, 1919, p. 1.
15. Walter Duranty account, *New York Times*, June 1, 1919, p. 1.
16. Ibid.

Chapter 12

1. Quoting Wilbur Wright article in *Scientific American*, James Tobin, *To Conquer the Air: The Wright Brothers and the Great Race for Flight* (New York: Free Press, 2003), 238–240.
2. Walter Hinton, interview, Oct. 27, 1967; Richard K. Smith, *First Across: The U.S. Navy's Transatlantic Flight of 1919* (Annapolis, MD: Naval Institute Press, 1986); *The Pathfinders*, Epics of Flight Series (Alexandria, VA: Time-Life Books, 1980), 23.
3. Steirman and Kittler, *Triumph*, 179–180.
4. C. G. Gray, "On the Defeat of the Atlantic," *The Aeroplane* 16, no. 2 (June 4, 1919): 2197–2202.
5. G. C. Westervelt, H. C. Richardson, and A. C. Read, *The Triumph of the NCs* (New York: Doubleday, 1920), 220–225.
6. *New York Times*, June 17, 1919, p. 5.
7. Letter from Capt. Craven to Kenneth Whiting, June 10, 1919, Smithsonian Museum Archives, Washington, D.C.
8. Telegram from *New York World* to Secretary Daniels, file 068-A-615, National Archives, Washington, D.C.
9. "Article Title," *Fort Wayne [IN] News Sentinel*, Sept 2, 1919.
10. Undated clipping and drawing from Hinton collection, Van Wert, OH.
11. Recruiting Flight NC-4 and itinerary, copy in Burns collection.
12. U.S. Operational Daily Aviation News Bulletin, Dec. 16, 1919, copy in Burns collection.

Chapter 13

1. "Safety," *Great Aviation Quotes*, 2011, www.skygod.com/quotes/safety.
2. This chapter is written from first-person interviews with Hinton, his various published accounts of the flight of the lost balloon, extensive coverage in *The New York Times*, *The Washington Post*, and *The New York World*, and the records of the Courts of Inquiry into the flight that crossed illegally into Canadian territory.
3. *The Exchangite* (March 1931): 4–5.
4. Walter Hinton, interview, June 19, 1967.
5. *Exchangeite* (March 1931): 22.
6. *New York Times*, January 11, 1921, p. 1.
7. Ibid.
8. Ibid.
9. Record of Proceedings in Revision of a Court of Inquiry Convened at the Naval Air Station, Rockaway Long Island, by Order of the Secretary of the Navy, Feb. 16, 1921, 56 pages plus attachments, copy in Burns collection.
10. *Washington Post*, Jan. 9, 1921; *New York Times*, Jan. 9, 1921; *New York World*, Jan. 9, 1921.
11. Walter Hinton, interview, May 19, 1967.

Chapter 14

1. Peter Bostock, *The Great Atlantic Air Race: The Adventure and Its Lessons* (New York: William Morrow & Col, 1970), 171.
2. "Nellie Bly: Around the World in 72 Days," *People and Events*, 2000, http://www.pbs.org/wgbh/amex/world/peopleevents/pande01.html.
3. Roberto Pires de Oliveira, "The Saga of Euclides Pinto Martins and his Friends," transl. Ralph Cooper, *The Early Birds of Aviation*, www.earlyaviators.com.
4. *New York World*, Aug. 18, 1922, p. 1, 3. Much of this chapter is based on Bye's reportage in *The World*. The *New York Times* during the period was also reviewed for stories on the trip.
5. *Washington Post*, Aug. 21, 1922, p. 7; Bye accounts in *New York World*.
6. *New York World*, Sep. 4, 1922, p. 1.
7. Ibid.
8. *New York World*, Sep. 8, 1922, p. 1.
9. Walter Hinton, interview, May 29, 1967.
10. *New York World*, Oct. 13, 1922.
11. www.mt-pelee.com accessed Dec. 20, 2010; *New York Times*, Oct. 12, 1922, p. 18.
12. *Washington Post*, Nov. 22, 1922, p. 6
13. *New York World*, Nov. 22, 1922, p. 1
14. *New York Times*, June 18, 1926, p. 6
15. *Christian Science Monitor*, Dec. 6, 1922, p. 1.
16. *New York Times*, Dec. 10, 1922, p. 4.
17. *New York World*, Dec. 20, 1922, p. 1
19. *New York World*, Dec. 22, 1922, p. 1, and Richard C. Knott, *A Heritage of Wings: An Illustrated History of Navy Aviation* (Annapolis, MD: U.S. Naval Institute Press, 1997).
19. *New York World*, Jan. 29, 1923, p. 1
20. *New York World*, Feb. 9, 1923, p. 1

Chapter 15

1. "Aviation Quotes," *Lone Star Flyers*, www.lonestarflyers.com/quotes. Day Lewis was an Irish poet and British poet laureate.
2. "Leaves of Wesley Heights," (July 1934): 10–11, partial article in the Hinton Collection, Brumback Library, Van Wert, OH. This chapter relies heavily on Hinton's various published accounts of the adventures, the Hinton 1967–1968 interviews, and Albert W. Stevens, "Exploring the Valley of the Amazon in a Hydroplane," *National Geographic* (April 1926).
3. "Leaves of Wesley Heights," (July 1934): 10–11, partial article in the Hinton Collection, Brumback Library, Van Wert, OH.
4. Canada Aviation and Space Museum, www.aviation.technomuses.ca (accessed Dec. 26, 2010).
5. *Washington Post*, March 30, 1924, p. ES-2.
6. Stevens, "Exploring the Valley of the Amazon in a Hydroplane."
7. Walter Hinton, "Flying over Brazilian Jungles," *The World's Work* 50 (May–Oct 1925), 625–638.
8. Ibid., 624.
9. Stevens, "Exploring the Valley of the Amazon in a Hydroplane."
10. Ibid., 360.
11. Tony Reichart, "Tales from the Eran When the Air Age Met the Stone Age," *Air & Space Magazine* (2004).
12. Stevens, "Exploring the Valley of the Amazon in a Hydroplane," 360.
13. Hinton, "Flying over Brazilian Jungles," 636.
14. Ibid., 636–637.
15. Reichart, "Tales from the Eran When the Air Age Met the Stone Age."
16. Hinton, "Flying over Brazilian Jungles," 638.

17. Walter Hinton, "Lost in the Jungles," *The World's Work* (New York: Doubleday, Page & Co, 1926): 85.
18. Ibid.
19. Stevens, "Exploring the Valley of the Amazon in a Hydroplane," 388–389.
20. Hinton, "Lost in the Jungles," 87.
21. Stevens, "Exploring the Valley of the Amazon in a Hydroplane," 393–395; "Brazilian Tapir," *Endangered Wildlife*, 1996, ladywildlife.com/animals/braziliantapir.html.
22. Stevens, "Exploring the Valley of the Amazon in a Hydroplane," 408.
23. Hinton, "Lost in the Jungles," 97.

Chapter 16

1. *Outlook Magazine* (June 27, 1927): 246–249.
2. Ibid., 246.
3. *The Exchangite* (Feb. 1929): 4.
4. Walter Hinton, *Aviation and You*, copy in the Brumback Library Hinton Collection, Van Wert, OH.
5. *New York Times*, Dec. 16 and 17, 1928.
6. Walter Hinton, *Opportunities in Aviation* (New York: W.W Norton & Co., 1929).
7. Ibid., x–xi, 6–7.
8. Ibid., 26, 84, 88, 185–186, 188.
9. Ibid.,196.
10. Ibid., 210.
11. *Exchangite* (June 1929): 10.
12. *Toledo Blade*, Nov. 29, 1930, p. 1.
13. *Exchangite* (Jan. 1931): 15.
14. *Exchangite* (April, 1931): 9–10.
15. *Exchangite* (Jan. 1931): 15, 32.
16. *Exchangite* (April 1931): 12, 13.
17. Ibid., 13, 22.
18. Ibid., 12.
19. Ibid., 12–13.
20. *Exchangite* (Jan. 1932): 17–24.

Chapter 17

1. Thomas Gray, "Elegy Written in a Country Church Yard." Gray was a British poet who lived from 1716 to 1771.
2. *New York Times*, Dec. 28, 1934, p. 26
3. *Washington Post*, Feb. 4, 1934, p. AU.
4. Walter Hinton, interview, May 29, 1967.
5. Hinton, interview; *New York Times* reference.
6. Script, Radio Department, Lennin and Mitchel Inc., New York, copy in Walter Hinton papers, Brumback Library collection, Van Wert, OH.
7. *New York Times*, Feb. 15, 1937, p. 2
8. *Lima* [OH] *News*, Nov. 1, 1940, p. 21; *Lima* [OH] *News*, Nov. 11, 1940, p. 2.
9. *New York Times*, May 9, 1949, p. 42.
10. Letter to Francis Tousley, Dec. 22, 1949, copy in Burns collection.
11. *New York Times*, Sept. 21, 1950, p. 46.
12. *New York Times*, May 1, 1969, p. 22.
13. Telephone interview, Theron Slade, 2004.
14. Postcards in Burns's Hinton collection.
15. Marjorie Tubbs, interview, Lansing, MI, May 2005.
16. Makara audio tape, Dec. 22, 1972, personal collection of Gwyn Makara.
17. Letter to Frank Tousley, Aug. 6, 1974.

18. *Newsweek*, Oct. 2, 1978, p. 19.
19. *Pensacola Journal*, Navy Museum Special (April 14, 1975).
20. Gene Baker, *Pensacola Journal*, Navy Museum Special, April 14, 1975. It should be noted that Hinton had no middle name so it is hard to figure where the K came from.
21. Bill Anderson, undated *Chicago Tribune* column, April 1975, Hinton Papers, Burns collection.
22. Letter from Smithsonian Secretary S. Dillon Ripley to Hinton, April 10, 1979, thanking him for the "generous gift," Hinton Papers, Burns collection.
23. Letter to Hinton from Frank Graham, March 29, 1979, Hinton Papers, Burns collection.
24. Phone interview with Hinton's friend Albert Bakker in Fort Lauderdale, Florida, June 28, 2000.
25. Ibid.
26. *News-Herald*, Jan. 10, 1979.
27. *Van Wert Times*, June 21, 1980.
28. *Miami Herald*, Dec. 17, 1980, p. 6BR.
29. Ibid.
30. Tubbs, interview, May 2005..
31. Richard Knott, telephone interview, July 9, 2003.

Epilogue

1. Amelia Earhart, *20 Hours, 40 Min: Our Flight in the Friendship* (New York: National Geographic, 1928).
2. Marjorie Tubbs, interview, May 2005.
3. Richard Knott, *A History of Wings: An Illustrated History of Naval Aviation* (Annapolis, MD: Naval Institute Press, 1997), 34.
4. "Flight into History," *Naval Aviation News* (Aug. 1986): 4–8.
5. Michael Ruane, "Model Builder's Trans-Atlantic Dream Taking Off," *Washington Post*, Aug. 7, 2002, p. B1.
6. "Model Plane Flies the Atlantic," *Science for Kids*, June 6, 2003, www.scienceforkids.org.
7. Ibid.
8. *New York Times*, March 6, 2005, p. A-11.
9. *New York Times*, Oct. 6, 2004.
10. Letter from Hinton to Francis Tousley, private collection of Gwyn Makara.
11. *Litton Avionics Newsletter*, undated.
12. Navy Office of Information, Biographies Branch, 27 January 1959.
13. Ernest E. Christensen Jr., "An Unlikely Naval Aviation Pioneer," *Naval History Magazine* (September 2008): 48–53.
14. Navy Office of Information, Biographies Branch, 27 January 1959; 1971 interview with Lavender by author in Washington, D.C.
15. Roberto Pires de Oliveira, "The Saga of Euclides Pinto Martins and his Friends," transl. Ralph Cooper, *The Early Birds of Aviation*, www.earlyaviators.com.
16. Theodore Taylor, *The Magnificent Mitscher* (Annapolis, MD: The Naval Institute Press, 2006).
17. Walter Hinton, interview, May 29, 1967.
18. *Raynham Family History*, 17 Oct 2007, www.raynham.org.
19. Letter from Eugene Saylor Rhoads to author, Nov. 16, 1967.
20. Navy Office of Information, Biographies Branch.
21. Ibid.
22. Richard K. Smith, *First Across: The U.S. Navy's Transatlantic Flight of 1919* (Annapolis, MD: Naval Institute Press, 1986), 106.
23. Walter Hinton, interview, June 19, 1967.
24. Don Kutter, "This Day in Aviation," *Aviation Safety Discussion from AVSIG*, avsig.com.
25. *New York Times*, Dec. 21, 1934.

Bibliography

Albion, Robert Greenhalgh. *Makers of Naval Policy 1798–1947.* Annapolis, MD: Naval Institute Press, 1980.
Alcock, Sir John, and Sir Arthur Whitten Brown. *Our Transatlantic Flight.* London: William Kimber, 1969.
Allen, Peter. *The 91 Before Lindbergh.* Shrewsbury, Eng.: Airlife Publishing Ltd., 1985.
The American Heritage History of Flight. New York: Simon & Schuster, Inc., 1962.
Arbon, Lee. *They Also Flew: The Enlisted Pilot Legacy, 1912–1942.* Washington: The Smithsonian Press, 1992.
Aymar, Brandt, ed., *Men in the Air: The Best Flight Stories of All Time from Greek Mythology to the Space Age.* New York: Crown Publishers, 1990.
Bach, Richard. *Biplane.* New York: Macmillan, 1966.
———. *Stranger to the Ground.* New York: Harper & Row, 1963.
Baker, B. Kimball. "Lieutenant Walter Hinton: A Naval Aviation Pioneer." Interview with Walter Hinton, University of Pittsburgh, Bradford, PA, 28 Oct 1981, Walter Hinton papers, U.S. Naval Air Museum, Pensacola, FL.
"Birdmen, Evolution of the Aeroplane." *Leslie's: The People's Weekly,* 9 May 1912.
Bostock, Peter. *The Great Atlantic Air Race: The Adventures and Its Lessons.* New York: William Morrow & Co., 1969.
Boyne, Walter J. "Standing on Orville and Wilbur's Shoulders." *Aviation History* (Nov 2003): 43–48, 64.
Brown, Sir Arthur Whitten. *Flying the Atlantic in Sixteen Hours.* London: Frederick A. Stokes, 1920.
Buck, Rinker. *Flight of Passage.* New York: Hyperion, 1997.
Burroughs, William J., Bob Crowder, Ted Robertson, Eleanor Vallier-Talbot, and Richard Witaker. *A Guide to Weather.* San Francisco: Fog City Press, 1996.
Byrd, Richard E. *Skyward.* New York: Blue Ribbon Books, 1928.
Callwood, June. *Portrait of Canada.* Garden City, NY: Doubleday & Co., 1981.
Campbell, W. Joseph. "'One of the Fine Figures if American Journalism': A Closer Look at Josephus Daniels of the Raleigh News and Observer." *American Journalism Review* 16, no. 4 (Fall 1999): 37–55.
Christman, Timothy J. "Cdr. Elmer Stone: Coast Guard Aviator No. 1." *Naval Aviation News* (May–June 1983): 36–38.
Coletta, Paolo E. *Patrick N. L. Bellinger and U.S. Naval Aviation.* Lanham, MD: University Press of America, 1987.
Collier, Peter, with David Horowitz. *The Roosevelts: An American Saga.* New York: Touchstone, 1994.
Collinson, Clifford, and Capt. F. McDermott. *Through Atlantic Clouds: The History of Atlantic Flight.* London: Hutchinson & Co., 1934.
Corn, Joseph J. *Winged Gospel: America's Romance with Aviation, 1900–1960.* New York: Oxford University Press, 1983.
Cronon, E. David, ed. *The Cabinet Diaries of Josephus Daniels, 1913–1921.* Lincoln: University of Nebraska Press, 1963.

Cunningham, Charlie, and Jackie Cunningham. *Putty and Bess*. Alexandria, VA: Association of Naval Aviation, 1997.
Daniels, Josephus. *The Wilson Era — Years of War and After, 1917–1923*. Chapel Hill: The University of North Carolina Press, 1946.
De la Croix, Robert. *They Flew the Atlantic*. Trans. Edward Fitzgerald. Derby, Ct: Monarch Books, 1960.
de Saint Exupery, Antoine. *Flight to Arras*. Trans. Lewis Galantiere. New York: Reynal & Hitchcock, 1942.
_____.*Southern Mail*. Trans. Curtis Cate, Orlando, FL: Harcourt Brace & Co., 1971.
_____. *Wind, Sand and Stars*. Trans. Lewis Galantiere. New York: Reynal & Hitchcock, 1940.
Del Giudice, Daniele. *Takeoff: The Pilot's Lore*. Trans. Joseph Farrell. New York: Harcourt Brace & Co. 1996.
Edgerton, Clyde. *Solo: My Adventures in the Air*. Chapel Hill, N.C.: Algonquin Books of Chapel Hill, 2005.
Ellis, F. H., and E. M. Ellis. *Atlantic Air Conquest*. London: William Kimber, 1963.
Erickson, Frank A. "The First Transatlantic Flight: U.S. Coast Guard Academy Alumni Association." *The Bulletin* 34 (May–June 1977): 18–23.
Fleischer, Suri, and Arleen Keylin, eds. *Flight, as Reported by the New York Times*. New York: Arno Press, 1977.
The Flight across the Atlantic. New York: Curtiss Aeroplane and Motor Corp., 1919.
Forsyth, Frederick, ed. *Great Flying Stories*. Rockland, MA: Wheeler, 1995.
Frazier, David. *ABCs of Safe Flying*, 3d ed. Blue Ridge Summit, PA: TAB Books, 1992.
Freedman, Russell. *The Wright Brothers: How They Invented the Airplane*. New York: Holiday House, 1971.
Gann, Ernest K. *Fate Is the Hunter*. New York: Simon & Schuster, 1961.
Goodspeed, M. Hill, ed. *U.S. Naval Aviation*. Pensacola, FL: Hugh Lauter Levin Associates, Inc., 2001.
_____. *U.S. Navy: A Complete History*. Washington Navy Yard, D.C.: Hugh Lauter Levin Associates, Inc., 2003.
Greenwood, John T., ed. *Milestones of Aviation, Smithsonian Institution National Air and Space Museum*. New York: Crescent Books, 1991.
Hagedorn, Ann. *Savage Peace: Hope and Fear in America, 1919*. New York: Simon & Schuster, 2007.
Hamlen, Joseph R. *Flight Fever*. New York: Doubleday, 1971.
Hawker, H. G., and K. MacKenzie Grieve. *Our Atlantic Attempt*. London: Methuen & Co., 1919.
Hawker, Muriel. *H. G. Hawker, Airman: His Life and His Work*. London: Hutchinson & Co., 1922.
Heinmuller, John P. V. *Man's Fight to Fly*. New York: Aero Print Company, 1945.
Hinton, Walter. "The First Trans-Atlantic Flight: The Annals of the American Academy." undated article, Walter Hinton papers, U.S. Naval Air Museum, Pensacola, FL.
Hoffman, Paul. *Wings of Madness: Alberto Santos-Dumont and the Invention of Flight*. New York: Hyperion Books, 2003.
Howard, Fred. *Wilbur and Orville: A Biography of the Wright Brothers*. New York: Alfred A. Knopf, 1987.
Jackson, Donald Dale. *The Explorers*. Alexandria, VA: Time-Life Books, 1983.
Johnson, Wayne. *The Colony of Unrequited Dreams*. New York: Anchor Books, 1998.
Junger, Sebastian. *The Perfect Storm*. New York: Harper Paperbacks, 1997.
Keefer, Louis. "Farm Boy to Famous Flyer — Walter Hinton." *Timeline* (Jan–Mar 2008): 38–51.
Knott, Richard C. *The American Flying Boat: An Illustrated History*. Annapolis, MD: U.S. Naval Institute Press, 1979.
_____. *A Heritage of Wings: An Illustrated History of Navy Aviation*. Annapolis, MD: U.S. Naval Institute Press, 1997.
_____, ed. *The Naval Aviation Guide*, 4th ed. Annapolis, MD.: U.S. Naval Institute Press, 1985.
Langewiesche, William. *Inside the Sky: A Meditation on Flight*. New York: Pantheon, 1998.

Lee, Chang-rae. *Aloft.* New York: Riverhead Books, 2004.
Lindbergh, Anne Morrow. *Listen! The Wind.* New York: Harcourt, Brace and Co. 1938.
Lindbergh, Charles A. *The Spirit of St. Louis.* New York: Charles Scribner's Sons, 1953.
Lubow, Arthur. *The Reporter Who Would Be King: A Biography of Richard Harding Davis.* New York: Charles Scribner's Sons, 1992.
MacMillan, Margaret. *Paris, 1919: Six Months that Changed the World.* New York: Random House, 2001.
Markham, Beryl. *West with the Night.* San Francisco: North Point Press, 1983.
Mason, Sammy. *Stalls, Spins, and Safety.* New York: McGraw-Hill, 1982.
McCutcheon, Marc. *Everyday Life from Prohibition through World War II.* Cincinnati: Writers Digest Books, 1995.
McDonough, Kenneth. *Atlantic Wings.* Hemel Hemstead, Eng.: Model Aeronautical Press, Ltd., 1966.
McMillan, Peter. "The Vimy Flies Again." *National Geographic* 187, no. 5 (May 1995): 2–43.
Miller, Bettina. *From Flappers to Flivvers: We Helped Make the 1920s Roar.* Greendale, WI: Reminisce Books, 1995.
Morrison, Joseph L. *Josephus Daniels, the Small-d Democrat.* Chapel Hill: The University of North Carolina Press, 1966.
Mosley, Leonard. *Lindbergh: A Biography.* Garden City, NY: Doubleday, 1976
Murphy, Charles, J. V. *Struggle: The Life and Exploits of Commander Richard E. Byrd.* New York: Frederick A. Stokes Co. 1928.
Neely, William. *Pilots: The Romance of the Air: Pilots Speak about the Triumphs and Tragedies, Fears and Joys of Flying.* New York: Simon & Schuster, 1991.
Nevin, David. *Architects of Air Power.* Alexandria, VA: Time-Life Books, 1981.
———. *The Pathfinders.* Alexandria, VA: Time-Life Books, 1980.
Nicolaou, Stephanie. *Flying Boats & Seaplanes: A History from 1905.* Osceola, WI: MBI Publishing Co. 1998.
O'Rourke, Debbie, and Jerome Kennedy. *To Learn about Our Heritage.* Grenfall, Newf.: Memorial University of Newfoundland, 1991.
Pearce, George F. *The U.S. Navy in Pensacola, from Sailing Ships to Naval Aviation (1825–1930).* Pensacola, FL: University of Florida Presses, 1980.
Poole, Robert M. "Canada's Place Apart." *National Geographic* 184, no. 4 (Oct 1993): 2–45.
Post, Wiley, and Gatty Harold. *Around the World in Eight Days: The Flight of the Winnie Mae.* Garden City, NY: Garden City Publishing Co., 1931.
Raddall, Thomas H. *Halifax, Warden of the North.* Garden City, NY: Doubleday & Co., 1965.
Reckner, James R. *Teddy Roosevelt's Great White Fleet.* Annapolis, MD: Naval Institute Press, Bluejacket Books, 1988.
Read, Albert Cushing. Original letters to Bess Burdine Read, April 1919 to June 1919, NC-4 Collection, Pensacola Naval Aviation Museum, Pensacola, FL.
———. "The First Trans-Atlantic Flight." In *Flying Officers of the United States Navy, 1917–1919.* 67–70. Atlen, PA: Schiffer Publishing Ltd., 1997.
Read, Bess Burdine. "The Private Letters of Putty Read, Written to His Wife on the Occasion of His Trans-Atlantic Crossing, May 1919." *Pensacola Naval Aviation Museum Foundation Magazine* (May 1986).
Reynolds, Clark G. *Admiral John H. Towers: The Struggle for Naval Air Supremacy.* Annapolis, MD: Naval Institute Press, 1991.
Roscoe, Theodore. *On the Seas and in the Air: A History of the U.S. Navy's Air Power.* New York: Hawthorne Books, 1970.
Rosenberg, Barry, and Catherine Macaulay. *Mavericks of the Sky: The First Daring Pilots of the U.S. Air Mail.* New York: Harper Collins, 2006.
Ross, Walter S. *The Last Hero: Charles A. Lindbergh.* New York: Harper & Row, 1968.
Rowe, Percy. *The Great Atlantic Air Race.* London: Angus Robertson Publishers, 1977.
Schwarzer, William. *The Lion Killers, Billy Mitchell, and the Birth of Strategic Bombing,* 2nd ed. Mt. Holly, NJ: Aerial Perspective Publishers, 2003.
Severy, Merle. "Portugal's Sea Road to the East." *National Geographic* 182, no. 5 (Nov 1992): 56–92.

Sheely, Lawrence. D., ed. *Sailor of the Air: The 1917–1919 Letters and Diary of USN CMM/A Irving Edward Sheely*. Tuscaloosa, AL: The University of Alabama Press, 1993.
Smith, Richard K. *First Across: The U.S. Navy's Transatlantic Flight of 1919*. Annapolis, MD: Naval Institute Press, 1986.
Steirman, Hy, and Harold Mehling. "They Showed Lindbergh the Way." *True Magazine* (Dec 1960): 58–61, 108–116.
____, and Gleen D. Kittler. *Triumph: The Incredible Saga of the First Transatlantic Flight*. New York: Harper & Brothers Publishers, 1961.
Stoff, Joshua. *Transatlantic Flight: A Picture History, 1873–1939*. Mineola, N.Y.: Dover Publications, Inc., 1999.
Swanborough Gordon, and Peter N. Bowers. *United States Naval Aircraft Since 1911*. New York: Funk & Wagnalls, 1968.
Taylor, Theodore. *The Magnificent Mitscher*. Annapolis, MD: Naval Institute Press, 2006.
____, and David Mondey. *Guinness Book of Aircraft Records: Facts and Feats*. New York: Canopy Books, 1992.
Tobin, James. *To Conquer the Air: The Wright Brothers and the Great Race for Flight*. New York: Free Press, 2003.
"Trepassey Made History on May 16, 1919, When the First Atlantic Flight Began." *The Daily News* (St. John's, Newf.), May 19, 1966, p. 15.
Van Deurs, George. *Anchors in the Sky: Spuds Ellyson, the First Naval Aviator*. San Rafael, CA: Presidio Press, 1978.
Van Dorm, William G. *Oceanography and Seamanship*, 2nd ed. Centreville, MD: Cornell Maritime Press, 1993.
Wallace, Graham. *The Flight of Alcock and Brown*. London: Putnam, 1955.
Westervelt, G. C., H. C. Richardson, and A. C. Read. *The Triumph of the NCs*. New York: Doubleday, 1920.
Wilbur, Ted. "First Flight Across the Atlantic, May 1919." *Naval Aviation News* (1969).
Wohl, Robert. *A Passion for Wings, Aviation and the Western Imagination 1908–1918*. New Haven, CT: Yale University Press, 1994.
Wolfe, Tom. *The Right Stuff*. New York: Farrar, Straus & Giroux, Inc., 1980.f
Woodhouse, Henry. *Textbook of Naval Aeronautics*. New York: The Century Co., 1917.
Wooldridge, E. T., ed. *The Golden Age Remembered, U.S. Naval Aviation, 1919–1941*. Annapolis, MD: Naval Institute Press, 1998.
Yeager, Chuck, and Leo Janis. *Yeager, an Autobiography*. New York: Bantam Books, 1985.

Index

A-5598 Navy balloon 132, 209
Alcock, John 41, 68, 109, 124, 225
America (flying boat) 26
Aroostook 64, 73, 154
Atlantic 101

Baltimore 61–62
Baltzel, John 157
Barin, Louis 41, 225
Barney 71–72
Bellinger, Patrick N.L. 25–26, 34, 41, 45, 225
Billingsly, William Devotie 24
Blériot, Louis 48–49
Bly, Nellie 159
Breese, James 42, 70, 111, 225–226
Brown, Arthur Whitten 68, 109, 124, 225
Bull, Dr. Charles 174
Bye, George 156, 194, 226
Byrd, Richard E. 33, 40, 41, 195, 226–227

C-4 (blimp) 43
C-5 60–61–62–63
Chatham Naval Air Station 51–60
Chew, Bob 201–204
Christensen, Rasmus 41, 227
Cochrane 102
Columbia 81, 110–111
Condon, Richard 193
Corvo 85
Cummings, Damon 140, 143
Curtiss, Glenn 21–22, 178

Daniels, Josephus 112–113, 146, 153
Delphy 60
Digby 41
Douglas, A.H. 145
Dumont, Santos 217

Eleanor III (flying boat) 172, 209

Ellyson, Theodore Gordon 22–23
Ely, Eugene 22
Evans, A.W. 143
Exchange Clubs 195, 204
Exchangite 200–203

Farrell, Stephen 133, 146, 151
Flores 80

Garber, Paul 130, 210, 221
Great Atlantic Air Race 39
Great White Fleet 18
Green, William 204

Handley Page bomber 110
Hangar fire 42
Hawker, Harry 41, 227
Hawker, Muriel 99–100
Hill, Maynard 224
Hinton, Effa Garrison 16
Hinton, Florence (Slade) 16–18, 210
Hinton, Lovinia 17, 209
Hinton, Millard Madison 16, 209
Hinton, Sally Adline 32, 133
Horta 81
Howard, Edward "Harry" 42–43, 125

Ionia 88, 111

Jackson, Adm. Richard 98, 112

Kerr, Adm. Mark 110
Kesler, C.I. 41, 227
Kimberly 50, 60
Kloor, Louis 133
Knapp, Carrie Susan 205
Knott, Richard 214, 217, 219
Koch-Grunberg, D. Theodor 178, 184

Lame Duck 54
Lavender, Robert A. 31, 41, 227–228

Index

Lindbergh, Charles 194–195
London Daily Mail 36, 39

MacKenzie-Grieve, Kenneth 99, 101, 103
Makara, Gwyn 212
Makara, John 212
Manteo, N.C. 162–163
Marks, Tom (Indian trapper) 142
Martinsyde 103
Mary 107
Mattice, Ontario 142
McCulloch, Dick 41, 228–229
McDermut 50, 60
Mitscher, Marc, 41, 229
Moore, Lloyd 41, 229
Moose Factory, Ontario 142
Morgan, C.W.F. 102, 104
Moulton, Harry D. (first stowaway) 39
Mt. Pelee 168
Muller, Jake 133, 159, 195, 207–208

NC-3 39
NC-4 41
NCs 36–37
Neuberger, Dr. Julius 150–151
New York World 156–159, 169

Olympia 19–21

Pensacola 31–32
Pensacola Naval Air Station 32
Pinto Martins, Euclides 156–159, 228
Plymouth, England 124
Ponta del Gada, Azores 98, 112

Rathburne 120–121
Raynham, Frederick 41, 102, 229
Read, Albert Cushing 28, 44, 60–64, 126, 210, 229–230
Read, Bess Burdine 55–56, 225
Rhoads, Eugene 43, 53, 58–59, 210, 230
Rhodes, Braxton 41, 74, 230–231
Rice, Dr. Alexander Hamilton 173, 176
Richardson, Holden Chester 24–25, 36, 92, 232

Rio Negro 180–181
Rochester 114–115, 124
Rockaway Naval Air Station 40
Rodd, Herbert 42, 54, 61, 231
Roosevelt, Franklin Delano 39, 61

Sadenwater, Harry 231
St. Johns, Newfoundland 41, 71
Sampaio Correia I 156, 160
Sampaio Correia II 164
Shattuck, Dr. George 178
Shawmut 115
Stevens, Capt. Albert 174, 178–179, 181–182, 186–188
Stone, Elmer 41, 231–232
Strong, Dr. Richard 183
Sunstedt, Hugo 38, 40
Swanson, John 178

Take off (May 8, 1919) 45–47
Tapir 188
Toledo Blade 201
Total passenger record 39
Tousley, Barbara 212
Tousley, Frank 212
Towers, John Henry 22–24, 44, 89, 112, 232
Trepassey, Newfoundland 69-
Tubbs, Marjorie Slade 210, 214

Van Wart, Isaac 16, 215
Van Wert, Ohio 15–17, 128, 222
Vera Cruz 25

Wells, N.Y. 135
Westerveldt, George 44
Whiting, Kenneth 28–29, 55, 232
Williamson, B.P. 146
Wilshusen, John 156, 177
Wright, Orville 21
Wright, Wilbur 21, 198

Zeppelin 124–126

www.ingramcontent.com/pod-product-compliance
Ingram Content Group UK Ltd.
Pitfield, Milton Keynes, MK11 3LW, UK
UKHW041937140426

5217IPUK00014B/523